Harwood Fundamentals of Pure and Applied Economics

ECONOMICS OF COOPERATION AND THE LABOR-MANAGED ECONOMY

ECONOMIC SYSTEMS & COMPARATIVE ECONOMICS I
In 3 Volumes

ECONOMICS OF COOPERATION AND THE LABOR-MANAGED ECONOMY

JOHN P BONIN AND
LOUIS PUTTERMAN

LONDON AND NEW YORK

First published in 1987 by
Harwood Academic Publishers GmbH

Reprinted in 2001 by
Routledge

2 Park Square, Milton Park, Abingdon, Oxfordshire OX14 4RN

Simultaneously published in the USA and Canada by Routledge

711 Third Avenue, New York, NY 10017

Routledge is an imprint of the Taylor & Francis Group

First issued in paperback 2013

British Library Cataloguing in Publication Data
A CIP catalogue record for this book
is available from the British Library

ISBN: 978-0-415-27467-8 (hbk)
ISBN: 978-0-415-86628-6 (pbk)

Economics of Cooperation and the Labor-Managed Economy

John P. Bonin
Wesleyan University, USA

and

Louis Putterman
Brown University, USA

A volume in the Economic Systems section
edited by
J. M. Montias
Yale University, USA
and
J. Kornai
Institute of Economics, Hungarian Academy of Sciences, Hungary

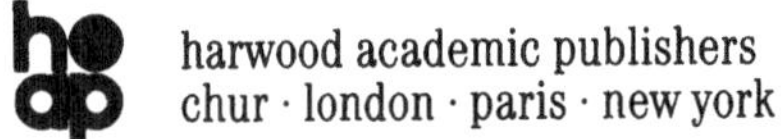

Harwood Academic Publishers

Post Office Box 197
London WC2E 9PX
England

58, rue Lhomond
75005 Paris
France

Post Office Box 786
Cooper Station
New York, NY 10276
United States of America

Library of Congress Cataloging-in-Publication Data

Bonin, John.
Economics of cooperation and the labor-managed economy.

(Fundamentals of pure and applied economics; vol. 14. Economic systems section, ISSN 0191-1708)
Bibliography: p.
Includes index.
1. Economics. 2. Cooperation. 3. Resource allocation. 4. Management—Yugoslavia—Employee participation. I. Putterman, Louis G. II. Title. III. Series: Fundamentals of pure and applied economics; vol. 14. IV. Series: Fundamentals of pure and applied economics. Economic systems section.
HB171.B545 1986 334 86-19563
ISBN 3-7186-0358-6

Contents

Introduction to the Series

Drawing on a personal network, an economist can still relatively easily stay well informed in the narrow field in which he works, but to keep up with the development of economics as a whole is a much more formidable challenge. Economists are confronted with difficulties associated with the rapid development of their discipline. There is a risk of "balkanisation" in economics, which may not be favorable to its development.

Fundamentals of Pure and Applied Economics has been created to meet this problem. The discipline of economics has been subdivided into sections (listed inside). These sections include short books, each surveying the state of the art in a given area.

Each book starts with the basic elements and goes as far as the most advanced results. Each should be useful to professors needing material for lectures, to graduate students looking for a global view of a particular subject, to professional economists wishing to keep up with the development of their science, and to researchers seeking convenient information on questions that incidentally appear in their work.

Each book is thus a presentation of the state of the art in a particular field rather than a step-by-step analysis of the development of the literature. Each is a high-level presentation but accessible to anyone with a solid background in economics, whether engaged in business, government, international organizations, teaching, or research in related fields.

Three aspects of *Fundamentals of Pure and Applied Economics* should be emphasized:

—First, the project covers the whole field of economics, not only theoretical or mathematical economics.

—Second, the project is open-ended and the number of books is not predetermined. If new interesting areas appear, they will generate additional books.
—Last, all the books making up each section will later be grouped to constitute one or several volumes of an Encyclopedia of Economics.

The editors of the sections are outstanding economists who have selected as authors for the series some of the finest specialists in the world.

J. Lesourne *H. Sonnenschein*

Economics of Cooperation and the Labor-Managed Economy

JOHN P. BONIN and LOUIS PUTTERMAN†

Wesleyan University, Connecticut, USA
Brown University, Rhode Island, USA

INTRODUCTION

The terms worker-managed, labor-managed, and self-managed firm or enterprise, and also producers' cooperative (PC), have sometimes been used interchangeably in the economic literature of recent years to denote the economic entities which, along with the (macro-)economies they may comprise, are the subject matter of this essay. What shall we understand by these terms? The theoretical economic literature on labor-managed firms usually distinguishes them from other firms by assuming them to have a distinct and particular objective function. The best known example is the tradition following Ward (1958), which distinguishes capitalist from L–M or "Illyrian" firms by assuming that the latter seek to maximize the dividend or net income per worker, while the former seek to maximize total profit. Since such an operating rule suffices to establish an enterprise's behavioral tendencies in the face of varying objective conditions, it has often appeared to be an adequate characterization of the worker-managed enterprise, avoiding the need for a descriptive and/or institutional definition. This parallels procedure in the theory of the conventional firm, where the assumed objective suffices as a basis for the characterization of

† We wish to thank the following for their comments on various sections of this manuscript: Will Bartlett, Avner Ben-Ner, Michael E. Bradley, John Burkett, David Ellerman, Saul Estrin, Norman Ireland, Peter Law, Bentley MacLeod, Michael McPherson, B. Milanovic, Deborah Milenkovitch, John Michael Montias, Dennison Rusinow, Stephen Sacks, Robert Stuart, Martin Swiecicki, Michael Wyzan, and members of the Department of Economics, University of Washington, and of the Colloquium on the Labor-Managed Economy, Institution for Social and Policy Studies, Yale University (May 3–4, 1985).

firm behavior, and no further information about what a firm *is* (e.g., the internal and/or contractual structure of the firm) is supplied.

While this practice is convenient and unobjectionable for purposes of specific investigations, broad discussion of the economics of worker-managed enterprises and economies demands a more general definition of terms. There is no unanimity as to the appropriate maximand or behavioral rule characterizing such enterprises. For example, Horvat has argued that the self-managed firm maximizes total profit; Sertel and others argue that the maximand is workers' expected utility; and Furubotn and Pejovich argue that a labor-managed enterprise's behavior may be affected by the conflicting interests of enterprise directors seeking to satisfy external authorities, and of groups of workers seeking to maximize the present discounted value of their projected earnings stream. To establish which of the competing operating rules most adequately characterizes the worker-managed firm in general, or whether several of these rules may be appropriate, each to a particular subclass of these firms or analytical situations, we must have reference to a primitive definition which tells us what is meant by worker-managed firm in the first place.

The most acceptable general definition would appear to be that a worker-managed firm is a productive enterprise the ultimate decision-making rights over which are held by member-workers, on the basis of equality of those rights regardless of job, skill grade, or capital contribution. A full definition would state that no non-workers have a direct say in enterprise decisions, and that no workers are denied an equal say in those decisions. This definition does not imply that any particular set of decisions must be made by the full working group, nor does it imply a particular choice rule, such as majority voting. It says nothing about financing structures other than that financiers are not accorded direct decision-making powers in the enterprise by virtue of their non-labor contributions, and it does not say anything about how income is distributed among workers. On all of these matters, all that is implied is that ultimate decision-making rights are vested in the workers, and only in the workers. Thus, the basic definition centers on an allocation of governance rights, and is simultaneously economic and political.

While quite general in that it permits great diversity of form, for example from the commune which is highly egalitarian in income distribution and leadership structures to the large industrial cooperative which may have quite differentiated wage scales and a highly hierarchical management structure, the definition remains rigid on the question of rights allocation. In practice, we find a substantially greater variety of enterprise types which *resemble* the worker-managed firm thus defined than of those that fully satisfy the definition, because many enterprises commonly treated as producers' cooperatives do engage in some short or long-term hiring of non-member labor, while still others allow non-workers, in particular share-holders, to enjoy some decision-making rights. We therefore propose to employ our definition both to identify the essential principle of workers' self-management in a pure form, and also as a benchmark allowing us to group other enterprises into a slightly looser worker-managed or participatory rubric according to their relative proximity to the ideal type, and distance from alternatives such as managerial capitalist corporations, state socialist enterprises, etc.

While the definition with reference to control-rights seems most apt for capturing the general meaning of self-management and for identifying more and less pure examples of the phenomenon, the formal economics literature continues to give pride of place to "dividend maximization" as the defining characteristic of labor-managed firms (LMF's). In our essay, the term LMF will be reserved for dividend-maximizing firms, exclusively.

It will be noted that all of the above definitions leave the terms "firm" or "enterprise" themselves undefined. This should not surprise the reader who is familiar with the literature on the conventional firm, where the problem of defining the proper boundaries of a given firm and of deciding what is and is not a firm remains unsolved. The literature on self-management has made no breakthrough here, and we continue to use the term in the same intuitive sense as employed both in "theory of the firm" in general and in the more specialized self-management literature.

The literature on workers' management

Whilst comments on producers' cooperatives can be found in the writings of 19th century economists such as John Stuart Mill, this essay looks at a burgeoning "modern" literature on self-management which was first inspired by the Yugoslav experiment with worker control of enterprises beginning in the 1950's, and which has its formal origin in a 1958 paper by Benjamin Ward. While we know of only a handful of important contributions in the 1960's (almost all at the end of that decade), the 1970's and the 1980's to date have found economists' interest substantial and continually increasing.

A check of the economic literature index data base,[1] available for the years 1969 to 1983, reveals that 63 papers were published in economics journals during 1969–70, 214 during 1971–75, 376 during 1976–80, and 240 during 1981–83, on the subject of producers' cooperatives, co-determination, and collective farms.[2] Filling in the incomplete five-year periods by assuming equal annual rates within those periods, we get 152, 214, 376, and 400 papers, respectively, for the four half-decades beginning 1965. Another gauge of the growth of interest is citations of Ward's paper in the *Social Science Citation index,* which is available on line from 1972 to 1983. This shows 9 citations of Ward (1958) during 1972–75, 30 citations during 1976–80, and 34 during 1981–83, which would correspond to approximately 11, 30, and 57 citations for the half-decades beginning 1970, by the same method of calculation. Finally, a large fraction of the papers published in the *Journal of Comparative Economics,* inaugurated in 1977, have concerned self-managed firms or economies, and by the 1980's, many textbooks on comparative economic systems treated labor-managed economies (usually represented by Yugoslavia) either on a par with or next in importance after capitalism and command socialism.

Sources of interest

Although enterprises fitting or approaching the pure definition of worker-managed firms can be found in a great number of countries

[1] The 'on-line' version of the *Journal of Economic Literature* index of articles in economics.

[2] A rather wide list of variants, too long to print here, was used for this search. For example: Illyrian, self-managing, enterprise democracy, participatory enterprise, etc. While some questionable titles were probably picked up, other papers clearly belonging in the literature were undoubtedly not identified by this list. In any case, it should be emphasized that papers in *non-economics* journals, and several important economics *books* on the subject, are definitely excluded.

and sectors, it is safe to say that intellectual and socio-political interest in the concept of workers' self-management outstrips the empirical prominence of these forms. It may therefore be useful to briefly explore the motivation for interest in this model. While our discussion will focus on reasons for favorable interest in self-management, we do not mean to imply that the economics literature just referred to is in all cases motivated by such concerns. Probably most work on self-management models attempts to be strictly analytical or descriptive. On the other hand, many contributions can clearly be seen to be motivated by the qualms, apprehensions, and outright opposition to the self-management concept elicited in response to arguments of the types to be surveyed here.

Several broad sources of interest in self-management can be identified. First, at an overarching philosophical level, interest in self-management can be related to questioning of quality of life, social relations, and personal development aspects of conventional patterns of work organization. Because work remains the single dominant activity to which most people devote their time, acceptance of hierarchical relations of subordination and authority, which may fail to promote interest in the job, development of problem solving and other productive powers, and self-esteem, are considered by many to be high costs of industrial civilization. It is also held that the democratic, egalitarian and cooperative values which are promoted as civic virtues in many contemporary societies are in practice eclipsed by competition in economic life and especially by top-down control in the workplace. Economic democracy in general and enterprise democracy in particular must be implemented, according to this view, before these values achieve full significance for society's members. Still more radical arguments view fundamental changes in work organization as but a part of an overall social revolution which is to end exploitation and unfetter the means of social progress.

A second set of motivations are more narrowly economic, and concern workers' interests in job security and/or an income distribution more favorable to them. First, there is the concern that under contemporary circumstances in which capital moves easily within and across national boundaries, workers may need to control their own jobs in order to preserve employment opportunities in their local communities and regions. Second, some workers may prefer jobs offering security of employment along with greater variability of earnings, as do some types of producers' cooperatives, rather than the conventional employment package providing fixed nominal earnings but cyclical lay-off possibilities that are outside of workers' control. Third, in the presence of firm specific rents, workers in self-managed firms might attain a better distribution of income towards labor as opposed to capital, by controlling the disposition of enterprises' residual earnings. Relatedly, self-management by its cooperative nature, internal politics, or constitutional constraints, might lead to a narrower and less skewed distribution of income between different grades of labor.

Finally, there are economic and social motivations which are concerned with workers' welfare principally from an *instrumental* point of view. A variety of analyses of methods for improving managerial performance and of combating observed or alleged "productivity slowdowns" in advanced industrial economies cite the worker's lack of identification with the firm, inadequate incentive to perform in more than a perfunctory fashion and to reveal information that may be of use in improving firm operations, and non-participation in decision-making, as sources of low productivity and unenthusiastic performance. More broadly, the face-off between labor and management typifying traditional industrial relations in capitalist economies is viewed by some as counterproductive and an obstacle to a well-functioning economy. To transform what is perceived as a zero or negative-sum game of industrial confrontation into a positive-sum game of cooperation, suggested reforms ranging from mild forms of participation, for example in quality circles, job enrichment, etc., to full industrial democracy have been widely discussed.

Not all proponents of the various arguments and approaches just reviewed identify full workers' self-management as a desirable element of reform. Among those who do, however, the moral and human developmental reasons for endorsing self-management may be rather similar. In the first place, the self-management concept embraces values of participation and equality of rights that are almost universal in modern socio-political rhetoric. Participation is viewed as both an inalienable right of those affected by an organization's behavior and as a means of raising the quality of decisions and their implementation as well as fostering personal development and community. Nothing need be said here about the normative justification of equality, but it is worth pointing out that what advocates of self-management desire is not necessarily a leveling of economic outcomes but rather equality of social and political status and of rights to influence social outcomes which may in turn govern the distribution of economic opportunities.

Secondly, the workplace is identified as a major arena within which application of participatory and democratic values ought to proceed. The centrality of the individual's role as worker, rather than citizen, consumer, etc., is underscored. In some presentations (for example Dahl, 1985, Pateman, 1970), failure to extend these values to the workplace earlier is identified as a shortcoming of classical liberalism, or even as revealing that the democratic claims of Western ("bourgeois") societies are false.

Finally and relatedly, a special status is accorded to labor as a contributor to the production process and as an activity. Co-equality of labor with other "factors of production," as in the conventional neoclassical terminology, may be rejected in favor of a humanistic view according to which labor, the productive activity of man, who is both the prime mover and the purpose of that activity, can not be placed on a par with the inanimate materials and tools that he uses. Similarly, moral and legal rights to *own* land, machines, finance capital, etc., and so to appropriate some part of their product, may be recognized but not placed on a full par with the inalienability of one's laboring powers[3] and of rights to share in their fruits. Ownership of non-labor factors, if sanctioned, is more likely to be seen as a means for spurring efficient resource utilization and incentives—including those associated with the freedom to utilize the earnings of labor itself—than as a fundamental human right; such ownership may be combined with a notion that non-labor productive resources are, at another level, social resources needed to fructify labor and to achieve community objectives.

These last points suggest that the attitude of proponents of self-management towards markets, while ordinarily far less antagonistic than that of state socialists, is sometimes more qualified

[3] That is, that they may not be bought or sold.

than that of free-market liberals. Those, in particular, who would make self-management an inviolable right, not even subject to the abridgement of consenting parties, are in practice favoring the abolition of that market in which, in conventional practice, workers trade their possibility of a say in the direction of their enterprise and their own labor, and of a claim on the disposition of enterprise net earnings, in return for a payment for fulfilling an employer's directives. Success in this program, which in philosophical terms might be referred to as the "decommodification of labor," has economic consequences in the resulting "incompleteness of labor markets" to which we will have several occasions to refer in what follows.

Questions raised by the incidence of cooperation in production

As we shall have occasion to remark in subsequent sections, contemporary discussion of enterprise self-management is frequently called to grapple with the question of whether the dominance of non-self-managed forms of enterprise in the industrial era is not *prima facie* evidence of the inferiority of self-management in efficiency respects. This question is sometimes tied to a broad historical view according to which property rights and forms of organization and contracting have evolved from less to more efficient kinds in either an absolute sense or with reference to changing technological possibilities. It is argued, for example, that private property rights have traditionally competed with joint forms of exploitation, and that it is only in the modern era that the former have become more prevalent than the latter, this predominance reflecting the greater efficiency of private over joint rights of resource exploitation.[4]

Against this particular phrasing of the matter, one can argue that in fact self-management envisions a no more collectivist approach to economic organization than that of the modern corporation—since ultimate control resides in both instances in a collectivity of individuals: in one case, the enterprise's personnel, in the other, its

[4] North, 1981; Demsetz, 1967; J. M. Montias, personal communication.

equity holders.[5] Nevertheless, the progressive elimination of communal forms of rural economy in both Europe and the rest of the world, and the relative rarity of self-management outside of controlled or legislated contexts (Yugoslav industrial firms, East European collective farms, West German co-determination) or particular lines of production and service (legal and medical partnerships, universities, and other activities in which human capital is the leading productive factor) is noteworthy. Responses to this observation range from its complete or qualified interpretation as evidence that expansion of self-management could carry heavy economic costs (Jensen and Meckling, 1979; Williamson, 1985; Pejovich, 1978), to scepticism regarding such inferences about efficiency (Vanek, 1970; Sertel, 1982; Putterman, 1984), as well as to approaches emphasing *rights* over and above allocative efficiency (Ellerman, 1984).

From a more positive standpoint, the above-mentioned issues suggest the desirability of increased attention to the legal, institutional, and policy contexts within which self-management and related forms of organization arise. Institutional restrictions undoubtedly explain the dominance of self-managed enterprises in Yugoslavia, but they also account for some of the handicaps of such enterprises in that country (Section 4, below). The kinds and the effects of policy tools used to encourage or aid producers' cooperatives in, say, Polish manufacturing and services (Section 6.b) or Cuban agriculture (Section 6.c), are also of interest. Finally, reasons why self-managed or participatory firms appear in specific sectors (e.g., law) or in clusters (the Basque Mondragon, U.S. northwest plywood firms, Israeli *kibbutzim*) are also worthy of investigation. We can attend to these questions, however, only to the extent that the existing literature and our personal competences allow.

[5] The question of the compatibility of self-management with hierarchy in operational management is examined briefly in Section 1.11, below. The uniquely "private" aspect of the capitalist firm, as opposed to its self-managed alternative, has been transformed, in the recent theoretical literature, from a matter of ownership to one concerning the right of a party outside of the producing *team* to claim residual income (Alchian and Demsetz, 1972) or to break the constraint that total net revenue be distributed in one way or another among team members (Holmstrom, 1982; Eswaran and Kotwal, 1984). Archibald and Neary (1983) argue that even "budget breaking" is accessible to the self-managed firm, however. (See Section 1.10)

Organization and scope of the paper

Our essay is divided into two major parts: theory, and applications, with each part further subdivided into three sections. As a whole, Part I provides an axiomatic development of the dividend-maximizing firm beginning in Section 1 with the simple benchmark case in which labor is the only variable input. We examine the robustness of the resulting comparative static propositions by treating the labor input from the perspective of the worker-members in the LMF. By identifying the membership as the appropriate decision-making body and consequently introducing quasi-fixed aspects to the labor decision, we immediately alter some of the effects of the variable labor case. The labor section continues with a consideration of government intervention to influence labor allocation between firms and of contractual arrangements within the LMF pertaining to the notions of egalitarianism and membership. The section concludes with a discussion of issues of internal organization, e.g., the incentives for members to provide effort.

Section 2 is concerned with decisions affecting the capital input in general and the financing of investment in particular. Initially, the Marshallian long run model without entry is developed as a long run planning problem. After a consideration of entry by including a summary of results from some general equilibrium models, the remainder of the section focuses on capital financing with special attention to property rights in the LMF and to agency and incentive issues. Section 3 is a review of other topics from the theoretical literature, grouped under four headings: internal bargaining and codetermination, the life cycle of a producers' cooperative, imperfect competition in product markets, and the macroeconomics of the labor-managed economy including aspects of growth.

Part II, applications, is a consideration of existing organizational forms of cooperation and labor-management, with the theory developed in Part I guiding our presentation and choice of institutional detail. Section 4 deals with applications of the theory of labor-managed firms to the economy of Yugoslavia. Section 5 treats collective farms and communes, and is largely devoted to the special branch of the theoretical literature that has been directed toward those institutions. Section 6 treats, in order: producers' cooperatives and other enterprises manifesting profit-sharing and/or workers' participation in decision making, in Western economies; non-farm producers' cooperatives in the East Bloc countries and China; and both agricultural and non-agricultural producers' cooperatives in the Third World.

In all of the areas just listed, our intent has not been to provide an exhaustive and all-encompassing survey of organizational alternatives to the capitalist firm; nor have we written definitive surveys of the material touched upon. Our coverage is necessarily selective and constrained by the limits of our expertise. Where possible, we have provided the reader with references to redress, at least partially, these limitations. However, even these are marred by omissions, especially with respect to non-English language sources.

Two further broad disclaimers are also required before we proceed. First, a number of topics in the economics literature which are suggested by the term "cooperation" are not covered in our essay. These include the joint exploitation of a common resource, or "the problem of the commons," the joint consumption of a common good, or the "theory of clubs," and the joint production and use of a public good (e.g. a community fire department), all areas in which alternative allocative and distributional principles are introduced to address special aspects of the economic environment. Also consciously omitted are detailed discussions of consumer cooperatives, trade unions, mutual organizations, and business partnerships in which the partners are not workers in the enterprise. Similarly, although some of the issues discussed in this essay may be related to the theory of the not-for-profit firm and to Martin Weitzman's recent theory of the "share economy," we do not consider these explicitly. Some of the topics just mentioned are likely to be covered by other essays in the larger project of which our paper forms a part. In any case, the literature on producers' cooperatives has developed with few references to or interactions with work on these other topics, and it would go beyond the knowledge of any one specialist to survey all of them. The "share economy" is not discussed in our essay because workers must be excluded from a decision-making role in that model if the macroeconomic benefits attributed to it are to be reaped, whereas we define the worker-managed firm or producers' cooperative as an enterprise in which decision-making status is accorded to labor.

The second general disclaimer concerns our failure to treat the less obviously "economic" facets of participation, including the voluminous literatures now available in other disciplines. Relatedly, our assessments of the performance of labor-managed firms generally assume the narrow model of human motivation that is conventional in economic theory, ruling out altruism, solidarity, and other sources of non-material satisfaction or incentives. At the end of his early and pathbreaking analysis of the producers' cooperative model (1966: 749), Evsey Domar commented:

> Judged by strictly economic criteria, the co-op has not come out well. But even on these grounds, it is quite possible that a co-op may be more efficient than a capitalist or a state-owned firm in societies where membership in the co-op, as contrasted with hiring out for a job, has a strong positive effect on workers' incentives[.]

One could go further and point out that even if productivity or allocative efficiency were deficient under workers' self-management, other factors contributing to total welfare might outweigh them. Similar cautions have been echoed by numerous subsequent writers and are no less relevant to our own survey. In a word, the literature that we survey remains by and large an analysis of cooperation among individualistic agents whose only objectives are to consume goods and services and to avoid effort.

PART I: THEORY

1. LABOR ALLOCATION AND INCENTIVES

1.1. Ward's Illyria: the short run Marshallian framework

The seminal microeconomic model of the labor-managed firm is due to Benjamin Ward (1958) who considers an "Illyrian" firm in which the objective is to maximize dividend rather than profit. In the Marshallian short run, dividend is simply value-added in production (i.e. the difference between sales revenues and material costs) minus fixed capital costs with the difference divided by the number of worker-members. In this egalitarian organization, dividend replaces wage payment or salary as remuneration for labor or managerial services provided. Conceptually, worker-members could receive a wage payment, or advance, initially and then share in net income after all costs including these wages have been subtracted. Then, the workers full wage would consist of the wage advance plus the dividend. In a deterministic financial environment, the objective of the firm in the short run is unaffected by this interpretation.

Specifically, Ward's basic model in the deterministic case postulates a single-output, single-variable-input firm with a fixed capital stock in the Marshallian short run. Dividend is written as:

$$y(L) = pQ(L)/L - C/L \qquad (1.1)$$

where: p is the constant output price,
L is the variable labor input,
$Q(L)$ is the short run Marshallian production function,
C is the fixed cost associated with capital input.

If wage payments are excluded from net income before dividend is determined, the accounting dividend would be written as

$$y(L) - w = pQ(L)/L - C/L - wL/L. \qquad (1.2)$$

Clearly, the worker's full wage would be the sum of the accounting dividend and the contractual wage, w, or simply $y(L)$. Furthermore, with labor as the only variable input, maximizing

$y(L)$ is equivalent to maximizing the accounting dividend. When the status of claimants to value-added becomes important in our discussion of financial responsibility in adverse economic situations, we will return to the issue of the significance of a contractual wage.

For this stylized model of a labor-managed firm in a perfectly-competitive environment, Ward's fundamental result is that the number of workers will decrease when price rises and increase when price falls. In the simple model, a unit of labor is identical to a single worker so that labor-leisure choice by the worker is suppressed and all workers are assumed to be homogeneous with respect to skill and seniority. Since $Q(L)$ is assumed to be a neoclassical short run production function with positive but decreasing marginal product over the relevant range, the marginal product of labor depends on the number of workers in the firm. The maximization exercise for the Illyrian firm is:

$$\text{Max: } y(L) \text{ with respect to } L. \tag{1.3}$$

We define the maximized dividend which results from this problem to be $y^*(L)$ which can be determined by solving the following first order condition:

$$pQ'(L) - y^*(L) = 0. \tag{1.4}$$

This equation has the natural interpretation of equating the value product of the marginal (last-acceptable) worker with his full wage, which is in this case the dividend due to the egalitarian distribution rule. Because the fixed capital cost is subtracted from value-added to determine the net income base for calculating the dividend, the optimal L for the dividend-maximizing firm is larger than the L which would maximize the average total product of labor, i.e., $Q(L)/L$. In order to maximize average *net* product of labor in the Illyrian firm, the average total product of labor will exceed the marginal product of labor when labor is chosen optimally in the short run.

Although the rule used to determine the optimal number of workers is rational in the same sense as is that whereby a profit-maximizing twin would adjust the number of workers in the short run to equate the value product of the marginal worker to his fixed wage, the resulting workforce differs. For example, take the case in which the profit-maximizing firm hires workers at a market wage, w, and positive profits over and above the fixed capital charge are made in the short run. In the profit-maximizing firm, these profits accrue to the shareholders, not the workers. However, in the Illyrian firm, the workers as a group receive the net income after capital costs have been subtracted. In the form of a dividend share, the worker's full wage exceeds the wage paid to the hired worker in the profit-maximizing twin because it includes a share of the positive profits. Moreover, this change in distributional arrangements has allocative implications.

The combination of a decreasing marginal product of labor and a higher full wage in the labor-managed firm which must be matched by the contribution of the marginal worker (i.e. his value marginal product to the firm) leads to an optimal number of workers which is smaller than the workforce in an equivalent profit-maximizing firm which hires workers at the lower market wage and distributes the profits to its shareholders. Consequently, the simple Illyrian model predicts that:

(i) labor-managed firms will be smaller than their capitalist counterparts in the short run when profits are positive.

Furthermore, the fundamental result indicates that the Illyrian firm's response to a product price change is opposite in direction to that of a profit-maximizing twin. An increase in product price raises value marginal product of labor less than it increases dividend at the previously optimal number of workers. Consequently, the marginal worker is no longer contributing an amount equal to his dividend share. In Ward's Illyria this is grounds for dismissing the marginal worker and any others who find themselves in such a situation. Of course, the profit-maximizing firm finds it in its self-interest to increase the hired workforce because the value product of the marginal worker now exceeds the going market wage.

We demonstrate the fundamental result formally by differentiating totally the left-hand-side of Eq. (1.4) with respect to the product price, p, as follows:

$$pQ''(L)\,dL/dp + Q'(L) - [1/L]\{[pQ'(L) - y(L)]\,dL/dp + Q(L)\}. \tag{1.5}$$

Setting (1.5) equal to zero and using (1.4), we derive:

$$dL/dp = [Q(L)/L - Q'(L)]/pQ''(L). \tag{1.6}$$

Now the numerator of the term on the right-hand-side is positive as mentioned above while the denominator is negative by the assumption of decreasing marginal product. Consequently, the optimal number of workers in the Illyrian firm responds inversely to changes in the parametric product price. So long as we maintain the simple objective of dividend-maximization and allow changes in the labor force, this result is remarkably robust and, hence, is differentiated from the others presented here.

Since labor is the sole variable input in Ward's short run Illyrian firm analysis, this fundamental result leads to a companion one; namely, that output responds inversely to product price changes. Consequently, the short run supply curve for the Illyrian firm is downward-sloping. This result is known in the literature as the perverse supply response of a dividend-maximizing firm; specifically,

> (ii) in the short run single product firm, output responds inversely and thus perversely to changes in the product price.

Ward also demonstrates that in the Illyrian firm an increase (decrease) in fixed cost leads to an increase (decrease) in the optimal number of workers. Intuitively, an increase in fixed cost decreases the dividend but has no effect on the marginal value product of labor so that the marginal worker is now contributing more than he receives as a dividend. Consequently, the number of workers is increased and the increased fixed cost is spread over a larger group, thus diluting the impact on any one individual.

Formally, differentiating totally (1.4) with respect to C yields:

$$pQ''(L)\,dL/dC - [pQ'(L)\,dL/dC - 1]/L + [y(L)\,dL/dC]/L = 0. \tag{1.7}$$

Using (1.4), we derive from (1.7) $dL/dC = -1/pQ''(L)L$, from which it clearly follows that:

> (iii) labor and, in the short run, output respond positively (negatively) to increases (decreases) in fixed cost.

Of course, the profit-maximizing firm changes neither the hired workforce nor output as fixed cost changes in the short run.

Considering the allocative implications of dividend-maximization in the Illyrian economy, Ward argues that labor will not be allocated efficiently across firms due to the rents earned by workers in individual firms. Suppose short run profits in differing amounts can be made by two profit-maximizing firms, each paying workers a parametric market wage, w. In order to maximize profit, each firm hires labor until the marginal worker contributes just his wage in additional value product. Since the market wage is the same for both firms, so too is the value marginal product of labor. This equality is a necessary condition for Pareto Optimality or efficient allocation of labor in the short run.

Now consider the implications of dividend maximization for these two firms. Because positive profits are earned in a profit-maximizing counterpart, each dividend-maximizing firm will use less labor and workers will receive a full wage (dividend) which exceeds the market wage, w, paid by each twin. Since it is the dividend to which the firm equates the value product of the marginal worker, the resulting allocation of labor is not efficient if dividend differs between the two firms. In this case, a reallocation of labor toward the firm with the higher dividend, and thus higher value marginal product of labor, from the other firm would increase total output in the economy. Therefore, dividend maximization in the short run does not lead to the equalization of value marginal products across firms because the full wage differs from the market wage paid by the profit-maximizer. Consequently, Ward claims that:

> (iv) labor allocation will be Pareto-inefficient in the Illyrian economy when short run profits are non-zero in profit-maximizing twin firms.

These four behavioral propositions and the fundamental result which are derived in Ward's seminal article provide the focus for much of the subsequent theoretical literature on the labor-managed firm (hereafter, LMF).

Before considering these contributions, we wish to emphasize the role played by rents and their distribution in the "perverse" Illyrian responses. Here, we use the term "perverse" to indicate behavior different from that of the profit-maximizing twin. If the maximum attainable profit in the short run for the twin hiring labor at the market wage is zero, then the dividend-maximizing firm would choose the same number of workers as the profit-maximizing firm and the resulting dividend would be exactly equal to the market wage. Furthermore, if negative profit results in a short run maximum for the twin, a larger number of workers would be optimal for the dividend-maximizing firm so that the fixed cost burden could be spread among more workers each of whom earns a dividend below the market wage paid by the twin to hired labor. The existence of positive short run rent is crucial to the first perversion, i.e., smaller output, and non-zero short run rent is essential to the fourth perversion, the short run inefficient allocation of labor.

It seems natural to ask why a distributional scheme which supports differential returns to capital in the short run is any more efficient than one which yields differential returns to labor. Again in the absence of short run profit for the capitalist twins, the dividend-maximizing firms would each pay a dividend equal to the market wage and thus achieve an efficient allocation of labor. In the traditional short run theory of the profit-maximizing firm, capital is assumed to be fixed. This immobility of capital insures that assigning unequal returns to this factor because of different rents does not cause an allocative disturbance by the very definition of the short run. Rather perfect mobility of labor in the short run and a parametric market wage lead to efficiency. One could take exception to such a characterization of the short run and argue that labor mobility may be costly and that welfare may be improved when labor stays put even if differential dividends result. What is more disturbing is the tendency of the Illyrian firm to respond to improvements in product markets by dismissing some of its workers, the fundamental result to which we turn for further analysis.

1.2. The fundamental result: decomposition and extensions

Hajime Miyazaki and Hugh Neary (1983) show that the perverse response of the demand for labor to changes in the parametric product price is due to an income effect attributable to the distribution of non-zero short run rents. Miyazaki–Neary decompose the effect of an output price change on the demand for labor into a "pure-price" effect and a "fixed-cost" effect analogous to the familiar Slutsky decomposition of consumer demand into a substitution and an income effect. The "pure-price" effect is equivalent to the labor demand response to a product price change in a profit-maximizing firm (hereafter, PMF) which is necessarily positive since an increase in price increases the value marginal product of labor. However, the "fixed-cost" effect is equivalent to response (iii) so that in the case of a decrease in fixed cost the improved profitability of the LMF leads to a decrease in the demand for labor and, in this context, a decrease in membership. The dominance of the income effect yields the fundamental result for the LMF.

The presence of such income effects and their negative influence on the demand for labor are pervasive in any decision in an LMF which is based on the objective of dividend-maximization. In his seminal contribution analyzing a multi-output, multi-factor, dividend-maximizing firm, Evsey Domar (1966) argues that an increase in the product price of one of the many outputs produced by the LMF would lead to a substitution in the product mix toward the output whose price increases and away from the other products. Although the supply response could easily be positive, Domar contends that the demand for labor is likely to respond inversely to a product price change. Thus a countervailing tendency to the product mix effect arises in the LMF due to the income effect on the demand for labor while, in the twin PMF, an increase in the price of one of its products would yield a corroborating increase in the demand for labor because of the increase in the value marginal product of labor. Domar concludes that supply curves are likely to be less elastic in a labor-managed economy (hereafter, LME) due to dividend-maximizing objectives than they are in the traditional capitalist-market economy (hereafter, CME). Nonetheless, Domar's consideration of the multi-product LMF leads to the reasonable expectation that supply curves in the LME would be upward-sloping.

Steven Rosefielde and William Pfouts (1986) challenge Domar's contention that the demand for labor responds inversely to a product price change in the multi-factor, single-output LMF. They demonstrate that the demand for non-labor inputs is also influenced by these "income effects" so that, in general, the responses of both non-labor and labor inputs to a change in the product price are ambiguous in sign. Furthermore, the supply response is indeterminate in the general case. Interestingly Domar claims that, for the case of radially-parallel isoquants, the supply curve is downward-sloping. Rosefielde–Pfouts provide a counterexample of a non-homogeneous production function with radially-parallel isoquants to disprove this assertion.

Since the multi-factor, single-output firm is a useful stylization for empirical work and since comparative static propositions are the basis for empirical testing, these issues are important. John Bonin and Wataru Fukuda (1986) validate Domar's claim that "radially-parallel" isoquants preserve the Ward results, namely, output and labor respond inversely to changes in the product price for all homogeneous production functions (the functional forms used most commonly in empirical work). Furthermore, Bonin–Fukuda show that, for any technology in which labor is an inferior input, the supply response is positively sloped while labor responds inversely to a change in product price. Finally, for the cases of a Hicksian-normal two-variable-factor production function (i.e., the second order cross partial derivative is non-negative), these authors demonstrate that the more intensive is the use of the non-labor inputs, both variable and fixed, the more likely are the two Ward perversions to occur. Somewhat counterintuitively then, LMFs with labor-intensive technologies tend to exhibit normal comparative static results.

The fundamental result that the demand for labor is inversely related to changes in output price is nonetheless somewhat robust. If we allow members to vary their labor input according to the usual labor-leisure tradeoff, Norman Ireland and Peter Law (1981) show that the response of a fixed membership LMF to an increase in profitability will depend in general on the countervailing income and substitution effects. However, when membership is adjustable, increased profitability will lead to a decrease in the optimal number of workers even though the remaining workers may work longer hours. The introduction of product price uncertainty does not eliminate the fundamental tendency either. John Bonin (1980) demonstrates that an increase in the expected product price leads to a decrease in the optimal membership if expected dividend is to be maximized.

One might usefully question the appropriateness of the Ward Illyrian objective of dividend maximization for most cooperative organizations as does Joan Robinson (1967) in a terse comment on Domar's paper. She asks: when profitability increases due to a change in a financial parameter, how shall the members choose whom among the brethren will be dismissed so that the remaining members will enjoy a higher remuneration? Considering the moral issue of group solidarity to be a basic foundation of the LMF, Jaroslav Vanek (1969) argues that it is nonsense to think that a working cooperative organization would "mutilate" itself for the sake of gaining a small additional increase in income per member. Branko Horvat (1971) claims that Yugoslav labor-managed firms maximize the residual profit after paying a contractual wage to the members so that dividend-maximization is an inappropriate objective for Yugoslavian firms.

Perhaps the strongest justification for continuing to consider the implications of dividend-maximizing behavior in an LMF comes from Vanek himself. Although he thinks that no LMF is a pure dividend-maximizer, Vanek acknowledges tendencies in that direction. For example, improved profitability could lead to nonreplacement of retiring workers so that in the longer term the contraction of the workforce occurs. Vanek has written a comprehensive treatise (1970) on the labor-managed economy, which is, essentially, a detailed development of traditional Marshallian microeconomic theory if dividend replaces profit as the maximand for the firm. Most of the economic literature on the LMF over the last decade and a half follows this Ward–Domar–Vanek (hereafter, WDV) tradition. No one denies that within an organization a simplistic objective like profit-maximization or dividend-maximization can not capture the richness of organizational goals and sub-goals. Yet simple models are the starting point for understanding the complex issues of real-world organizations. For the LMF and the LME, dividend-maximization has important implications for studying the economics of cooperation and labor-management.

1.3. Property rights, labor mobility, and egalitarianism

In his comprehensive paper, Domar also introduces the supply of labor to the theory of the LMF by considering a labor supply curve which is upward-sloping in wage/labor-offered space for a fixed membership LMF. Although Domar does not consider explicitly labor/leisure decisions, he assumes that members can find alternative employment so that labor offered is positively related to the dividend earned in the LMF. Domar discusses two cases; one in which supply constrains the attainment of the dividend-maximizing labor force, and another in which the LMF would demand a smaller labor force at the dividend-maximum than would be supplied (unemployment). In the supply-constrained case, the Ward comparative static results are reversed as increased profitability due to an increase in product price or a decrease in fixed costs leads to an increase in labor (members) along the upward-sloping supply curve. The unemployment case corresponds to unconstrained dividend-maximization as discussed above but it also provides the motivation for a consideration of contractual arrangements which benefit those in the firm at the expense of those excluded by an egalitarian sharing rule.

Denote by y^* the dividend-maximum for the LMF for some specifications of product price and fixed costs and consider the unemployment case. There are more people willing to work at y^* in the LMF than are demanded; denoted by L^* (the dividend-maximizing labor force). Because Domar assumes that the labor supply curve is upward-sloping, the L^* people who are accepted by the LMF earn rents. It would be possible to increase these rents by offering some of the excluded workers employment at a wage below y^*. By the properties of the dividend-maximizing solution developed earlier, the value marginal product of an additional worker can be approximated by y^* so that such an offer would increase the rents shared among the L^* members and be acceptable to a previously excluded worker whose reservation wage is met. Clearly, however, we would now have an inegalitarian firm since workers performing the same tasks would receive different remunerations.

The explicit characterization of membership rights is the major contribution of an insightful review of Vanek's book by James Meade (1972). Once a LMF is formed, Meade argues, members have certain rights and responsibilities. Regarding short run adjustment to changes in financial parameters, Meade considers the rules appropriate for permissible membership changes. The first rule proposed is that no member may be dismissed involuntarily, nor may any member leave the cooperative without the permission of the remaining members. Although the second part of this rule may appear coercive as stated, the idea is that a member should not be able to abdicate responsibility for commonly incurred obligations, e.g., enterprise debts, without a mutually acceptable arrangement. The second rule proposed by Meade is that no one may be conscripted, so that any additions to the membership must be voluntary, and that any new members are added with the consent of the original members.

The introduction of these memberships rights and responsibilities have important allocative consequences. As profitability increases, due for example to a price increase, the LMF can not contract the membership in the short term since all existing members have a right to the new higher dividend. So long as the LMF was in equilibrium prior to the change in a financial parameter in the sense that no member wished to leave and was prevented from leaving by the other members, the LMF will exhibit group solidarity when output price increases to yield an increase in the dividend. Of course, the increase in dividend might attract new applicants to the LMF but the existing members would not be willing to take them on because additions would decrease their own now higher dividend. Hence, the egalitarian LMF in which any member shares equally in value-added will exhibit a solidarity response to increased profitability.

To see this result formally, let p be the original product price and p' be a new higher price. In the tradition of the literature, assume that the maximized dividend in the original equilibrium is a market-clearing one, denoted y_0. In the initial situation, with y^* indicating the dividend maximum and L^* the accompanying optimal membership,

$$y^*(p) = pQ(L^*)/L^* - C/L^* = y_0. \tag{1.8}$$

Now, let L' be the labor force which maximizes dividend at the new price, i.e.,

$$y^*(p') = p'Q(L')/L' - C/L'. \tag{1.9}$$

If the LMF exhibits group solidarity and does not dismiss any members, the total income to be divided among the L^* workers can be written as;

$$Y(p', L^*) = p'Q(L^*) - C. \tag{1.10}$$

The solidarity dividend $Y(p', L^*)/L^*$ is larger than $y^*(p)$, which is equal to y_0, but smaller than $y^*(p')$, the maximized dividend for p'.

However, if the alternative earning opportunity is y_0, the reduction in membership required to earn $y^*(p')$ can not be achieved by voluntary withdrawal. Furthermore, although others would wish to join to earn the higher dividend, the existing members would not approve their membership as the dividend decreases with increases in membership for any level above L'. This latter condition follows from the properties of the dividend-maximizing solution since value marginal product of another worker is below the corresponding egalitarian dividend at membership levels higher than the optimum.

Alfred Steinherr and J-T Thisse (1979) rationalize further this solidarity result by considering the self-interest maximizing behavior of the individual member of an LMF in which any dismissals will be undertaken by randomly laying off workers who will then receive the alternative dividend, y_0 which is smaller than the dividend earned by those still employed in the LMF after the price change. They correctly assert that if an individual member is risk-neutral or risk-averse, he will prefer the certain outcome of the solidarity dividend to the probability weighted average of the higher maximized dividend and the alternative dividend. However, they also argue that the LMF will respond to price decreases with solidarity as well so that no quantity supply response would be observed in response to any price change.

Meade, on the other hand, takes a different view of the response in an egalitarian LMF to a decrease in price from its initial equilibrium level. He states that the supply response will be perfectly inelastic above the initial price but he argues that it will be perfectly elastic at the equilibrium price up to the initial quantity level. This "backwards-L-shaped" supply curve seems suspect. What are the consequences of all members agreeing to disband the cooperative and join other firms paying y_0 when price falls below p? The "rats leaving a sinking ship" solution would ignore the debt burden, presumably leaving it to be borne by others (who are unspecified). However, since the members incurred collectively the short run debt burden, this solution seems inappropriate.

1.4. Shutdown and temporary hiring: short run equivalence

John Bonin (1981) argues that a proper shutdown condition can be specified if, when some members leave to earn the alternative dividend available elsewhere, y_0, they also retain their responsibility for the collective debt. Formally, denote as Y the total income earned by members when N are employed in the LMF so that:

$$\begin{aligned} Y(p'', N, L^*) &= Ny(p'', N) + (L^* - N)y_0 \\ &= p''Q(N) - C + (L^* - N)y_0. \end{aligned} \tag{1.11}$$

The first component of total return to the membership is the product of those members working in the LMF, i.e., N, and the appropriate evaluation of the dividend, i.e., $y(p'', N)$. The second component is the earnings of those members working outside the LMF at the going market dividend y_0. Since membership status is unaffected by this price decrease, the appropriate maximand is total income which is then divided equally among the L^* members. As Bonin demonstrates, this portion of the supply curve is equivalent to the Marshallian counterpart in the PMF when the alternative dividend y_0 is equated to the market wage, w, paid by the PMF.

Formally, maximizing $Y(p'', N, L^*)$ with respect to N yields the first order condition:

$$p''Q'(N^*) = y_0. \tag{1.12}$$

Intuitively, labor is employed in the LMF to the point where the value marginal product is equal to its alternative wage. Since $Q''(N)$ is negative and $pQ'(L^*) = y_0$, employment outside of the LMF of some members will be optimal when price falls to p'' below p. By replacing y_0 with w, the employment condition is made equivalent to the hiring condition for labor in the PMF. This same condition would apply to price increases above the initial level if the LMF could hire workers at y_0 leading to full equivalence between the two firms, an issue we take up in the next section.

To demonstrate the equivalence of the shutdown decisions of the PMF and the LMF, consider a technology which generates U-shaped short run average variable cost curves. For the PMF the shutdown price, therefore, is the price which just covers average variable cost at its minimum point. For the LMF, the shutdown price occurs where revenues generated by production in the LMF exactly equal the income that the members employed in the LMF, according to equation (1.12), could earn elsewhere. Revenues are used in this comparison because the members will share the fixed cost burden regardless of the source of income.

Formally, let p^s be the shutdown price and N^s the corresponding employment level, then:

$$p^sQ(N^s) = N^s y_0 = N^s w. \tag{1.13}$$

Clearly, algebraic manipulation yields,

$$p^s = wN^s/Q(N^s). \tag{1.14}$$

The expression on the right hand side is average variable cost and the equivalence of the two shutdown points is demonstrated.

Brewer and Browning (1982) extend the Steinherr–Thisse approach to the case of multiple outputs and multiple inputs. For the situation in which the price of one output increases, the supply response is positive due to changes in the output mix. However, decreases in output price lead to discontinuities in supply curves and irreversibilities. These abnormalities are traceable to the assumption made by Brewer and Browning that the LMF may be dissolved costlessly with no remaining financial obligation to the members if product markets deteriorate sufficiently to make the alternative return more attractive to all members. Consequently, the specification of the members' responsibility for debt incurred influences significantly the predicted short run behavior of the LMF.

1.5. Inegalitarian firms and temporary hires

To this point, we have considered formally only the egalitarian LMF in which members receive equal shares in total income regardless of their place of employment. The introduction of alternative employment possibilities for members when product market conditions dictate such relocation allows the possibility of temporary hiring if product market conditions improve. Such temporary work arrangements lead to inegalitarian remuneration within the LMF. Suppose that temporary workers who themselves may belong to other firms can be engaged by the LMF at the prevailing market dividend. Reconsider the situation of an increase in product price from p to p'. Although it is not optimal for the L^* original members to expand membership, total income can be increased by engaging temporary workers at the rate y_0. So long as the value marginal product of labor exceeds the compensation for temporary workers, the income shared by members can be increased by the addition of these workers. Consequently, the condition for optimal employment will be equation (1.12) above for all prices either above or below the initial equilibrium value p. In the case of price increases, the LMF consists of two types of workers, i.e. members and temporary workers. Remuneration for equal work is now unequal with members receiving a share in the total income of the LMF while temporary workers receive the prevailing market dividend.

As Bonin (1981) argues, temporary work arrangements may yield full equivalence of the short run Marshallian supply curves in the LME and the CME. The difference is distributional in that short term rents accrue to capital in the CME while the members receive the rents in the LME. This reconciliation of dividend-maximization with short run efficient allocation of labor (temporary workers move to equate the value marginal product of labor across firms) has been criticized as sacrificing equity for efficiency. However its inegalitarian nature depends to some extent on one's frame of reference. A simple example will help to make the point.

Consider an LME consisting of two firms, each of which produces a single product, and denote these LMF(X) and LMF(Y) to correspond to their respective products. Suppose that an initial equilibrium is disturbed by a change in consumer preferences and that the demand for X increases. The price received by LMF(X) for its product increases as a result of the demand change while the price of the product of LMF(Y) decreases. In the short run, temporary workers will be engaged by LMF(X) and voluntarily supplied from the membership of LMF(Y) until value marginal products are equated between firms. All members in LMF(X) are treated equally in that each receives a dividend share larger than y_0 and all members in LMF(Y) are treated equally in that each receives a dividend share smaller than y_0. However, the difference between the remuneration of the two sets of workers is not due to differences in work skills or intensity. Rather the difference could be considered as an entrepreneurial rent paid to the members of LMF(X) because they are producing a product the demand for which has increased (they bet on the right product).

In the CME an equivalent scenario would have all workers receiving the market wage, w, and the capitalist in industry X earning rents while the capitalist in industry Y suffers a short term loss. The temporary work solution when it involves transfers among LMF's of members on temporary work assignment is inegalitarian in the same sense that entrepreneurial rents (losses) differ among firms. Stephen Sacks (1977) discusses these transfer arrangements and relates the efficiency results to the Yugoslav institution of BOALS (Basic Organizations of Associated Labor).

Many of the proposed solutions to an incomplete labor market in the LME involve inegalitarian treatment of this sort in the short run. James Meade's inegalitarian cooperative is similar to his joint-stock organization in that the dividend which any member receives depends upon when his membership began. Consider again the case of two firms in which dividends and thus value marginal products are unequal. If the members of LMF(X) can offer to workers in LMF(Y) membership at a lower dividend than they themselves receive, efficient contracts which satisfy Meade's rules for admittance can be arranged. A new member from LMF(Y) will be paid a dividend below his value marginal product in LMF(X) but above his value marginal product (and dividend) in LMF(Y). Therefore, the dividend for the original members of LMF(X) increases and they welcome the new member. Similarly, the new member joins voluntarily because his earnings are higher in LMF(X). Although paying the new member less than his value marginal product may seem like exploitation in Joan Robinson's terms, this relocating worker receives more than his value marginal product in his previous firm.

This suggests the important question: will the remaining members of LMF(Y) agree to this transfer? By leaving, the exiting member generates an increase in the value marginal product of labor in LMF(Y) but also imposes a higher debt burden per member on those remaining. Without compensation paid by the departing member, the members of LMF(Y) will not willingly release the person requesting withdrawal. Since the difference between value marginal products indicates that total revenue can be increased by a reallocation of labor from LMF(Y) to LMF(X), the departing member can purchase his release from LMF(Y) and still receive a net increase in income which makes him willing to move. Clearly, so long as any such difference in value marginal products is expected to persist, some mutually agreeable arrangements are possible with side payments and the resulting differentiated dividends. As Meade concludes, the inegalitarian cooperative economy organized in this way can achieve a Pareto efficient allocation of labor in the short run.

Meade's resolution of this fundamental inefficiency differs from temporary work arrangements in one important way; namely, members actually leave one cooperative and join another. Clearly, this movement of labor is an appropriate permanent adjustment to any long-term change in market conditions. On the other hand, when workers retain their membership in a parent LMF while on temporary assignment in another LMF due to short term market conditions, no such adjustment occurs. Temporary arrangements of this sort are more reasonable when the fluctuations in product prices are likely to be transitory. However, if the change in consumer preferences between the outputs produced by X and Y described above is permanent, some mechanism encouraging the production of X and discouraging the production of Y is necessary. In the LME, labor must move from less profitable to more profitable ventures in the longer term.

Murat Sertel (1982) analyzes a competitive market for worker-partnership deeds which completes the labor market by establishing transaction prices for membership in all LMFs based on the discounted present value of their expected future returns. Sertel's solution assures an efficient allocation of labor since the membership price captures fully any expected future rents in an LMF when the market is competitive. Gregory Dow (1986) formalizes the general equilibrium notion of the worker-partnership deeds economy. Meade's rules of permissible membership change are incorporated into this economy as workers make capital gains or suffer capital losses when they sell their membership rights in the competitive market.

The practicality of the Sertel–Dow solution to incomplete labor markets in the LME may depend upon arrangements in financial capital markets. For example, the eventually high cost of membership shares in some successful plywood cooperatives in the Pacific Northwest of the U.S. is often cited as a reason for their conversion to the more traditional form of capitalist organization. Unless workers have access to perfect capital markets in which they can borrow against the future profitability of the membership share to be purchased, financial barriers to entry may arise in worker-partnership deeds markets rendering suspect their competitiveness. Further research integrating capital and labor markets in an LME seems important to a full resolution of the issue of selling membership rights. Some of the relevant financial issues will be discussed in our next part of the essay entitled "capital".

1.6. Fiscal intervention and labor transactions

Another possible way to complete the labor market is through government intervention. Norman Ireland and Peter Law (1978) propose an adjustment mechanism in a mixed LME which achieves the efficient allocation of labor and reverses the Ward perverse supply response through an enterprise incentive fund which specifies transfer payments, either a tax or a subsidy for each LMF. The transfer payment is based on the relationship between the value marginal product of the membership in an LMF, the dividend after any membership adjustment and a macroeconomic shadow wage, W. If we take M to be the initial membership before the introduction of the fiscal scheme, the transfer is calculated to be:

$$[pQ(L^*) - C - WL^*][(L^* - M)/M]. \tag{1.15}$$

The first bracketed term is the "profit" earned by the LMF after adjusting its membership if labor is "costed out" at its shadow wage, W the macroeconomic parameter. The incentive fund then subsidizes (taxes) a "profitable" LMF which expands (contracts) its membership.

Similarly, an "unprofitable" LMF which contracts (expands) its membership is subsidized (taxed). By combining this fiscal transfer with the definition of dividend, income per member for any LMF can be written as:

$$W + [pQ(L) - C - WL]/M. \tag{1.16}$$

Clearly, if L is chosen to maximize income per member, the value marginal product of labor will be equal to the shadow wage in each LMF. Therefore, the incentive fund of Ireland and Law leads to a Pareto-efficient allocation of labor in the LME as long as the shadow wage maintains full employment by equating exactly the aggregate demand and the aggregate supply of labor. Furthermore, an increase (decrease) in the product price for a LMF will lead to an increase (decrease) in the optimal membership thus assuring the positively-sloped supply response.

In the Ireland–Law proposal, membership responds to market forces in the appropriate Pareto-optimal way while the full wage received by members in different firms may differ because of the fiscal transfer. Starting from an equilibrium in which there are no rents, consider an increase in product price for LMF(X) and a decrease in price for LMF(Y). LMF(X) will expand and LMF(Y) will contract until the value marginal product of labor is equalized between firms and the shadow wage is adjusted, if necessary, to achieve full employment. However, all members in LMF(X), not just the original members, will receive a higher full wage than all members in LMF(Y). Furthermore, since subsidies will be paid to both firms even though LMF(Y) is "unprofitable" in the sense described above, the incentive fund will not be running a balanced budget. The rents shared by the "lucky" workers who leave LMF(Y) for LMF(X) may lead to distributional equity concerns. The resulting imbalance of the fiscal budget should be considered if such a scheme is proposed to complete the labor market. A possible solution to both issues is to impose a lump sum tax on LMF(X) to cover fully the deficit and provide additional revenues to LMF(Y) in a lump sum fashion if this would be necessary to equalize the full wage in both firms after the relocation of workers.

In addition to the unbalanced budget problem, William Thomson (1982) notes two other limitations of the Ireland-Law scheme; namely, the necessity of the center being able to observe the output of the firm to determine the appropriate transfers and the assumption of competitive price behavior on the part of the firms. Using analysis familiar from the theory of incentives, Thomson shows that the observability of output is a necessary condition for any centralized incentive scheme to achieve an efficient allocation of labor in the LME. Such an impossibility result is in sharp contrast to the decentralized price solutions commonly found in incentive theory. However, once observability of output is assumed, Thomson shows that schemes can be designed which do not require firms to exhibit price-taking behavior (in the incentive theory language, the schemes are strategy-proof as the desired result is a dominant strategy equilibrium) and which are assured of running a balanced budget. These schemes are more complicated than the Ireland–Law scheme (they require a message space of more than the one dimensional space of Ireland-Law). Furthermore, in the class of schemes comparable in communication complexity to the Ireland-Law scheme, an impossibility result is shown regarding the incompatibility of a balanced-budget solution with even weaker (Nash) incentive properties.

1.7. Implicit contracts; membership and employment

The decision-making environment of the implicit contract theory literature (see Martin N. Baily (1974) or Costas Azariades (1975)) is used by John Bonin (1984) and Hajime Miyazaki and Hugh Neary (1983) to analyze employment and membership decisions in the LMF. We follow Bonin and distinguish short run employment decisions from medium term membership determination for risk-neutral workers in this section. We return to a consideration of risk-averse workers and risk-sharing arrangements, which is the central focus of the implicit contract theory literature, in part three after our discussion of capital in the next part. The LMF is characterized as a group of members who take financial responsibility for a fixed debt obligation in return for the use of a short run production technology. When the group is formed, the market price of the single output good produced by this technology is assumed to be unknown. Membership constitutes a claim to uncertain net income, i.e., revenues minus the fixed debt obligation, of the LMF.

After the number of members is decided, the output price becomes known. In this temporal sequence of events the members then determine employment in the LMF taking into consideration any available alternative sources of income for members who are not employed in LMF production. Although membership is decided before employment in a chronological sense, the need for potential members to evaluate expected income before applying for membership necessitates the determination of an employment policy for the LMF before optimal membership can be considered.

To simplify the exposition, we require each member either to work full-time in the cooperative or to be engaged full-time in an alternative activity. In reality, labor-leisure concerns may be important for determining the response of the LMF to changes in price and other financial parameters. We shall treat this matter in a later section which deals with the general issue of internal incentives. As is customary in the literature, we assume that all workers (i.e., potential members) are equally skilled and that there is no internal ladder ordering cooperative members (for, example, according to seniority). The results would be essentially unchanged if differential claims to membership earnings were to be based on seniority and skill differences. Complications would occur however if such concerns were relevant to the formation of the group (e.g., if certain skill requirements were included in the technology).

We define the egalitarian cooperative as an organization in which members share equally in net income from all sources once the group is formed. This notion of egalitarianism differs from that found in Steinherr–Thisse (1979) and Brewer–Browning (1982). In a fixed membership cooperative, these authors treat differently members who are excluded (furloughed) from LMF production and involved in an alternative activity in the short run. Following Ward, they define the LMF dividend as value-added minus the fixed debt obligation with this difference divided by the number of members actually employed (involved in cooperative production). If the dividend is greater than the income received by excluded members, either as compensation for being furloughed or as payment for labor services provided elsewhere, rents accrue to members employed in the LMF. We consider such an LMF to be *ex post* inegalitarian. However, since each member faces the same probability of being employed in or excluded from LMF production, it is *ex ante* egalitarian.

An LMF will be defined to be *ex post* egalitarian if income is initially pooled, the fixed debt obligation is then paid, and the resulting residual is shared equally among all members regardless of employment status. Notice that when the dividend calculated on the basis of employed members exclusively falls short of the alternative payment, income-pooling and this sharing rule imply a symmetric treatment of membership rights and responsibilities. The same worker/members who share in cooperative rent when market conditions are good also bear collective responsibility for the debt obligation when market conditions are poor. As Meade (1972) suggests, if the cooperative is truly egalitarian, all members should sink or swim together.

A contractual employment rule, $n(p)$, is derived as a function of the output price, p, when an initially fixed membership, m may participate in an alternative activity which returns w. A short-run Marshallian production function, $f(\ )$, is used and a fixed cost, R, is incurred as the rental charge for the single period. Due to the egalitarian nature of our LMF, the objective is to maximize pooled earnings so that the problem is written:

$$\text{Maximize: } [n(p)/\bar{m}]y(p) + [1 - n(p)/\bar{m}]w \tag{1.17}$$

$$\text{with respect to } \quad 0 \leqq n(p) \leqq \bar{m} \tag{1.18}$$

$$\text{where } \quad y(p) = \{pf[n(p)] - R\}/n(p). \tag{1.19}$$

We denote as $\hat{n}(p)$ the solution to the above problem and notice that it yields a supply relationship and a shutdown price $\hat{p}$ equivalent to those discussed in Section (1.5). Using this solution to characterize the optimal membership decision, we let $\bar{p}$ denote the minimum price at which it becomes optimal to employ fully the membership, $\bar{m}$, in LMF production. When only the distribution of output price, $g(p)$, is known, the first-order condition for optimal membership m^* is given by:

$$\int_{\hat{p}}^{\bar{p}} \left[\frac{pf\{\hat{n}(p)\} - \hat{n}(p)w}{m^*}\right] g(p)\, dp + \int_{\bar{p}}^{\infty} \left[p\left\{\frac{f(m^*)}{m^*} - f'(m^*)\right\}\right] g(p)\, dp = \frac{R}{m^*}. \tag{1.20}$$

The first term on the left-hand side of (1.20) is expected revenue minus opportunity cost in LMF production where the opportunity cost is measured as payments foregone in the alternative activity by members employed in the LMF. Taking the second term on the left-hand side, by itself, and equating it to the right-hand side indicates that the LMF acts like a dividend-maximizing firm when the membership is fully employed in the LMF with no member taking part in the alternative activity.

Equation (1.20) is the basis for Bonin's sensitivity analysis and his discussion of the policy implications, a summary of which follows:

(i) the availability of a monetary return to the alternative activity which can be pooled with revenues from LMF production is preferable to having only an individual-specific return (utility or a non-marketed-in-kind return) with respect to encouraging membership and promoting a non-perverse short-run supply function.

(ii) the subsidization of capital costs to the LMF (a policy prescription contained in the Industrial Common Ownership Acts in Britain) generates negative incentives to membership and yields less expected output.

(iii) to encourage formation of LMFs, public policy should focus on Keynesian short-run demand management prescriptions for stimulating aggregate demand (contrary to the implications of the simple Ward model).

(iv) a balanced budget fiscal policy can be designed (which taxes the LMF in a lump-sum way and distributes the tax revenue through an unemployment compensation scheme for furloughed members) to increase both membership and expected output in the LMF.

Result (i) indicates that the non-existence of an alternative employment outlet for members may lead to overemployment in the LMF compared to the PMF efficiency benchmark in the short run. Bonin derives a downward-sloping segment of the short run supply curve which arises due to the need to meet the debt obligation even during periods of low market demand. Low output prices require increased production to generate sufficient revenues to cover the debt obligation with further product market implications. A criticism sometimes levied against the plywood cooperatives is that they "dump" during periods of low market demand to maintain the income levels of the members.

Result (iv) indicates the feasibility of designing a self-financing support scheme which will encourage membership. Suppose that the alternative payment to members who are temporarily unemployed is public unemployment compensation. By judiciously levying a lump sum tax on the LMF, the government can finance these payments by running a balanced-budget on average. Furthermore, this combined tax-subsidy program will increase the optimal membership in a LMF although it will have an ambiguous effect on expected output and a depressing effect on LMF employment. However, by considering individual product market characteristics (i.e., specifying $g(p)$ more concretely), the government can assess the relative expected costs in terms of employment and output of this program across various markets.

Completing the labor market in the Marshallian short run is possible with many suggestions in the literature concerning temporary work arrangements. However, Avner Ben-Ner (1984) argues that a successful LMF faced with the possibility of hiring labor on a temporary or spot market will eventually return to the traditional capitalist organization of production. Ben-Ner develops the incentives for replacing members with hired labor whenever possible (due to retirement or other voluntary leave) because of positive rents. With dividend above the market wage, the LMF can always increase the return per remaining member by replacing members with equally skilled hired workers. He argues that such a process will continue logically until only a single member (the capitalist) remains and all other workers are hired hands.

In a subsequent part of this essay, we return to the behavior of an LMF in an economy with a spot labor market and treat the life cycle of the LMF from birth to death as conceived by Hajime Miyazaki (1984b). What is developed in this part is the close relationship between incomplete labor markets in the LME and the distinctive behavior of the LMF. As Jacques Dreze (1976) argues, when rents are competed away, organizational form becomes irrelevant. With labor "de-commodified", the LMF behaves differently from its PMF counterpart as much of the economic literature demonstrates.

1.8. Incentives and internal organization under self-management

In addition to investigation of the implications of workers' self-management for factor and output levels and mix, and for industry structure, in the various 'runs' (membership variable, capital fixed; all factors variable, industry structure fixed; all factors variable, entry and exit permitted; etc.), theoretical understanding of the self-managed work organization requires examination of the internal organizational and incentive attributes of the enterprise. To make such an analysis tractible, membership and non-labor inputs are often taken in it as given.[6]

[6] Some exceptions are Sertel, 1982, and Ireland and Law, 1985a.

This part of our discussion will be pursued in two sub-sections. In the present one we investigate incentive structures and the variation of real effort or labor input levels of an existing membership under an implicit assumption that inputs of homogeneous labor by individual members are accurately measurable at zero cost. In later sub-sections we drop the measurability assumption and investigate questions of monitoring and hierarchy, along with more general issues of organization, decision-making, and implementation.

Effort supply under self-management

This analysis is motivated by the observation that the number of workers does not determine effective labor input to an enterprise, even if hours of labor are fixed.[7] With effort a variable,[8] the effective labor input will depend on worker motivation, the incentive structure internal to the enterprise, and perhaps external labor-market factors. We assume that there is no production uncertainty and, for the time being, that labor is homogeneous and costlessly measurable, and we focus on incentives internal to the enterprise in order to clarify the properties of alternative payment schemes.[9]

Proponents of workers' self-management have sometimes argued that whereas capitalist firms offering a fixed wage in exchange for fulfillment of minimal expectations provide no incentive to greater effort, the profit-sharing producers' cooperative rewards more (and smarter) effort and permits workers to reach their most preferred effort/income positions.[10] From an opposite standpoint, detractors

[7] Inclusion of "effort" or "efficiency labor" as a distinct variable in recent neoclassical discussions parallels the labor power/labor distinction in Marxian approaches. Compare, for example, Shapiro and Stiglitz, 1984, with Bowles, 1985 and Lazonick, 1982.

[8] Alternatively, much the same analysis applies if effort and time are simultaneously variable, or if effort is viewed as constant and only hours are chosen by the worker.

[9] While measurement problems are assumed absent in the present section, it should be pointed out that some kind of uncertainty, asymmetric or incomplete information, or labor market imperfection may be required to motivate the analysis. Without such realistic elements the internal incentives problem could be obviated by simultaneous choice, at the outset of membership, of a contractual effort level for all states of the world, along with a wage vector or distribution rule, and with reference only to the alternative opportunities provided by the external labor market.

[10] Vanek, 1970, Chapter 12.

of cooperation frequently suppose that only the profit-oriented firm, which pays workers their value marginal product, generates ideal individual work incentives, whereas by their income-sharing nature producers' cooperatives must dilute work incentives and thus generate strictly sub-optimal effort equilibria.[11]

Each of the above arguments relies on a caricature of the denigrated enterprise type, although one to which some members of the respective species may more or less conform. In the first argument, the capitalist firm is viewed as having no flexibility in its contractual offerings, and a labor market in which workers have a variety of effort-wage options from which to select is assumed absent. In the second argument, the idea that producers' cooperatives might (like the idealized capitalist firm) also tie individual reward to individual effort is passed over on the assumption that such behavior is foreign to the character or values of cooperation.

Formal analysis beginning with the assumption of perfect monitoring ability supports neither position. Taking working conditions and other possibly relevant factors as given and focusing upon the effort-income trade off, we begin with the proposition that an individual's work incentives are optimal when they lead him to perform only such labor, on the margin, as generates additional value at least as great as the value of leisure foregone, and to allocate effort between income-earning activities[12] in such a way that the value of labor's marginal product is equal across them. In equilibrium, the worker's marginal rate of (indifferent) substitution between income and leisure would be equal to the marginal social product of labor. This outcome obtains only when the marginal product coincides, at least locally, with the marginal private return to the worker. Such coincidence is expected, for example, when the worker is self-employed, when the social and market value of the product are the same, and when there is no marginal tax on income. The same will hold when the worker is employed by an enterprise which monitors and pays out his individual marginal product—i.e.,

[11] E.g., Williamson, 1980.

[12] I.e., where more than one job can be held or where there is more than one income earning activity, as in the collective farms discussed in Section 5.

the increment in the value of firm output due to this one worker's effort, with all other labor and non-labor inputs held constant.[13]

While neoclassical economics conventionally maintains that the worker is paid the value of his marginal product by the competitive capitalist enterprise facing a perfect labor market, this proposition usually arises in expositions where the quantity of labor provided by an additional worker is taken as a datum. Payment of the value of marginal product for variations in effort by a worker, once on the job, requires implementation of a payment scheme going beyond the fixed contractual wage of the ordinary textbook model. One theoretical possibility is that the worker simultaneously selects his effort level and employment contract, in which case the conventional supposition that wage equals marginal product might continue to be maintained under ideal conditions. Another possibility is to pay a per unit (e.g., hourly) wage equal to the value of the incremental product of some small labor unit times the number of such units contributed, which will give a close approximation to strict VMP payment if the units are reasonably small and the VMP schedule is continuous and not precipitously steep.

Whether the capitalist enterprise is able to attain the latter standard is an empirical question. Conceptually, the outcome should depend upon the competitiveness of the labor market and the monitoring capabilities of the firm, among other factors. At the present level of theoretical discussion, given the assumption of perfect and costless monitoring, we could for argument's sake take literally the firm's payment of a marginal product wage hypothesized in neoclassical theory, whence we could assume that the incentive optimality of self-employment and of employment by the conventional firm are equivalent.

For the worker-managed firm, theoretical investigations have often begun by assuming that a distribution rule will be chosen from a constrained set of ideologically or organizationally determined possibilities, and have gone on to investigate both the positive implications of such rules and their degree of approximation to a

[13] In this case, each worker receives what he contributes when viewed as the marginal worker, although not when seen as an *infra*marginal member of the labor force.

marginal product payment outcome. The rules examined have been suggested either by self-management practice or by values assumed compatible with the self-management concept or socialist theory.

From the standpoint of values, the egalitarian strain in self-management[14] has suggested that all workers would have equal claims to enterprise net earnings, or at least equal claims for equal work. The residual-claimancy status of the workforce, given uncertainty over actual distributable income, also implies, from this same standpoint, that the payment rule will tend to define shares rather than fixed sums and will thus assign to each worker some type of proportional entitlement. Socialist theory, on the other hand, supplies the Marxian concepts of "to each according to his needs" and "to each according to his work," which have nominally underlain practice in collective farms and other socialist producers' cooperatives. Finally, the "needs" and "work" distribution systems have gained currency through adoption in theoretical models of the Chinese agricultural production team of the 1960's and '70's, the Soviet collective farm, and pure communes such as the Israeli *kibbutz*, some historical Mormon producers' cooperatives, etc. The practice of establishing pay scales and distributing dividends proportionate to base pay, widespread in Western, Yugoslav, and other industrial cooperatives, may be interpreted as a form of work-proportionate payment. Where this practice is accompanied by maintenance of a welfare fund or provisions for community goods without reference to the pay scale, an element of "needs" distribution is also seen to be present. In view of the concentration of existing theoretical literature on the two pure systems of "distribution according (or proportionate) to work" and "distribution according to need," and on systems mixing both principles in varying proportions, our discussion proceeds by considering the incentive characteristics of these idealized systems.

"Distribution according to work"

What is perhaps most interesting about incentives under systems of payment proportionate to labor input is that, assuming perfect measurability of labor, it appears just as likely (*a priori*) that

[14] See "Sources of Interest" in the Introduction, above.

incentives will be *excessive* (from a welfare standpoint) as that they will be insufficient (from the same point of view). Optimality of incentives can be approached by (a) scaling nonlabor factors so that labor's marginal and average net products are equal, or (b) subtracting some net income from the amount to be distributed in proportion to labor. Optimality will also be achieved if (c) effort choices are made on the assumption, by each worker, that other workers will respond proportionately to changes in his/her own labor input. In the absence of (a), (b) or (c) (which are discussed further below), incentives will be non-optimal because the incremental returns to labor will be influenced substantially by labor's average net product, which will usually diverge from marginal product.

Specifically, letting l_i be worker i's effective input of (homogeneous) labor, letting $i = 1, 2, \ldots, n$ index the enterprise's N members, $L = \Sigma_{i=1}^{N} l_i$ be the total labor input, $Q = f(L, \cdot)$ be the value of output (where $\cdot$ represents all nonlabor factors, here assumed fixed), and C be nonlabor costs, we have (as our definition of "distribution according to work")

$$y_i = (l_i/L)(Q - C) \tag{1.21}$$

as worker i's income, and

$$dy_i/dl_i = \eta_i f_L + (1 - \eta_i)(Q - C)/L \tag{1.22}$$

as i's incremental return on labor, where

$$\eta_i = (dL/dl_i)(l_i/L) \tag{1.23}$$

is the elasticity of aggregate with respect to individual labor input. When $dL/dl_i = 1$ by the Cournot assumption that $dl_j/dl_i = 0$ all $j \neq i$, and when l_i/L is small, dy_i/dl_i is close to $(Q - C)/L$, or the average net product of labor. In this case, in the range of a short-run production function in which both marginal and average net product of labor are declining, dy_i/dl_i will exceed f_L, labor's marginal product, so the work incentive will be excessive. Indeed, dy_i/dl_i can be positive and substantial even when marginal product is zero. Collective income distribution thus displays a built in externality, a "tragedy of the commons" in which workers may on the margin seek to lay claims to a positive average product, governing "workpoint" value, even though their incremental labor does not increase real output. The assumption that $0<\eta_i<1$ also implies that work incentives are *inadequate* in the range of the production function (where such a range exists) in which average net product of labor is below marginal product.

"Distribution according to needs" and mixed systems

Unlike collective or work-proportionate distribution, communal or needs-based distribution performs, upon formal investigation, much as is expected on the basis of casual thinking. In "needs" distribution, the individual's income may be determined as an assessment of his particular consumption needs, or incomes within the enterprise may simply be equal—what is crucial is that incomes are not differentiated with respect to work contributions. Following the standard format of modelling "needs"-based incomes as equal,[15] and retaining previous notation, we have

$$y_i = (1/N)(Q - C) \tag{1.24}$$

and thus

$$dy_i/dl_i = (1/N)f_L(dL/dl_i). \tag{1.25}$$

Here, incremental return is related entirely to marginal and not at all to average product, yet the sharing formula assures that work incentives are suboptimal in all ranges unless dL/dl_i is close to N.

The term dL/dl_i is presented without restriction in the above equations because, while it is plausible to suppose that a worker will make the Cournot assumption that his incremental effort has no effect on that of fellow workers in a large enterprise, the effects of one worker's decisions upon those of fellow workers could in some cases, most obviously those involving small teams, be nontrivial. If workers include an estimate of these effects in their calculations of incremental return to labor, incentives will be changed accordingly. In particular, as Eqs (1.22) and (1.25) show, incentives will become more sub-optimal as dL/dl_i approaches 0 from above, corresponding to a net "free-rider" effect, and more optimal as dL/dl_i approaches L/l_i, which has been called the "perfect cohe-

[15] Sen, 1966; Chinn, 1979; Israelsen (who calls an enterprise practicing this system a "commune"), 1980; Putterman, 1980, 1981; Ireland and Law, 1981.

sion" or "complete emulation" value (Chinn, 1979; Ireland and Law, 1981). At the latter value, indeed, incentives would be optimal under either payment scheme and regardless of the relationship between marginal and average products at equilibrium.

In view of the structural significance of the reaction term dL/dl_i, it is perhaps not surprising that a number of authors have proposed arguments to the effect that the "complete emulation" value may or must hold in equilibrium.[16] However, Putterman (1985b) argues that where reactions are based on utility maximization in the face of an aggregate labor input which is varying but given to the individual worker, and where such reactions are not strategic choice parameters in their own right, then this result is most improbable—and particularly so when the requirement of rationality, or of consistency between anticipated and observed reactions, is imposed. Only by virtue of repetitiveness and/or other conditions making it possible for workers to communicate threats or commitments might it be possible to generate an equilibrium of positive, rationally anticipated reactions that are themselves strategic choices to which each worker binds him/herself by precommitment.[17]

Cognizance by team members of the interdependence of their outcomes and effort decisions suggests another solution to the incentive problem, namely that of collusion, which may be either explicit or implicit. Although invocation of cooperative optimization over effort levels has been casual in some of the literature, especially when large teams are at issue, some concept of collusion in this sphere appears helpful in explaining apparently successful outcomes in cases of essentially "communal" (or "needs"-based) income distribution, such as the Israeli *kibbutz*. Implicit collusion may be generated by optimization over strategies of precommitment to contingent behaviors in one period games or in supergames in which penalties for breach of commitment are entailed (Archibald and Neary, 1983; MacLeod, 1984; Putterman, 1983).

With the incentive externality in the case of collective or

---

[16] See, e.g., Bradley, 1971; Bonin, 1977; Berman, 1977; Markusen, 1975, 1976; and the discussion in Putterman, 1985b.

[17] The distinction between these two kinds of reactions is precisely parallel to that between passive reactions, associated with the conventional idea of "conjectural variations," and strategically chosen reactions, in oligopoly. See Guttman and Miller, 1983.

work-based distribution being traceable to divergence of marginal from average net product, three further possibilities for assuring incentive optimality present themselves. First, the producers' cooperative can simply choose levels of factor inputs and of membership such that labor's marginal and average net product are equal in equilibrium, which makes dy_i/dl_i equal to marginal product in (1.22). As Ireland and Law point out, this results directly from those longer-run adjustments that bring labor to the top of the average net revenue (or profit per worker) curve.[18] Second, when incentives are excessive because average net product is above marginal product given forthcoming effort supply, just enough of net output can be deducted from the portion to be distributed according to the work input so that marginal return is again made equal to marginal product. Although if Pareto-optimality of work incentives is the only concern the deducted portion could simply be buried or given away, more likely enterprise members would prefer to apply it to the provision of public goods or to distribute it according to some principle independent of labor input. Under such conditions, Sen (1966) has shown that an optimal incentive system can be attained for a cooperative composed of identical individuals by mixing "needs"- and work-based distribution, and Putterman (1981) and Putterman and DiGiorgio (1985) have shown that Sen's mix would be chosen by self-interested majority voting if the distribution of members' labor inputs is symmetrical about its mean. However, no single mix of linear egalitarian and work-based distribution rules could simultaneously provide *precisely* optimal incentives to all cooperative members if preferences between labor and leisure differ across members, because the work-proportionate component of distribution causes the marginal return to labor to differ across workers when workers anticipate heterogeneous levels of own labor input, as will be the case under heterogeneous preferences. This non-optimality of simplified systems mixing "work" and "needs"-based distribution rules when workers differ in their preferences for leisure and income has been generalized by Browning (1982) who shows that no pre-specified distribution rule can produce Pareto-optimal incentives under heterogeneous pre-

[18] Ireland and Law, 1982, pp. 78–79.

ferences unless the production technology meets a highly restrictive requirement labelled "$(n-1)$-additivity."

"Internal wages" and "value-added sharing"

A third method of achieving optimal work incentives under "distribution according to work" is to specify and enforce a ceiling on remunerable labor input. This result arises in a body of research on incentives in worker-run firms that is *not* posed explicitly in terms of "distribution according to work" or "according to needs": namely the work of Sertel and colleagues, much of which is collected in Sertel (1982). The two main kinds of incentives employed in the enterprises modelled by Sertel are (a) "internal wages" amounting to fixed pre-announced payments per unit effort input, and (b) "value added sharing" schemes, where net revenue is divided among workers according to a pre-determined sharing formula. Since the sharing formulae of (b) do not adjust *ex post* to reflect actual effort inputs, "value added sharing" may be seen as part of the general family of incentive systems that also includes "needs" or "egalitarian" distribution. It can accordingly be expected to behave much like "distribution according to needs" as analyzed above. "Internal wages," on the other hand, are a variation on "distribution according to work," but one in which the proportionality factor $(Q-C)/L$ (from (1.21)) has been replaced by a constant, w_i, which is by assumption the correctly anticipated value of that expression.[19]

Two results demonstrate the equivalence of the incentive systems just described. First, Dirickx and Sertel[20] and Sertel, Basar and Selbuz[21] show that enterprises using "internal wage" schemes perform optimally only when internal wages are supplemented by quotas specifying maximum rewardable effort inputs. When workers choose the most remunerative *feasible* set of internal wages *without* specifying maximum effort by quotas, these incentives "lead them to *over* work themselves."[22] "Internal wages with quotas" achieves

[19] That the apparently fixed wage must equal the proportion is a result of requiring that total wage payments exhaust enterprise surplus.

[20] Chapter 3 in Sertel, 1982.

[21] Chapter 7 in Sertel, 1982.

[22] Dirickx and Sertel, p. 44, emphasis original.

optimality by specifying wages sufficient to elicit *at least* the optimal effort levels (equivalent to those obtained in hypothetical capitalist enterprises with marginal product wages), but setting a ceiling on effort levels at precisely those optima. The excessive effort response to internal wages is attributable to the wedge between payments based on average net revenues (which w_i must be equal to due to feasibility and the pay-out constraint) and marginal product, the same wedge observed under "distribution according to work." Imposition of work quotas is thus an alternative to the incentive diluting device of the "mixed distribution" system discussed above.

Second, Dirickx and Sertel (op. cit.) and Basar, Selbuz and Sertel,[23] find that optimal effort levels can be obtained under value added sharing schemes only when workers select effort *cooperatively*—i.e., so as to maximize aggregate as opposed to individual utilities. This result parallels those from the analysis of "needs" distribution, such as Sen (1966).

1.9. Imperfect measurement and monitoring issues

The somewhat unexpected result that in a neoclassical framework with no attention to group solidarity or to the morale effects of participation and profit sharing, collective internal distribution rules may generate *excessive* work incentives, may be seen to hinge critically upon the assumption of perfect and costless measurability of labor input. Suppose that a high degree of imperfection in monitoring is unavoidable. Then in distribution according to work, one receives a portion

$$\hat{l}_i/L$$

of the net income, where

$$\hat{l}_i = l_i + \epsilon_i, \tag{1.26}$$

ϵ being a random error term with $\mu(\epsilon)=0$, $\sigma^2_\epsilon \geqq 0$, and ϵ_i a realization.[24] The utility-maximizing effort level of a risk-averse worker-member will now in general depend upon the variance of ϵ

[23] Chapter 8 in Sertel, 1982.

[24] The denominator of the ratio introduced just above might be written $\hat{L} = \Sigma \hat{l}_i$, but L can be substituted if (a) it is directly inferred from output Q, although the individual $\hat{l}_i$ is not, or (b) the approximation $\hat{L} \cong L$ is assumed, based on ϵ having mean 0, and on N being large (and, thus, on the law of large numbers).

(inversely, on the accuracy of $\hat{l}_i$ as a measure of l_i), although a negative relationship between l_i^* and σ_ϵ^2, meaning that better monitoring elicits greater effort, need not follow. For example, with a quadratic utility function $U^i = ay_i - b(y_i)^2 + u(T - l_i)$ where T is available time and u is a concave function of its argument, l_i^* will vary negatively with σ_ϵ^2 only when the marginal product of labor is greater than its average net revenue product. However, if each worker expects to be paid on the basis of observation $\hat{l}_i$ only if monitored during the period in question, to be paid as if he worked L/N units otherwise, and to be monitored with probability ρ which is an increasing function of the overall level of monitoring in the enterprise, then the utility-maximizing effort of risk-neutral workers would be an increasing function of monitoring under more general conditions.[25] If distribution according to work input would otherwise have generated excessive incentives, measurement error may serve as an offsetting factor, compensating for the original incentive externality or even turning the hypothetically excessive incentives into sub-optimal ones.

If measurement error increases with size of enterprise, and declines to zero (or, more precisely, loses its relevance) for a one-man enterprise, it could operate also to offset the advantages of technological scale economies. This might, for example, account for the attractiveness of household level peasant farm production over group (collective) farm production even where technical scale economies turn out to be present. However, when comparing enterprises of given size *across organizational form*—e.g., in the comparison of large capitalist and large cooperative firms—whether measurement problems should be viewed as a particular disadvantage of producers' cooperatives is unclear.

It is often supposed, for example, that because of cooperative principles or philosophy—perhaps translating into less hierarchical decision-making or management structures (see below)—producers' cooperatives must tend to reward different work contributions with insufficient discrimination. A well-known example is the argument by Alchian and Demsetz (1972) that because a cooperative team lacks an exclusive residual claimant, no member has an adequate incentive to monitor the (work) contributions of the others. A key

[25] Putterman, 1986b.

assumption in this argument is that monitoring effort is itself unmonitorable and thus cannot simply be purchased on a payment for service basis. The Alchian–Demsetz argument does not imply that measurement is perfect in capitalist firms, but it does assert that when claims to enterprise income above contractual payments are concentrated in an owner-manager, that individual has optimal incentives to monitor and to attempt to pay out the marginal products of other team members, measured up to the point at which the incremental returns on and costs of monitoring are equated. To date, this argument has not been formalized, and it remains unknown under what (if any) specifications of worker utility functions, of the process generating observational error, and of payment rules, the model would hold true.

In order to fully establish the Alchian–Demsetz argument regarding incentives to monitor,[26] it is necessary to further specify the technology of monitoring, how competitive the market for manager-owners is, and related matters. Assuming it to be possible to identify plausible conditions that suffice to validate the argument, it remains the case that Alchian and Demsetz's hypothesis is limited to the effects of a particular specification of property rights on *incentives to monitor* but not on the ability to observe accurately. Additional factors affecting the accuracy of monitoring, and the optimality of the level of monitoring, are the technology of monitoring, which will be a function of spatial and technical characteristics of the work process, and workers' abilities to impede or distort observations. It is possible, for example, that while concentrated residual claimancy creates heightened incentives to monitor, this factor could be partly or wholly offset by reduced efficacy of monitoring when much information concerning workers' real productivities cannot be easily observed from "above".

To establish an optimal level of monitoring it would further be necessary to account for workers' tastes for being monitored or for freedom from monitoring. The level of monitoring required by a given organization is likely to depend also on social and interpersonal relations characteristics of that organization, for example,

[26] This paragraph follows Putterman, 1984, pp. 172–175.

whether its "atmosphere" is cooperative or antagonistic.[27] Cable and FitzRoy (1980), Bradley and Gelb (1981) and other authors have suggested that profit-sharing can set in place incentives for "horizontal monitoring" that could be reinforced by a broad social dynamic, whereas hierarchical monitoring and competition within organizations generate both counter-productive behavior and specific attempts to thwart monitoring. To quote Cable and FitzRoy (p. 103):

> If the numbers involved are not too large and shirking imposes perceptible losses on co-workers with whom there is some personal interaction, then "positive collusion" and "horizontal monitoring" to encourage effort is the rational response by the peer group. This represents a reversal of the widely observed "negative collusion" to restrict output under traditional piece-pay schemes, where informal social sanctions and even violence against "rate-busters" have a lengthy history.

Many production enterprises are probably characterized by a situation in which there are significant economies to be captured if agents cooperate in an ongoing fashion in the pursuit of production, innovation, cost-control, marketing, and related goals, yet precise monitoring of individual contributions is prohibitively costly or informationally infeasible. To avoid individualistic "sub-goal pursuit" which might undermine the organization's ability to return benefits to participants and to society, it is then necessary to find ways of aligning workers' interests with organizational performance. Williamson (1975), for example, looks at a long term employment relation incorporating potential promotion up vertical job ladders with pay attached to jobs rather than to the individual worker, and more intermittent and qualitative assessment of performance. According to Williamson, this relationship, said to characterize some sectors of the U.S. labor market, economizes on low

---

[27] In producers' cooperatives, the ideological suppositions of participants (and also, in some cases, of influential external agents such as leaders of the cooperative movements, or political authorities) may significantly affect the legitimacy with which discrimination in reward assignments, and hence the process of monitoring itself, is viewed. The social and political dynamics of the organization may also impact on its effectiveness at developing and implementing incentive schemes. Many historical producers cooperatives may have performed poorly or failed due to factors inhibiting the development and operation of material incentive systems, as argued (with respect to collective farms in Tanzania and China) by Putterman, 1985a.

productivity monitoring, reduces irritating supervision, and inculcates loyalty or at least greater congruence of individual and enterprise goals. The result is said to be more "consummate" as opposed to "perfunctory" job performance.[28]

Workers' cooperatives may benefit from the availability of their own characteristic strategies for aligning individual and group interests in job performance. In an examination of share-cropping which makes an explicit analogy with profit-sharing, Stiglitz (1974) found that when monitoring of individual inputs was prohibitively costly, output-sharing could be superior to paying fixed wages and attempting to measure performance. To the extent that exact contributions are not ascertainable, especially on a short-term basis, the shared residual claimancy of workers in producers' cooperatives may help to motivate cooperative attitudes toward work (including innovation). Unmeasurability of inputs creates an *ex post* "communal" element in the cooperative, in the sense that the benefits of one worker's effort are likely to be captured in part by other group members. This observation suggests that examination of incentive issues in pure "communes", an an ideal type, may have usefulness beyond the limited incidence of communes themselves. In particular, it may be useful to examine the conditions under which "collusion" in determining effort and, more generally, performance levels, is likely to come about. Shared residual claimancy may provide a material basis for the "collusion" phenomenon, but a wide variety of other factors, including size of the operating/accounting unit, continuity of membership, and kinship, cultural, ideological, or other ties, may help determine whether effective "collusion" occurs.

Efforts to formally model the monitoring problem for cooperatives include Bradley and Gelb (1981), FitzRoy and Kraft (1984), Ireland and Law (1985), and Putterman (1986b). Ireland and Law avoid part of the problem posed by Alchian and Demsetz by

[28] Other theorists have argued that the incentive to work must be to some degree internalized rather than based upon strict marginal calculations. As A. K. Sen writes: "It is certainly costly and may be impossible to devise a system of supervision with rewards and punishment such that everyone has the incentive to exert himself. Every economic system has, therefore, tended to rely on the existence of attitudes toward work which supersedes the calculation of net gain from each unit of exertion." (1977, pp. 333–334) See also Arrow, 1974, and Leibenstein, 1982.

assuming that monitoring is an ordinary input that can be purchased, as opposed to an unobservable factor the outright purchase of which would be uninforceable. Their model assumes payment "according to work" (1.21), with $\hat{l}_i$ (1.26) substituted for l_i when a worker is monitored and payment according to average net revenue (resembling (1.24)) when a worker is not monitored.[29] The variance of the error term in $\hat{l}_i$ declines with monitoring frequency, which is a parameter selected by the cooperative. The cooperative also chooses the proportion of the workforce that is monitored.

In Ireland and Law's model, worker utility functions embodying risk aversion via a mean-variance formulation (utility is a positive linear function of expected income and a negative linear function of the variance of income) generate positive effort responses to monitoring frequency. Allowing membership, effort, and monitoring coverage and frequency to vary, Ireland and Law find "the Illyrian response to price change . . . robust despite the inclusion of monitoring" although "effort is unaffected by [an increase in fixed costs] where the membership can freely adjust the proportion to be monitored." They also find that while "[i]n zero-profit long-run equilibrium both [capitalist and LM] firms would produce the same level of output, assuming the identical costs of monitoring and the same production function . . . because of its choice of monitoring parameters, the capitalist firm is likely to have a smaller labor force and a higher level of effort per worker." (p. 31)

Putterman's paper considers the cooperative team only, and assumes that payment follows a convex combination of (1.21) and (1.24). The analysis, summarized at the beginning of this section, shows that with $\hat{l}_i$ (1.26) substituted for l_i, and with error in the observation of each l_i assumed to have a mean of zero and a variance that approaches 0 as a scalar monitoring variable approaches infinity, risk-neutral workers will be unresponsive to monitoring and risk-averse workers may respond either positively or negatively, depending upon their utility functions and the technology. It is suggested that models in which monitoring determines not only the variance but also the mean of the distribution of payments

[29] In each instance, monitoring costs are deducted before determining net revenue. As in Calvo and Wellisz (1978), observations from those periods in which a worker is monitored do not affect pay in periods in which he is not monitored.

conditional on effort will tend to be more consistent with conventional notions of the monitoring-effort relationship.

In the papers by Bradley and Gelb and by FitzRoy and Kraft, each worker is assumed to earn a fixed share of the cooperative's income, a situation assimilable to "needs" or "communal" distribution as discussed above. For both sets of authors, also, "monitoring" (also referred to as "encouragement" and "cajolement"[30]) is assumed to influence the choice of effort level not by changing the monetary return to labor, but rather by altering the disutility of effort. Bradley–Gelb and FitzRoy–Kraft assume (in conventional fashion) that workers engage in monitoring of fellow workers up to the point at which the marginal disutility of the monitoring effort equals the marginal utility of the increment to their individual profit shares. While Bradley and Gelb do not attempt to solve for or characterize the equilibrium choice of monitoring levels, FitzRoy and Kraft are able to show how a worker's own monitoring effort, which brings him or her disutility, would be chosen as a function of the actual variation of co-workers' effort levels in response to it.

1.10. Self-policing incentive models

In both Bradley–Gelb and FitzRoy–Kraft, as just seen, monitoring is modelled as affecting choice of effort level by a direct effect on utility, rather than by influencing material reward. In the Ireland–Law and Putterman models, in which monitoring affects effort by generating reward adjustments, the problem posed by Alchian and Demsetz with respect to the motivation of monitoring is not addressed. However, the Alchian and Demsetz hypothesis, according to which optimal monitoring is motivated by exclusive residual claimancy by a capitalist, and in which labor input by workers responds positively to improved monitoring, has itself not been formalized. The formal principal-agent, incentive, and hierarchy literatures (see, e.g., Holmstrom (1982), Mirrlees (1976), and Malcomson (1984)) focus on the properties of incentive schemes, and usually do

[30] Bradley and Gelb in addition refer to monitoring as "control." In FitzRoy and Kraft's model the activity of monitoring includes "material assistance to help in adverse circumstances."

not explicitly model the monitor's choice of monitoring level.[31] Where the issue of observability of effort arises, it is often addressed, as in Holmstrom's paper, by characterizing payment schemes that elicit efficient effort choices in the absence of observability, circumventing Alchian and Demsetz's monitoring problem.

A discussion in this spirit with respect to workers' self-management has been provided by Archibald and Neary (1983). These authors begin by confirming Browning's (1982) finding, reported earlier, that a fully efficient incentive outcome is unattainable in "a one-stage game with Nash behavior." They argue, however, that Pareto-efficient vectors of effort and income can be attained in cooperatives through a two-stage process. This process begins with a tantonnement bidding procedure through which an efficient agreement point is arrived at. The problem is to find a means of assuring that the optimal effort vector, once identified, is achieved even when individual effort inputs are unobservable. Like Holmstrom, Archibald and Neary show that a reward scheme in which all members of the self-managed enterprise are penalized when any member performs sub-optimally, will effectively assure the efficient outcome in the face of individualistic behavior.

As with Holmstrom, Archibald and Neary find it necessary that an agent outside of the working group be the recipient of any surplus over the minimal payments specified for the case in which there are defections from the effort vector that has been agreed upon. A problem arises since, if producers' cooperatives are defined as groups of workers who have exclusive claims to their net revenue and always exhaust it by some sharing procedure, then Holmstrom's result seems to show the necessity of a capitalist residual claimant or some similar external "principal." Archibald and Neary, however, argue that the analogous function (i.e., of a "sink" for absorption of revenue extracted in a collective penalty) can be performed for workers' cooperatives either by associated self-managing accounting units of larger worker-run enterprises (e.g., the Yugoslav BOALs) or by banks entering into special agreements with them.

[31] Partial exceptions in this regard are Mirrlees's paper, some of the radical literature including Bowles (1985), and in the recent tournaments literature, O'Keeffe, Viscusi, and Zeckhauser (1984).

A similar but distinct approach is taken by MacLeod (1984), who supposes that a self-managing team selects its income-sharing formula so as to maximize an internal social welfare function, which might (as in his example) be Rawlsian. MacLeod argues that the problem posed by Holmstrom can be answered through a cooperative solution to the repeated "game" of effort allocation, in the spirit of Friedman's (1977) oligopoly solution and Tyson's (1979) discussion of effort in labor-managed firms. One period departure from first-best optimal behavior temporarily rewards the defector with a net utility gain due to higher leisure and only slightly reduced income. However, if all workers are committed to reverting to (Cournot-) Nash or free-rider effort levels in all periods following a defection, then, given that defections will become known through their effect on output, the defector suffers in the long run because his or her action destroys the cooperative equilibrium. With a sufficiently long horizon and low discount rate, it is never optimal to defect (or "shirk").

In MacLeod's model, as he notes, individual workers may have incentives to leave their cooperatives for alternative employment if the "social welfare function" determining the payment scheme is too egalitarian. MacLeod argues that if cooperatives generate higher labor productivity and have other desirable features, society may be better off when these workers are induced to stay with their teams by exit barriers such as forfeiture of a capital stake. The recommendation of exit barriers and emphasis on distributive justice determinants of internal distribution in self-managing teams seem to stand in partial opposition to efforts to increase the competitiveness of the "quasi"-market for labor in LMEs by facilitating enterprise creation and dissolution, since greater competitiveness would undercut the possibility of internal incentive schemes based on SWFs not unanimously shared by an enterprise's workforce.

1.11. Self-management and decision-making

Another aspect of internal organization that may be central to the relative efficiency of different organizing modes is the structure of information collation, processing, and decision-making both with regard to such conventional theory of the firm variables as the levels of various inputs and outputs, and to the internal allocation of the enterprise's resources among various activities and tasks (following the view of the firm as an *internal market,* proposed by Alchian and other authors). Simon (1971) and Williamson (1975, 1980) have argued that efficient decision-making in large organizations must be hierarchical, because (according to Simon) hierarchy is a means of economizing on the management of complex information in the face of bounded rationality, and (according to Williamson) the alternative to hierarchy is a multi-channel communication network which must become overloaded when the number of agents becomes large. Williamson (1980) also contends that "peer groups" (a construct presumably akin to producers' cooperatives[32]) will be less efficient than hierarchical firms in decision-making respects, both because inferior decision-making will fail to assign individual workers to their most productive tasks, and because cooperative principles will oppose the emergence of stable management ranks.

In the absence of further definitional strictures on self-management, it is impossible for us to know whether the Williamson and Simon concerns constitute a general problem for producers' cooperatives. That is, assuming that a certain amount of hierarchy and specialization in decision-making is conducive to more efficient enterprise operations, all else being equal, we cannot rule out the adoption of hierarchical forms by self-managed firms, provided that ultimate control resides in the working body, as opposed to an owner-manager, financial shareholders or the state. The picture of the democratic cooperative holding meetings late into the night to make detailed management decisions, as for example in the production teams of Chinese communes during certain radical campaigns, appears to merely caricature the worker-managed firm as a general phenomenon. Although some producers' cooperatives may be constrained to follow particular decision-making procedures due to external directives, constitutions, or ideological requirements, the self-managed firm in general can be assumed to choose its organizational structure, and the level of participation in decision-making by average workers, in much the same way as it makes other decisions—that is, so as to satisfy the preference of members. If detailed participation in decision-making is not desired,

[32] But see Putterman, 1981 and Russell, 1985.

for whatever reason, delegation remains consistent with the principle of ultimate democratic control by the workforce.[33]

The question is whether the decisions made democratically by members, whether over an investment strategy, over the details of organizational structure and delegation of authority, or over working conditions, can be efficient in view of the fact that (a) ultimate decision-making rights are dispersed through the workforce and (b) there are limits to the acquisition of managerial experience and training by the workforce as a whole. In contrast to Simon and Williamson, McCain (1973: 386) has proposed the counter-claim that " 'collective entrepreneurship' is a powerful means of conserving entrepreneurship, a resource which other systems waste." Jensen and Meckling's (1979) charge that "none of the advocates (or analysts) of the ... labor-managed firm have suggested ... a well-defined set of procedures for solving the decision-making problem within the firm when the preferences of the workers are not all identical (p. 488)" is correct insofar as it points out the paucity of attention to the decision-making function in the theoretical literature.[34] If decision-making is ultimately by majority vote, then it would be subject to the many serious problems of rationality and consistency which have become familiar from the public choice literature of recent years.

2. CAPITAL ALLOCATION AND INVESTMENT

2.1. The long run planning problem

The long run planning problem for the LMF can be considered in the usual Marshallian context in which labor and capital are the

[33] Williamson's (1985, chapter 11) distinction between strategic and operating decisions might be relevant here.

[34] E.g., the Ward model assumes the existence of a manager who manipulates variables so as to maximize profit-per-worker, but what makes the manager adhere to this goal is not made explicit. Semi-formal discussion of member decision-making with respect to investment was introduced by Furubotn and Pejovich (1970) and Neuberger and James (1973). See also the just cited discussion of the collective choice problem by McCain (1973). A formal model of democratic voting in a hypothetical semi-collective farm is presented by Putterman (1980, 1981) and Putterman and DiGiorgio (1985).

only two inputs both of which are freely variable. For this problem, entry is precluded so that the full market effect of Marshall's long run analysis are not considered. The time period is taken to be of sufficient length so that the user cost of capital, denoted r, can be treated as a fixed parametric price per unit of use by the LMF. Initially, we use the same framework developed in the first part of this essay but replace the fixed cost, C, with the capital expenditure, rK, in the determination of dividend.

Long run dividend is written:

$$y(L, K) = pQ(L, K)/L - rK/L \tag{2.1}$$

where $Q(L, K)$ is the long run neoclassical production function. Examining the first order conditions for dividend-maximization with respect to both inputs in the planning problem, we have:

$$pQ_L(L^*, K^*) - y(L^*, K^*) = 0, \text{ and} \tag{2.2}$$

$$pQ_K(L^*, K^*) - r = 0. \tag{2.3}$$

Taken together to represent the optimal choice of technique by the dividend-maximizing firm, we have:

$$Q_L/Q_K = y^*(L, K)/r \tag{2.4}$$

where the numerator on the right hand side of (2.4) indicates the maximum dividend, which acts as a shadow price for evaluating labor, and the marginal products of labor and capital on the left hand side are evaluated at optimum levels of both inputs.

Suppose initially that $y^*(L, K)$ is equal to the wage rate, w, paid to workers in a PMF twin. Then, Eqs (2.2), and (2.3) would be analogous to the appropriate first order conditions for profit maximization. In such a case, we would observe again an equivalence between the input choice of an LMF and the twin PMF (facing the same capital user cost, r). If, on the other hand, the twin PMF is profitable; i.e., $pQ - wL^* - rK^*$ is positive, the maximized dividend, $y^*(L, K)$, will exceed w as the workers in the LMF share the rents. Consequently, the choice of technique characterized in (2.4) will be more capital-intensive than the profit-maximizing one which considers w to be the factor cost of labor. In essence, the shadow factor cost of labor is higher in the LMF due to the higher dividend paid to workers.

Analogous to the fundamental result in the WDV short run problem, the LMF will be more capital-intensive than the PMF twin when the latter earns positive profit in the long run. Determining the optimal long run scale of operation of the LMF is more complicated. As Saul Estrin (1982) demonstrates formally, a dividend-maximizing optimum for the LMF facing parametric prices for output and capital and using a variable-returns-to-scale, homothetic production technology occurs at the critical isoquant where returns to scale change from increasing to decreasing. If constant returns to scale were assumed throughout, dividend would be invariant to scale since profit would increase in exactly the same proportion as each input.

Both Meade and Vanek consider the significance of this result for the dividend-maximizing LMF in the Marshallian context. In the CME, entry leads to a zero profit long run competitive industry equilibrium in which each PMF produces at the minimum point of a U-shaped average cost curve and the industry technology exhibits constant returns to scale. In the LME, dividend-maximization is consistent only with constant returns to scale in the long run if prices are parametric. As Meade and Vanek observe, the LMF exhausts economies of scale but never produces in a region of decreasing returns. Rather, if the PMF twin could earn positive profit before entry occurred and thus maximize profit by operating in the decreasing returns region, the LMF would produce on a smaller scale, i.e., that represented by the minimum point of the PMF's average cost curve, and choose a more capital intensive technique in the homothetic case.

The comparative statics of the planning problem depend on the way in which the slope of the isoquants change with respect to scale along rays from the origin (c.f., Norman Ireland and Peter Law (1982)). In the homothetic variable returns case, the slope of the isoquants is invariant to scale and therefore output is determined by the critical isoquant for any value of the product price. An increase in price leads to a higher dividend and a more capital-intensive technique only as labor becomes more expensive due to its increased shadow price. With a parametric unit price for capital, a higher dividend induces a substitution towards the relatively-less-expensive input, capital. In this case, the absence of a scale response in the long run leads to the continuance of the short run labor perverse result and a perfectly price-inelastic supply curve.

As Ireland and Law demonstrate for the general case in which the slope of the isoquants may vary with scale, if the ratio of the marginal product of capital to the marginal product of labor increases (decreases) with scale so that a change in the product price will lead to a more capital (labor) intensive technique chosen by the PMF with given input prices, the supply response of the LMF is positive (negative). Nonetheless, the optimal amount of labor responds inversely to a price change so long as the PMF twin is earning positive profit, a result which follows as a special case of the multi-input LMF discussed in Section 1.2. Because negative profit would result in long run shutdown by the PMF, we consider only non-negative PMF profits in our long run cooperative analysis.

To summarize, with a homothetic variable-returns-to-scale technology, if output price increases the LMF will continue to operate at the same scale. Retiring (departing) members will be replaced by machines so as to achieve the long run optimal input mix. If, on the other hand, output price decreases the LMF will attempt to substitute new members, in excess of simply replacing departing ones, for capital so as to reduce the per-member burden of capital costs. Therefore, under these stylized conditions of no entry (by which we mean the formation of new firms in response to product market "profitability") and the existence of a parametric price for capital, the perverse labor movements in response to price signals continue and the perverse supply response is countervailed only to the extent that capital is substituted for declining labor. As a result if we assume equal fixed stocks of capital in an LME and a twin CME benchmark along with complete rental markets for capital, the LMF planning problem indicates that a Pareto-inefficient input mix will result in the LME if the rents earned by labor are not competed away by entry.

2.2. Entry and efficiency in the LME

Jaroslav Vanek (1970) discusses the crucial role played by entry in the LME. If entry of any sort is sufficient to dissipate rents, the equilibria in the LME and the CME are equivalent; in other words, the maximum dividend in the LMF is exactly equal to the competitive wage paid to workers hired by the PMF. In the LMF's planning problem the shadow price of labor and the unit capital charge are then equivalent to the factor prices faced by the PMF so that the LMF chooses the same input mix and the same scale of output as the PMF. Equivalence between the two organizational forms is due to the absence of any rents to be distributed between the two factors, capital and labor.

For Vanek, the mechanism for rent dissipation is the entry of newly-formed LMFs into profitable markets. Costless formation of new firms insures a continual state of full employment in the LME with workers earning dividends equal to market equilibrium wage rates in the CME. This result follows from the tendency of workers seeking the best income-earning opportunities in the LME to found firms in areas which generate the highest potential profit thus insuring that all rents are dissipated. Vanek likens this phenomena to a "bee-swarm" effect and views it as a natural long run consequence of differentiated short run dividends across LMFs.

Formal models of long run general equilibrium in the LME begin with the work of Tatsuro Ichiishi (1977). Drawing on the literature in game theory on coalition formation which uses the core as an equilibrium concept, Ichiishi supports Vanek's intuition about entry leading to equivalent equilibria in the CME and the LME so long as equilibrium exists in the LME. Elaine Bennett and Myrna Wooders (1979) extend the coalition formation analysis in the LME to situations in which the formation of firms is costly and the existence of equilibrium is not assured in the LME. These authors show that equivalence of equilibria depends on the magnitude of formation (transaction) costs and discuss the implications of their results for income distribution by including the possibility of lump-sum transfers in the LME. Joseph Greenberg (1979) studies the sufficient conditions for equivalence between the CME and the LME in two different environments, one allowing workers to belong to more than one firm (moonlighting and sunlighting) and the other in which a worker may belong to only one firm. Any tendencies toward non-optimality of LME equilibria are traced to the indivisibility of a firm in the core into divisions which could produce and share total output in these subgroups.

This technical literature suggests the importance of size of the decision-making, dividend-sharing group and its relevance to internal incentive issues when efficient allocation of resources is a desirable goal in the LME. It perhaps also suggests a rationale for the separation of Yugoslav firms and Chinese collective farms into smaller evaluation units, BOALS and teams respectively. Although coalition formation is an appealing way to think about entry in the LME, the rental capital market is too simplistic to capture many of the important issues of capital financing in the LME to which we now turn.

2.3. Capital financing and workers' management

The early development of the theory of LMFs assumed rental of capital goods in stylized depiction of the relationship between Yugoslav firms and the state, which "granted" them their initial stocks of capital equipment and "set each year the rate to be paid to the state as interest on fixed capital (Ward, 1958: 568)." Rental is only one of several paths of access to capital, however, and its prevalence in market economies is widely believed to be limited by the costs of monitoring the utilization, in an enterprise, of equipment and facilities belonging to outside parties. The alternative to rental is ownership by the enterprise or by its financiers. The financial capital making possible such asset ownership, in the latter case, is typically obtained in one of four ways, namely, (a) by the direct contributions of a proprietor or proprietors—i.e., owners who are also among the operating personnel of the enterprise; (b) by the subscriptions of outside (equity-)owners to issued shares in enterprise assets; and by two types of borrowing: (c) from banks and similar financial institutions, and (d) from other creditors, via the issue of debt. Investment from retained earnings and replacement of assets out of funds earmarked for depreciation may be listed as additional means of financing the acquisition of capital goods, although they can be grouped with sources (a) and (b) when the retained earnings are the property of the proprietors or equity owners prior to the retention decision.

In principle, all of these ways of financing investment are open to the LMF provided that, for the pure LMF at least, the principle of worker sovereignty and equality in ultimate control rights is safeguarded by ruling out forms of equity or debt that give voting say to the investor or lender.[35] It is of great importance to recognize, in addition, that ownership by proprietors, which here corresponds to ownership by the worker-members, may have quite different implications depending on the degree to which such ownership takes the form of an individualized saleable asset or (on the other hand) of assets collectively owned by the workforce.

Two of the key issues in the finance of LMFs are those that revolve around the importance of the restriction on investor or lender participation in enterprise control, which is definitional, and of any possible collective ownership, which is not required but is an observed feature of several species of LMFs. The theoretical literature to date has been largely preoccupied with issues of collective or even 'social' ownership of capital, as well as of capital book value maintenance rules, administered interest rates, and other aspects of the policy environment of *Yugoslavia.* A more general approach to the financial theory of LMFs will begin with the theory of finance in capitalist market economies.

Ownership and control rights

While gathering sufficient financial capital to allow the purchase (rather than rental) of enterprise fixed capital may circumvent the problem of monitoring equipment utilization, it is widely perceived as raising another monitoring problem, namely that concerning the management of the financial capital itself and the alignment of managers' incentives with the interests of owners, often summarized in the notion of "wealth maximization." The modern corporate manager utilizes financial means largely provided by other parties, raising the central question: what assures that the manager will

[35] We do not address here philosophical questions regarding the compatability of various ownership forms with self-management. For pure self-management, as we have defined it, all that is strictly ruled out is for individuals or institutions to be accorded decision-making or membership rights in the firm by virtue of an ownership or creditorship relationship. Worker-members might own unequal shares of enterprise capital, and are not by our definition prohibited from receiving unequal income streams on that account. However, our definition does rule out any association between the number of shares or amount of firm capital owned by a worker, and his or her weight in enterprise decision-making. Of course, as before, we will continue to give some consideration to forms of partially worker-managed enterprises that violate these restrictions in one respect or another, including firms in which financiers and workers *share* decision-making rights.

pursue maximization of the wealth of equity owners and will not improperly risk the capital provided by lenders and/or pursue individual goals such as increased salary, leisure on the job, power over subordinates, or market share? The main answer provided by modern finance theory is that *capital markets monitor managers* by tracking managerial activity and by forcing managers to bear the costs of opportunistic behavior in the form of a higher cost of capital to the firm plus value revisions in their own equity shares and salaries. The most influential statement of this theory is by Jensen and Meckling (1976).[36]

To see whether the same principle might apply to the financing of LMFs, it is important to look more closely at the role of decision-making rights in this model of the capital market. The modern finance literature by Jensen, Meckling, Fama, and others, is in part a response to the argument raised by Berle and Means (1932), according to which diffuse equity ownership made the modern corporation an instrument of wealth utilization without control by the owners of wealth. While a possible response would be to argue that the voting mechanism gives shareholders ultimate control over management since voting rights can be used to displace the latter in cases of inappropriate managerial behavior, this approach has been thought subject to serious weaknesses.[37] Instead, the majority of responses to Berle and Means rest on the argument that the market causes the manager to internalize the costs of opportunistic behavior by way of more or less automatic value adjustments, due to the capturing of such information in stock and bond prices, which raise the cost of finance to management. Complementing this factor may be the acceptance, by managers, of a portion of their direct compensation in the form of equity shares

[36] This paragraph should not be taken as implying unanimity of theoretical positions on the efficiency of capital markets. For some reservations see Stiglitz (1981) and sources cited therein.

[37] If all shareholders hold insignificant fractions of the total share value, none has much incentive to monitor the firm's performance or expend resources on voting. A "raiding" firm or management team that believes itself capable of raising the firm's (equity) value by better management could buy a controlling fraction of shares at a premium, but the raider's gains can be appropriated by hold-out shareowners, limiting the incentive for raids, as shown by Grossman and Hart (1980). The problem is also discussed by Stiglitz, 1981, with even stronger conclusions regarding the limits to the efficiency of shareholder control.

and the returns on such shares. Additional ways of attenuating the agency problems of external finance are for lenders to be given access to enterprise accounts and other assistance in scrutinizing enterprise operations, and for firms to commit themselves to certain policies or investment decisions in advance of loan agreements. None of these devices is in principle closed to an LMF.

However, more direct control rights by the outside financier are not entirely eschewed in the literature. For example, Manne (1965) has argued that take-over bids, while relatively infrequent, are a control device of central importance.[38] And from a strictly theoretical standpoint, Drèze (1976) has stated that

> [g]iven the existence of a stock market, efficiency of prodution decisions requires that control rights be vested with the shareholders.

Unlike the more indirect agency approaches of Jensen, Meckling, *et al.*, the direct control arguments of Manne and Drèze, if accepted, do present obstacles to efficiency that the pure LMF could not, by definition, overcome.

A problem with Drèze's statement is that to apply to capital alone the principle that control rights must be accorded to the bearer of risk is improperly asymmetric. There is widespread agreement that a common feature of labor contracts is the imprecision with which the exact set of tasks to be performed is specified. Unless workers do not care how their labor is used, submission to the authority of an employer is itself an acceptance of risk. A still more obvious form of risk-bearing by labor is the uncertain prospect of being laid off, which under conventional employment arrangements, is outside of the control of the worker. Drèze's statement, taken at face value and in its apparently strict sense, implies an inefficiency unless workers are also granted a share in the control of their activities.

The combination of Drèze's point and our "counter-point" leads some authors (such as Steinherr) to conclude that only co-determination (between capital and labor) satisfies both efficiency requirements. Yet most economic theorists infer from market outcomes (and contrary to Steinherr) that what workers receive in the conventional employment bargain in the form of wage guarantees, a

[38] See, again, the footnote above, however.

restricted domain on employer discretion (Simon, 1951), etc., outweighs the loss due to sacrificing control over the risky utilization of their labor factor. If this possibility can be admitted with regard to labor participation and risk, then Drèze's point about capital participation and risk may also be less than fully general. That the loss or diminution of financiers' control would entail welfare losses that could not be outweighed by the benefits both to the financiers themselves—e.g. were they to be financially compensated for the added risk—and to the full coalition of agents connected with the enterprise, is accordingly an inference from observed institutional outcomes, rather than a result that follows of necessity on *a priori* grounds. The informational, institutional, and distributional bases of that inference remain to be investigated systematically.

Worker-ownership, debt, and equity

If the possibilities of debt and non-voting equity finance are admitted alongside those of finance by the worker-members, the question of the proportions between each source has still to be addressed. The theoretical literature on LMFs has made no advance over the general finance literature in providing either a positive or a normative theory of the debt-equity ratio, and only some general comments are available here. McCain (1977), for example, has argued that the level of debt financing of enterprise investment would be limited by a "principle of increasing risk," according to which it becomes more and more costly to borrow capital at fixed rates of return since such arrangements permit the lenders to share in the lower tail of the distribution of possible enterprise outcomes, namely the risk of bankruptcy and default, without any claim on the upper tail of higher than expected profits. This reasoning, which might explain the mixing of debt with equity in the financing of PMFs, leads McCain to conclude that LMFs could achieve more efficient financial performance if they issued an equity-like instrument giving its owners a share, alongside workers, in enterprise revenue net of payments to non-labor costs including interest to debt-holders. He provides a mathematical analysis from which he concludes that the LMF whose objective is to maximize profit-per-worker, and which issues both ordinary bonds and the equity-like "risk participation bonds," would "attain the same allocation of resources as would a capitalist corporation, under comparable circumstances and informationally efficient markets (1977: 382)." Unfortunately, McCain's model does not specify the order of claims to the revenue and assets of a bankrupt firm, a necessary element of a full analysis, and no further work along these lines has been presented.

In the general finance literature, as indicated above, it is frequently stated that ownership of some equity shares by managers might be imposed as a precondition for external finance, and that in any case it might make public equity purchases more attractive. The reason is that covariance of managerial and shareholder incomes serves as a signal of "commitment" to profit-maximizing behavior on the part of managers whose actions remain imperfectly monitored by outside shareholders. The same reasoning has been applied by Schlicht and Weizsacker (1977) and by Gui (1985) to argue that LMF borrowing in external capital markets will require some participation in ownership by the worker-members. Although perhaps not as the result of market pressures strictly speaking, this phenomenon already appears to explain some of the internal investment observed in Yugoslav firms, where "social" ownership probably generates counter-incentives to such reinvestment (see below and the sub-section on Yugoslavia).

Another consideration likely to affect the proportion of member versus non-member financing is the size of the firm. In practice, only the largest 10 or 15% of capitalist enterprises—although these control well over 90% of industrial assets in their economies—have access to public capital markets, a likely explanation being that there are economies of scale in capital market monitoring of corporate performance and prospects. Size should also make for more restrictive financing possibilities for small LMFs. Small LMFs solely owned by worker-members and their families, with limited access to bank loans, are the rule in Western market economies today. Similar firms might predominate in such market LMEs as might arise in the future, although financial constraints can be partially alleviated by cooperative federations and networks of the type discussed in Section 6a, below.

Given that some degree of member financing is likely to be necessary or at least efficient in even large LMFs, the question of the form of internal financing must arise. As we develop in what follows, the literature on finance and LMFs is dominated by discussion of the disincentives to internal investment of funds that arise when individual ownership claims are dissolved in the investment act and when the membership right is not marketable, so that each member benefits from the stream of higher productivity resulting from investment only insofar as it raises his share of enterprise earnings, and thus only for the duration of his tenure as a working member. This facet of Yugoslav institutions, plus the Yugoslav rule that the enterprise must maintain the book value of all (including incremental) capital in perpetuity, will be addressed in the succeeding subsections. For the moment, we may state that there is no reason why worker-members cannot be given equity shares in their firms' assets without violating the principle of basing control upon working rather than owning status, and yet also without creating any of the above-mentioned disincentives of collective ownership. What remains as a system-specific problem of self-management is this: if workers must substantially finance their own firms, then they are forced to bear more enterprise-specific risk than would be the case were they to work for fixed wages in capitalist firms and to invest their savings in financial intermediaries or diversified portfolios (Neuberger and James, 1973). Worker-managers may presumably proceed further to insure enterprise-specific risks with institutions specializing in such functions but, due to the unavoidable moral hazard problem, the costs are likely to become prohibitively high before much insurance of this type is issued.

2.4. Incomplete capital markets: the property rights approach

The property rights literature stresses the incompleteness of the capital market in the LME based on Yugoslav-type socialist property rights. It is argued that the long-run planning problem for the LMF treated by Vanek, Meade, and Estrin does not capture the essence of capital decisions according to this school. Eirik Furubotn and Svetozar Pejovich, the most frequent contributors to the literature, stress a fundamental disincentive to accumulate internal funds to finance investment by a socialist labor-managed firm (hereafter, SLMF). This point is also noticed by Vanek (1970) so that we will refer to this lack of self-financed investment in the LMF as the FPV effect.

When funds are available from financial intermediaries, Furubotn and Pejovich conclude that only external funds will be used to finance investment (e.g., Pejovich, 1973 and Furubotn, 1974). Drawing economy-wide conclusions from his work, Furubotn (1976 and 1980b) argues that aggregate savings will be smaller in the LME than in the CME due to the limitations placed on the set of financial instruments. The property rights literature concludes that underinvestment and exclusive reliance on external financing will result from worker-management of capital in the LMF and that too little aggregate investment and a misallocation of capital will plague the LME. Critical of applying these results to LMFs in general, Stephen (1980) argues rather that the FPV effect and the attached corollaries are due to a peculiar capital maintenance requirement imposed on Yugoslav firms.

In an attempt to review concisely and critically this voluminous literature, we adopt some definitions and appeal to the standard capital budgeting approach to analyze investment decisions in the LMF. In a SLMF, the social nature of the property rights over capital further distinguishes the LMF from a capitalist profit-maximizing firm (CPMF). By a SLMF, we mean an organization which is restricted from issuing tradeable private ownership claims on its assets. Although they do not own the physical assets of the firm, the worker-members still hold some "equity" in the SLMF since their current income fluctuates with firm performance. They are also the directors of the firm since their preferences form the basis for decision-making. However, social property rights can prevent the workers from capturing fully the stream of returns to all investment projects. When an obligation to maintain capital in perpetuity is imposed on the SLMF, the resulting organizational form is commonly taken to be representative of a Yugoslav firm.

The fundamental conclusion of the property rights literature is that this Yugoslav usufruct law which combines the right to use social capital with an obligation not to abuse it leads to underinvestment in capital. With respect to the provision of internal financing, this result is shown initially in Svetozar Pejovich (1969) and the implications for resource allocation in the LME discussed earliest by Eirik Furubotn and Pejovich (1970) and Jaroslav Vanek (1971). The scenario is the following: workers have available only two assets, namely, reinvestment in their own firm and savings deposits held in financial intermediaries, over which they make a portfolio choice.

Furubotn and Pejovich (1970) distinguish between the two by calling the latter an owned asset and the former a non-owned asset. The property rights structure dictates that deposits in a savings account earn interest and the principal may be withdrawn at any time; thus, they are perfectly liquid. However, earnings reinvested in the firm rather than paid out as current wages entitle a member to share in incremental value-added for only as long as he works in the SLMF. Not only is investment in this asset illiquid, but the member loses his entitlement to the returns upon leaving the firm; i.e., the limited appropriability property.

Although the worker owns fully the principal in his savings account, funds reinvested in the firm are used to finance capital over which the worker has only an incomplete ownership claim. Members are entitled collectively to "use the fruits" (*usus fructu*) of capital acquired by internal funds but this entitlement cannot be traded nor, in this context, does it include any individual retirement benefits. Consequently, Furubotn and Pejovich argue that the riskless return to self-financed investment within the SLMF will have to be substantially higher than the interest rate on savings to induce workers to allocate funds for reinvestment. Furubotn (1980), in the self-financed case, and Nicos Zafiris (1982), in the external-financed case, link investment disincentives in the Yugoslav-type SLMF to a capital maintenance obligation imposed by the government.

In the literature, uncertainty with its consequent risk premium are usually considered only after the fundamental result is developed and group decision-making issues with any resulting incentive problems are suppressed. Furthermore, most complicating real world factors like indivisibilities, liquidity (especially bankruptcy provisions), inflation accounting (book value vs. replacement cost) are normally ignored. Rather a representative worker is considered, either because a median voter result can be appealed to or because workers have preferences which are sufficiently alike so as to be modeled as if they were identical. This representative worker is assumed to have full information on which to base his portfolio choice between the bank deposit account and self-financed investment projects. Implicitly then, the consumption-savings decision, or choice between current and future income, is already made. This distinction is not always clear in the literature and confusion may arise when the worker's preference for the bank deposit is referred to as a preference for current income.

A final assumption is made so that the representative worker's investment decision is comparable to the investment decision in a CPMF. In the SLMF, the individual member's income shares from an investment project may be different from the usual CPMF cash flows from this project. For simplicity, take CPMF cash flows to be constant per period over the given life of some asset which has no salvage value. Cash flow is defined as the difference between increments to revenues and increments to production costs. In the CPMF, the sum of discounted cash flow over the life of the asset would determine the present value of the investment project. A comparison of this present value with the cost of the asset would lead to a calculation of its internal rate of return (hereafter IRR). Since production costs include labor costs, cash flow nets out any change in the wage bill in the CPMF.

However, in the SLMF, the member/worker is not a wage earner but rather a residual claimant to the incremental value-added (i.e. revenue minus both material costs and financing costs when relevant) associated with any investment project. He receives a share of net production income rather than a wage. Consequently, the returns to any investment project in the SLMF will be a combination of returns to labor and a return on investment. For the representative worker, the relevant return to investment is his share of this incremental value-added, i.e., the discounted difference between his own future earnings with and without the project, less his share of the cost of self-financing.

In the literature on the investment behavior of a SLMF, cash flows are used as an appropriate measure of net return so that wealth maximization by a representative worker affords direct comparisons with the CPMF. In essence, input interrelationships are not considered explicitly. For example, if an investment project involves additional labor, these requirements are not met in the same way by the LMF and the PMF. In the latter, labor is hired and cash flow accounts for the incremental labor cost. In the former, membership or hours worked per member or both must be increased. If membership is increased, new members share not only in the returns to this investment project but also in the net income produced by all assets (i.e., all previous investment projects). A potential exists for share dilution due to membership increases, not to mention the possibility of shifts in the control over decision-making in the SLMF.

It is the loss of decision-making power by the initial membership group which concerns Furubotn (1976) when membership is expanded. Consequently, Furubotn considers dilution costs to be dichotomous by assuming a critical level of membership expansion above which dilution costs are infinite but below which they are zero. However, it seems equally reasonable that an interest group with initial voting control, although perhaps not a majority of the members, could strengthen its decision-making position by hiring like-minded individuals. Expansion of the membership would then yield political benefits to the controlling group.

Strictly speaking, in the SLMF, any membership dilution costs along with the costs related to any change in hours worked per member should be subtracted from incremental value-added when the net return to an investment project is calculated. Similar considerations apply if the investment project is labor-saving so that much of the net return accrues from decreased labor costs. The rules governing the provision of internal funds must also be designed carefully. In the egalitarian situation, every dollar provided by the representative worker for self-financed investment must be matched by a dollar from every other current member. Otherwise, gaming strategies and incentive problems further complicate the problem.

By assuming, with the literature, that these aspects can be incorporated properly into a cash flow calculation for the SLMF which is then directly comparable to that in the CPMF, Bonin (1985) examines the conditions required for the property rights results and their general applicability. Referred to as the horizon effect as well, the FPV effect depends on the representative worker's inability to appropriate any returns from investment projects which accrue after his membership tenure expires, either because of retirement or a change in jobs. As Zafiris (1982) demonstrates, this limited appropriability is strongly related to social capital. Clearly, if a worker could sell his membership right to returns on investment projects financed and undertaken during his tenure to a new member or to the remaining members, a perfect capital market would allow him to capitalize fully the expected future returns. Under these circumstances, the investment behavior of a PMF and a LMF would be equivalent.

Once social capital is imposed so that the capital market is no longer complete, Bonin shows that the SLMF will rank investment projects differently from the CPMF unless a strong capital maintenance requirement (hereafter, SCMR) is imposed. The SCMR is defined by Bonin as an obligation to maintain, in perpetuity, the *real* value of all capital assets so that inflation cannot render ineffective an obligation based on book value. The SLMF without an SCMR will exhibit a preference for liquidity by ranking some projects with shorter payback periods above others with higher IRR if the projects under consideration have life expectancies greater than the membership tenure of the representative worker. With an SCMR, all projects become infinitely long-lived in the financial sense.

A SLMF with a SCMR will always exhibit the FPV effect because of the finite membership tenure of the representative worker. Then the critical rate of return applied to projects which are to be self-financed will reflect the requirement that any project accepted must earn an annuity sufficient both to match the interest foregone on the alternative savings asset *and* to recoup fully the principal over the future tenure of the representative member. This critical annuity, or hurdle rate as Bonin calls it, will exceed the savings deposit interest rate which would itself be the opportunity cost applied to any investment project financed by internal funds in a PMF. When self-financing alone is considered for the SLMF, a SCMR is a sufficient condition for the FPV effect to obtain with its accompanying underinvestment as compared to a PMF. Furthermore, the hurdle rate is inversely related to the expected tenure of the representative member of the SLMF so that the marginally acceptable investment project will have associated with it an IRR which is firm-specific. Different expected tenures for representative workers across firms will lead to a misallocation of capital, according to the Pareto criteria, in the LME.

2.5. Financial intermediation in an LME

Furubotn and Pejovich consider the possibility of banks providing financial intermediation and conclude that then the SLMF would use external funds only to finance investment projects. In this scenario, the representative worker would make his saving/ consumption decision based on total dividend income from the

SMLF with no deductions for self-financed investment (no funds retained for investment). Savings would be put in a bank in the form of a Furubotn–Pejovich owned asset. The bank(s) would lend money to SLMF's for the purpose of financing investment, and Furubotn–Pejovich claim that the opportunity cost of external funds would be the bank lending rate, just as would be the case for the traditional PMF.

However, Bonin argues that the situation in the SLMF is not identical to that in the PMF because the term of the bank loan as well as the lending rate will influence financing decisions. When external financing is available, the representative worker in the SLMF must calculate the appropriate cost of capital schedule to determine the mode of financing investment. For comparison, we note that in the PMF the cheapest-source-first rule applies so that when the bank lending rate, b, exceeds the bank deposit rate, i, internal funds will have a shadow price or opportunity cost lower than the cost of borrowing so that internal financing is used before any external financing is sought. Borrowing will be considered only if the *IRR* of investment projects remaining after internal funds are depleted exceeds b.

The literature on the investment behavior of the SLMF contains some disagreement over a comparable cost of capital schedule. Frank Stephen (1980) claims that the cheapest-source-first rule will apply also in the SLMF and that, in the above case, self-financing may be used first. Eirik Furubotn (1980b) replies by claiming that the hurdle rate applied to self-financed investment will normally exceed the bank lending rate, and, consequently, the Furubotn–Pejovich external financing only result will hold. The contention is a good example of the importance of distinguishing a general model of an LMF from one which relies more heavily on Yugoslav-type institutions.

In the absence of a SCMR, perfect financial intermediation (i.e., $b = i$) can support an efficient investment equilibrium in the LME equivalent to the one in the CME. As Bonin (1985) shows, this is achieved when repayment schedules for the LMF are structured to reflect the value of the real asset held as loan collateral. Furthermore, this result is consistent with some projects being self-financed. However, once a SCMR is imposed so that the organization is a Yugoslav-type SLMF, efficient investment can be supported only if no principal is ever repaid to financial intermediaries.

Then external financing is used exclusively by applying the cheapest-source-first rule.

If, on the other hand, principal repayment is required by the bank and an SCMR is imposed, the SLMF is charged twice as Zafiris and Furubotn argue. Revenues must be set aside to replace the asset after its useful life has expired while, at the same time, deductions from revenues are required to meet principal payments on the bank loan. When principal repayment is demanded of the Yugoslav-type SLMF, cost of capital calculations depend on the term of bank loans and the hurdle rate applied to self-financed investment. Bonin derives a cost of capital schedule for the SLMF with a SCMR in which long term debt is used first, followed by self-financing and then short term debt. As in the case of exclusive self-financing, the critical annuity which in turn determines the hurdle rate for internal funds depends on firm-specific characteristics. Thus, internal price considerations remain relevant and under-investment problems and a misallocation of capital are likely to continue to plague the LME even in the presence of financial intermediation.

The debate between Stephen and Furubotn concerns the generality of the results for LMFs without an SCMR and even non-socialist LMFs. Stephen considers it important to clarify the dependence of the results on the assumptions of Yugoslav-type property rights. The only way in which financial intermediation can support an efficient allocation of resources in the case of the Yugoslav-type LMF with an SCMR is for banks to refinance continually the loan principal. If perpetual "rolling over" of loans is required for an efficient allocation of resources in the LME, this raises serious concerns. On the one hand, the SCMR means that the life of real assets in the LMF is infinite. If loans are secured by the value of the real assets of the LMF, no principal need be repaid so long as the asset's value is maintained in perpetuity. On the other hand, such a resolution involves the banking system in the financial analogue of a pure rental solution so that the agency criticism of Jensen–Meckling would need to be considered.

2.6. Capital financing: risk and agency issues

In his general equilibrium model of the LME, Jacques Drèze (1976) assumes a perfect (rental) capital market and proves an equivalence between equilibria in the LME and the CME. Since the welfare theorems of the competitive equilibrium would then apply to the equivalent LME equilibrium, it is crucial to consider whether or not the classic agency confrontation between the owner of an asset and its user is more likely to lead to incomplete market arrangements in the LME than it would in the CME. According to Jensen and Meckling, as a user of nonowned social capital, the SLMF will not husband resources properly but rather the workers will attempt to appropriate social capital for private gain by misuse and improper maintenance. In their critique, Jensen–Meckling also claim that it would be infeasible to monitor a SCMR in the real world. However, capital maintenance requirements seem peculiar to Yugoslav-type SLMFs so that this comment is directed to only one particular form of an LMF. To argue that a capital maintenance requirement of some sort is a natural governmental response to workers' incentives to consume enterprise capital seems asymmetric since capital maintenance rules are not imposed on managerial corporations in the literature discussed above. Of course, there may be other incentives to maintain capital in the managerial corporation, for example, the threat of takeover or the difficulty of obtaining external financing.

In order to broaden our treatment of capital financing issues to more general LMF forms, we introduce uncertainty explicitly and focus on the residual claimancy status of the worker in a LMF. According to Drèze, in an uncertain world, it may be difficult to find institutional arrangements which are both compatible with labor-management and supportive of efficiency. The latter requires that production decisions conform to the preferences of those bearing the risk while the former requires decision-making status for worker-members only. Consequently, production decisions may reflect too little risk-taking if workers are unable to diversify efficiently their earnings risk.

To clarify this point, we consider the tension between risk-sharing and moral hazard using the framework of the principal-agent literature and discuss the application of incentive contracts to the LMF. James Markusen (1976) provides a simple specification of the moral hazard problem in the revenue-sharing context by abstracting from risk-sharing concerns. Workers as a group are involved in supplying effort, which can neither be costed out financially or monitored by the principal. The principal provides capital to the firm and the contractual form of payment for capital and remuneration for the workers is the only issue. If Pareto-efficient outcomes are sought, workers in the LMF must be accorded complete residual claimancy status and the principal given a fixed payment which does not depend on the LMF's net revenue. Such a contract provides the group with the appropriate incentive for supplying the efficient amount of effort. If the principal were to share in revenues, some portion of the benefit of effort would not be retained by the workers; hence, they would have an incentive to "shirk" by supplying less than the Pareto optimal amount. A further problem arises in individualizing the group incentive to avoid the "free rider" effect, a topic taken up in Section 1.8.

In an uncertain world, the reverse insurance result of Markusen would violate the optimal conditions for risk-sharing by shifting the entire burden of risk to a risk-averse party, the workers. The recent literature on implicit contracts concludes that optimal risk-sharing leads a risk-neutral entrepreneur to insure fully worker's remuneration across states of nature because the worker is risk-averse. However, such contracts are fully Pareto optimal only if incentive problems are absent (e.g., moral hazard and asymmetric information). The extent to which these results concerning risk-neutral entrepreneurs or financiers hiring risk-averse workers can be borrowed and applied directly to the LMF where risk-averse workers attempt to finance investment is discussed in Section 3.2.

Stephen Ross (1974) specifies the necessary conditions for optimal risk-sharing when both parties to the contract are risk-averse. Building on this foundation, the principal/agent literature assesses the full optimality of contractual arrangements and relates this characterization to environmental circumstances. If the principal has perfect information about the agent's choice variable (in our context, the workers' effort), James Mirrlees (1976) demonstrates that the optimal contract is dichotomous with a very low payoff to the agent unless he chooses the action which will maximize the net payoff exclusive of his private cost and a risk-sharing contract according to Ross' conditions if the agent chooses this first best action. If the principal can obtain only imperfect information about the agent's action, either through monitoring some result of this action or by sampling directly through supervision, information is clearly valuable but its use is risky due to its imperfectness.

Steve Shavell (1979) and Bengt Holmstrom (1979) show that in this case only second best contracts are possible, these contracts use the information about the agent's action which is known only imperfectly by the principal as well as the result which is observable costlessly by all (in our context, this result would be the output or net revenue of the LMF), and these contracts have no simple characterization properties (for example, they are not necessarily simple linear sharing rules nor are they always concave or convex functions of decision variables).

These negative results are corroborated by Tracy Lewis (1980) in a situation in which the principal knows the agent's reaction function to any particular contract specification but can not monitor perfectly the agent's action. Lewis provides an example in which a dichotomous contract dominates the best linear sharing rule but he concludes that no general second best contract can be specified because the size of the gain to both parties depends on the exact magnitude of the moral hazard problem. To summarize, the principal/agent literature demonstrates the impossibility of constructing a contract which will both provide optimal incentives to the workers and share risk optimally when both parties are risk-averse and moral hazard problems occur because of imperfect information.

Benedetto Gui (1985) analyzes the effects of asymmetric information on bankruptcy decisions in an LMF by considering contractual arrangements between a risk-neutral financial market and the risk-averse workers. Physical capital has a one period effective life in the firm and a salvage or resale value if the firm is dissolved. A contractual debt repayment with an accompanying interest (service) charge is determined in the capital market depending mainly on the portion of the capital costs which are externally financed (conceivably, this portion could be the entire value of the capital). Workers have limited liability to shareholders in the sense that they may dissolve the firm and avoid the contractual payment at no cost above the loss of their own stake of financial capital. If the firm is dissolved, financiers recoup the entire salvage (or resale) value of the firm's physical assets but nothing more.

The agent/workers liquidation decision depends on the realization of a stochastic variable, gross income from production consisting of value-added inclusive of capital costs, which is observed by them alone. The probability distribution of this variable is known completely to both parties at the time the contract determining the debt payment is negotiated. In a perfect capital market, the principal/financier requires that the expected value of his return (interest and principle if the LMF operates but only the liquidation value if it is dissolved) be equalized to the value of his financial stake (due to risk-neutrality).

Gui shows that, under reasonable conditions on the probability distribution of gross income, the possibility of bankruptcy leads the self-interested workers to finance some of the capital themselves rather than opt for the full external financing strategy suggested by Furubotn/Pejovich and Vanek. Situations are characterized in which the workers' decision to liquidate is not socially optimal because gross income exceeds the salvage value but also falls short of the contractual debt. Gui shows that the workers bear completely this social loss through the determination of the terms of the debt contract. He argues that, if gross income is observable or monitorable by the financiers, the optimal contract is to make the debt payment contingent on the realization of the stochastic variable, a solution similar to the McCain "participation" bonds proposal.

Gui focuses on the possibility of a reorganization of the firm, or a takeover, to eliminate the social loss and thus increase expected wealth. In principle, such a solution requires zero reorganizational costs or its equivalent, perfect information. In the case of asymmetric information concerning the realization of gross income, Gui's analysis indicates why McCain "participation" bonds (or non-voting stock) may not be equivalent to the voting equity shares of a PMF as the latter allow for takeovers. Since only workers have the decision-making authority in the LMF, a reorganization or takeover is precluded. In Gui's model, the workers alone decide on liquidation based on their private information about gross income possibilities. Consequently, workers can influence the payments to bond holders by increasing the probability of liquidation after the contract is negotiated (or in a more complicated environment, workers can shirk taking non-monetary remuneration at the expense of monetary income which is shared with the financier).

Gui demonstrates how the percentage of the workers' own wealth that is invested in the LMF provides an important signal to the financier because it indicates the amount the workers stand to lose by dissolving the firm. As such it creates a constraint on opportunistic behavior in the moral hazard situation. Since the workers' wealth is likely to be small vis à vis the financier, Gui argues that the commitment burden may be a heavy one for the workers and thus still not alleviate completely the effects of moral hazard on the contractual arrangements. As a potential remedy to this problem, Gui suggests that both workers and the financier share decision-making status so that what was private information to one party would become public. Such an organization would resemble a codetermined firm which we shall discuss more fully in the next section. However, to the extent that information asymmetries persist, the party with better access to the information can benefit from strategic behavior regardless of the organizational form.

When markets are complete and all rents are "competed away" in equilibrium, the LMF and the PMF behave equivalently since all organizational forms are indistinguishable. On the other hand, if firm-specific rents are present, the "sharing" of these rents between capital and labor is an appropriate issue for organizational design. The property rights literature and the agency incentive issues considered in this part suggest reasons why the LMF may be expected to pay a risk premium in capital markets so that the workers cannot capture fully all firm-specific rents. Economic theory leads us to conclude with Gui (p. 117) that

> worker-managers will be required to save and bear risks to a greater extent than subordinate workers. Their autonomy does have a cost.

3. OTHER THEORETICAL ISSUES

3.1. Internal bargaining and codetermination

The possibility of constructing a spectrum along which organizational forms can be placed according to the relative bargaining strengths of labor and capital with the traditional PMF at one pole and the LMF at the other is attracting much attention in theoretical economics. Hajime Miyazaki (1984a) analyzes bargaining over firm-specific rents, the existence of which can be justified by the acquisition of firm-specific human capital by the workforce or other such idiosyncratic relationships. The relationship between Benjamin Ward's seminal model of the LMF and traditional collective bargaining models is recognized by Peter Law (1977). The case in which the union has maximal bargaining power and management no bargaining power characterizes the LMF. William Fellner (1947) suggests that the appropriate utility function for the union in collective bargaining models would have two arguments, the wage and the number of workers employed. As Law argues, the Ward model is equivalent to including the wage only in the union's utility function (Fellner's case of horizontal indifference curves in the quadrant with wage on the y-axis and employment on the x-axis).

When employment is introduced into the union's utility function, Robert Solow and Ian McDonald (1981) examine the efficient contracts that can be negotiated between a monopoly union and a profit-maximizing firm. These contracts are characterized either by a wage above the worker's marginal revenue product at any given level of employment or, by more job security for any given wage. A further interesting aspect of these contracts is an asymmetry between the polar cases. When the workers have maximal bargaining strength, wage maximization does not lead to Pareto optimal contracts because employment levels are too low. This reflects the fundamental result first shown by Ward for the LMF. However, if the workers have no bargaining strength, profit-maximizing behavior leads to Pareto Optimality.

Masahiko Aoki (1980) models the bargaining problem as a cooperative game in which stockholders and employees bargain over their respective shares of the rent. For Aoki, quasi-rents are organization-specific and shared by shareholders and employees with a manager acting as an arbitrator in formulating corporate policy. Once the internal distribution is determined according to a Nash–Harsanyi solution to a cooperative game, allocative decisions are equivalent to those made in a capitalist counterpart (in his case a Marris-type firm). Aoki defines the poles of his spectrum by considering the traditional firm in which the employees receive a market-determined wage on one side and the Ward firm in which the entire organizational rent is controlled by the workers on the other.

Roger McCain (1982) argues that collective bargaining and codetermination are distinct organizational forms because the set of variables determined in the bargaining process differs between them. The subtle differences resulting from changes in organizational form should not be obliterated in overly simplistic economic models. In the transition from the individual bargaining of untrammeled capitalism to collective bargaining, a new choice variable, employment level, is introduced to organizational decision-making. This is well-handled in the Fellner tradition discussed above. However, codetermination allows for further cooperation in decision-making because of the joint administration of all the variables under the employer's control (shared decision-making). To take an example, workers would have a voice in capital decisions. Perhaps not as obvious is the closer connection between the supplier and user of capital which may make proper husbanding and monitoring potentially less costly in the codetermined firm. Although the properties of these simple models lend themselves to a treatment of the polar extremes of the spectrum as limiting cases where bargaining power is fully vested in one of the two parties, some important subtleties might be overlooked in the process.

A useful way of categorizing the models of the codetermined firm is proposed by Norman Ireland and Peter Law (1985b) who distinguish between models for which the Nash cooperative maximand is defined over total payments to factors or over rates of return. The latter case, which Ireland and Law consider, makes wage and the profit rate the relevant shares so that employment concerns are suppressed. Jan Svejnar (1982) considers both criteria in a Nash model with predetermined fixed bargaining power. Bargaining over rates of return yields Ward-type behavior on the part of labor and a distribution of rent in which the ratio of total factor payments in excess of opportunity costs (or Nash threat point utility levels) is equal to the proportion of the two factors' respective bargaining strengths.

As McCain reports in his summary of the empirically testable propositions derived from these theories, one would expect to find under codetermination higher wages as a proportion of profit, a positive correlation between above-normal wages and profit, a positive correlation between wages and capital intensity and a negative correlation between both of these and output. If, on the other hand, bargaining takes place over total factor payments, i.e. the wage bill and total profit, Svejnar concludes that the optimal decision is to maximize total rents and determine shares again according to relative bargaining strengths but with a more complicated formula. In this case, workers bargain on behalf of the entire workforce, including those outside of the firm. In essence, the firm is considered to be a source of income for the entire workforce, some fraction of which will be employed therein. Obviously, allocative decisions are equivalent to those of a PMF since, with bargaining strength fixed, the workers wish to maximize the total rents to be distributed. Because the wage bill is simply the product of wages and employment, this criteria is a special case of Fellner's utility function for the union with wage and employment as arguments.

As Svejnar points out, an important difference between the two models arises with regard to exogenous changes in the relative bargaining strengths. When rates of return are the relevant concerns, changes in bargaining strength have both allocative and distributive effects. When total factor payments are at issue, such changes have distributive consequences only. Using a different approach in which a homothetic organizational utility function with wage and rate of return on capital as its arguments is assumed, Ireland and Law demonstrate that the codetermined firm will be factor stable in the face of a fluctuating product price; i.e., employment and capital usage will remain stable while the returns to each factor will respond to changes in product demand. Both capital and labor will share the risks of total income fluctuation without any allocational effects.

Roger McCain (1982) stresses the productivity-enhancing aspect of the stability of the relationship between factors in cooperative decision-making organizations and codetermined firms. Any such productivity improvements may be more than sufficient to offset the Wardian tendency to restrict membership (and hence output levels) so that effective capital-labor ratios (i.e., measured in efficiency-labor units as opposed to numbers of workers) may be no different than in the PMF. McCain also sees a potential for the codetermined firm to avoid any of the investment disincentives attributed to the LMF by Furubotn–Pejovich.

Since labor and capital jointly determine the use of inputs, McCain argues that any inefficiencies derived from workers' taking too short a planning horizon will be eliminated. Norman Ireland (1983) disagrees; he claims that the horizon problem will persist, leading both to an FPV disincentive because workers will not contribute to capital financing and to a preference for short duration capital projects by workers, so long as the capitalist has a longer horizon (the life of the project) than the group of workers with whom the present bargain is struck. Ireland models the codetermined firm as a sequential game between the capitalist and successive generations of workers. Once commited to the firm, capital will have a lower threat point value in the next round of bargaining because it is more valuable in its firm-specific use than in some alternative one. McCain, on the other hand, looks at the problem as a single bargaining game, the outcome of which is binding on all future generations of workers. This interpretation seems more appropriate if we consider the Yugoslav-type LMF with a capital maintenance requirement. Both McCain and Ireland deal only with the situation in which workers have no recoupable ownership claims over capital; hence, they ignore other property rights structures, like internal capital accounts à la Mondragon, which may attenuate the strong conflict of interest between capital and labor.

In economic models, codetermination is treated as a convex combination of two polar forms, the dividend-maximizing Wardian LMF and the PMF. However, the possibility of productivity improvements based on a reduction of opportunistic behavior on the part of both parties may be a more important consideration. Labor productivity and working conditions may improve together as public good aspects of the work relationship (e.g., effort, job rotation) are decided jointly as opposed to opportunistically in the PMF. Investment incentives and proper capital husbanding may be encouraged by joint decision-making rather than pure worker control. The general indeterminacy of any bargaining problem taken together with the results from the theory of the codetermined firm indicating the sensitivity of allocational decisions as well as distributional ones to the relative strengths of the bargaining parties suggests the importance of empirical work in this area. The Federal Republic of Germany provides the data base for a study of codetermination while many European countries have large numbers of firms which involve the workers to varying degrees in decision-making and income-sharing. We survey the empirical literature in this area in a subsequent section (Section 6a) of this essay.

3.2. The life cycle of the cooperative: an implicit contract theory approach

The economic viability of the producer cooperative in competition with traditional profit-maximizing firms has been long debated. One scenario begins with an ailing capitalist firm faced with expected bankruptcy being turned over to the workers. A restructuring of the debt then leads the worker-managers to accept the wage cuts necessary to avoid bankruptcy. If the newly-organized firm becomes a successful LMF and earns "profits" which are shared among the workforce, a dissolution phase may result from worker-members hiring labor as needed and replacing exiting members with hired labor in order to maximize the *per capita* rent. As the number of members dwindles over time, the successful LMF reverts back to its traditional PMF form. An empirical documentation of this type of life-cycle is traceable to Sidney and Beatrice Webb (1920) and Mikhail Tugan-Baranovsky (1921).

Hajime Miyazaki (1984) models this particular life-cycle hypothesis in a mixed economy in which the representative worker has two options due to the existence of a spot market in which labor can be hired by PMFs and LMFs in the short term. A worker may join a LMF and become contractually obligated to accept some risk associated with firm-specific value-added. Otherwise, the worker can hire out his labor services in each period on the spot market which is assumed to clear at a wage related to the aggregate economic conditions in the period. Miyazaki's model provides a utility-maximizing rationale for births and deaths of LMFs in the mixed economy.

Suppose that the LMF participates in the spot market by either hiring temporary labor or supplying some of its members' labor services temporarily to other firms, depending on its own short term needs. In this framework, the short run opportunity cost of labor to the LMF is the *ex post* spot market wage. Once membership is set, the objective of the LMF is to maximize the total return from value-added in production in the firm and earnings from members on temporary work assignment. Membership is contracted prior to the realization of the stochastic economic conditions when the expected utility of a representative member across a state of nature variable is the relevant concern.

As discussed in Section 1.7, a risk-averse worker will prefer to insure his *ex post* income across employment assignments. For members in the LMF, this is equivalent to pooling income from *ex post* sources, i.e., the revenues of the firm and wages earned from temporary assignment on the spot market. Since an individual member will receive a share of this pooled income regardless of his employment status in the LMF, such an arrangement makes each member indifferent to his work assignment. Labor allocation is Pareto Optimal in the *ex post* state since each firm bases its own use of labor (either hires or furloughs) on equality between the spot market wage and the internal ex post marginal product of labor.

The existence of the spot market as a source of income for an unattached (newly entering) worker imposes a rationality constraint on membership in the LMF. For the representative worker, the LMF must promise expected utility as least as great as the expected utility of selling labor on the spot market. The state of nature variable, denoted s, influences the spot market clearing wage, denoted $w(s)$, through the effects of economic conditions on the aggregate demand for and supply of labor. Examining a single LMF which is itself a participant in this market, we capture the effect of product market uncertainty based on economic conditions by defining "shadow quasi-rent", denoted $P(s)$, as follows:

$$P(s) = R(s) - w(s)[m(s) + n(s)], \tag{3.1}$$

where $R(s)$ is value-added or sales revenues minus materials cost,
$w(s)$ is the spot market-clearing wage,
$m(s)$ is the supply of labor from the membership, and
$n(s)$ is labor hired on the spot market.

In the LMF, outside labor is hired only when economic conditions are good enough to first employ fully the membership so that $n(s) = 0$ unless $m(s) = M$ where M denotes the total amount of labor services available from the membership.

As given by (3.1), $P(s)$ is value-added net of the "shadow cost" of using members' labor in the firm (the opportunity cost of which is given by the spot market wage, $w(s)$) but gross of capital charges. Miyazaki considers two polar cases for the financial environment in which the firm operates; one a capital market in which the debt payment is contingent on the state of nature and the other a capital market in which the firm is required to meet a fixed debt requirement regardless of the state of nature. Allowing for the possibility of a state-contingent debt payment, denoted $D(s)$, we define $z(s)$ as follows:

$$z(s) = [P(s) - D(s)]/M, \tag{3.2}$$

that is, the per capita membership dividend after capital charges and all production costs, including the opportunity cost of "in house" labor, are met. Notice that $z(s)$ may be negative in which case the full membership "wage", i.e., $w(s) + z(s)$, is less than the spot market clearing wage. Regardless of employment assignment, each member receives this full wage because of the income pooling arrangement.

If the capital market is perfect, the LMF can arrange a state-contingent debt contract with payment shortfalls in bad economic times compensated for by surplus payments in good economic times so that it meets on average a "normal" debt payment per period, denoted D. Miyazaki, following the implicit contract theory, argues that the risk-averse member will wish to insure his income across states. By "laying-off" all risk, the representative member receives a constant full wage, denoted v, regardless of economic conditions. All the variation in value-added is borne by the capital market. In good economic times, $D(s)$ exceeds D; in bad economic times, $D(s)$ is less than D. To compensate for this risk-shifting, the risk-averse worker is willing to accept a fully insured wage v which is less than the expected value of $w(s) + z(s)$. From (3.2), v will depend on M.

The rationality condition for membership in the LMF facing a perfect capital market is:

$$u(v) \geqq E[u(w(s))], \tag{3.3}$$

where $u(\cdot)$ is the utility function of the representative worker. Miyazaki uses the perfect capital market characterization to stylize the life-cycle of producer cooperatives. Beginning with the rationality condition (3.3), consider the case of a successful LMF in which v exceeds $E[w(s)]$ so that rents are positive *on average*, i.e., $E[P(s) - D(s)]$ is positive. In this case, the optimal membership is one, by assumption the smallest possible number of members. The result follows by noticing that taking on an additional member would require the single initial member to share some of the average rent whereas hiring someone to provide the same labor services allows the initial member to retain all the rents. As discussed above in Section 1.7, Ben-Ner shows an analogous result for the deterministic case in the Ward–Domar–Vanek tradition. If, on the other hand, v is less than $E[w(s)]$, the LMF is ailing in the sense that it earns negative rents or losses *on average*. In this case, the optimal membership is infinite which follows from an attempt to increase membership indefinitely so as to make the per capita loss as small as possible.

Of particular interest is the consistency between the rationality condition (3.3) and the birth condition that v be less than $E[w(s)]$. The possibility of these two conditions being satisfied simultaneously follows from Jensen's inequality; i.e., $u(E[w(s)])$ exceeds $E[u(w(s))]$. Therefore, $u(E[w(s)])$ can be greater than $u(v)$ which can in turn be greater than $E[u(w(s))]$. Consequently, worker risk-aversion can explain a willingness on the part of labor to take over an ailing firm and reorganize it as a LMF rather than face the vagaries of hiring-out on the spot labor market.

The perfect capital market case allows each worker to insure fully his wage rather than share the risks in fluctuating firm-specific value-added. If the state of the firm's product market is not verifiable externally or if the workers can substitute nonmonetary return for effective labor input by shirking, such a contract involves moral hazard. A polar alternative examined by Miyazaki is a state by state bankruptcy constraint which forces the LMF to meet exactly the normal debt payment D per period. The member's full return in the LMF can then be written as the sum of the spot market wage $w(s)$ and $z(s)$ where $z(s)$ is defined by (3.2) with $D(s) = D$. The full wage now depends on the state of the economy as it affects both the spot market and the "quasi-rent" of the firm. Of course, $z(s)$ will be negative in bad economic times.

Miyazaki considers two possibilities for firm-specific "quasi-rents;" $P(s)$ is either procyclical or countercyclical. A procyclical LMF is one for which the covariance of $w(s)$ and $P(s)$ is positive. Aggregate economic conditions which lead to a high demand for labor in the spot market and thus a high equilibrium wage also make the procyclical firm more profitable. The rationality condition for a procyclical LMF is that $E[P(s)]$ be positive. The worker's motivation for joining the procyclical LMF stems from receiving a return, i.e., $w(s) + z(s)$, which on average exceeds the spot market wage. If this were not the case and $E[P(s)]$ were nonpositive, the positive covariance would increase the total variance of the return in the LMF over that in the spot market with no increase in mean return. The optimal membership, M^*, is larger than one as more members reduce the variability in the member's full wage, $w(s)+z(s)$, and the number of members is chosen to strike the optimal balance between risk and expected return.

In this financial environment, optimal membership will realistically be greater than one but finite. Hence, the knife-edge result on membership size in the perfect capital market scenario is blunted. If the LMF's product market is more stable than the spot labor market so that $\operatorname{cov}\{w(s), P(s)\}$ is negative, the LMF is defined to be countercyclical. Then rationality is consistent with $E[P(s)]=0$ so long as $\operatorname{cov}\{P(s), P(s)+w(s)\}$ is positive. The motive for joining such a LMF is to reduce the variability in earnings only, since rents on average are zero. Consequently, Miyazaki's work is suggestive of the conditions under which risk-averse workers will be willing to join a LMF even if capital bears no risk and a spot market equilibrium insures that there is never any voluntary unemployment. Expected rents suffice but even if there are no expected rents to be made, risk reduction may induce workers to join the LMF.

Nothing precludes the spot market from effectuating temporary work assignments among LMFs only, a practice which seems to have some empirical relevance in Yugoslavia where BOALS subcontract with each other for temporary labor (cf. Sacks (1977)). On the positive side, the spot market insures *ex post* Pareto optimality by establishing a macroeconomic "shadow price" for labor which both clears the market so there is no involuntary unemployment and equalizes the marginal product of labor across firms for the *ex post* realization of the economic state. As we discuss more fully in Section 2.6 above, incentive problems may arise if LMF members receive fully insured wages rather than share to some extent in value-added. The polar alternative offered by Miyazaki is for this group of risk-averse workers to make a fixed payment to capital financiers, a solution which cannot be optimal on risk-sharing grounds. Somewhere in between these two poles lies the relevant characterization of the financial environment faced by LMFs. Work to date provides a contractual (incentive-compatible) justification for the existence of LMFs in a capitalist environment.

3.3. Imperfect competition in product markets

In much of the theoretical literature on the LMF, the market in which its product is sold is assumed to be competitive and, consequently, output price is parametric to the firm's decision-making problem. Jaroslav Vanek (1970) considers the long run optimal choices of labor and capital for a monopoly LMF in which capital is rented and labor is remunerated according to the dividend share. The only difference in first order conditions from our earlier specification is that labor is taken on up to the point where its marginal revenue product is equal to the dividend. Since the LMF is assumed to have a monopoly in its product market, the marginal revenue product is less than the value marginal product for any membership level. Consequently, the monopoly LMF restricts membership in order to earn more rents than its LMF competitive counterpart. Therefore, the welfare costs attributed to capitalist product market monopoly would pertain to the LMF as well.

A long run comparison between a monopoly LMF and a monopoly PMF indicates that the LMF chooses a smaller labor force than the PMF. As long as labor is a non-inferior input, the monopoly LMF produces less output than a monopoly PMF twin as shown in Ireland–Law (1982). The monopoly LMF produces an output level for which both demand elasticity and returns to scale exceed one. That increasing returns to scale is a necessary condition for dividend-maximization follows from noticing that constant returns to scale renders the dividend invariant with respect to changes in scale when all prices are constant and all factors are variable. For the monopolist, a reduction in output leads to a higher product price along a downward-sloping demand curve. Such an output reduction in the region of constant returns must lead to a higher dividend due to this price increase. As Saul Estrin (1985) shows, the monopoly LMF chooses optimal scale by equating the Lerner coefficient of monopoly power, i.e., the ratio of price to marginal revenue, to the returns to scale parameter in the variable returns, homothetic technology specification.

The comparative static analysis in the monopoly case is similar to that in perfect competition, as Saul Estrin demonstrates, with results depending on returns to scale, the possibility of rents, and the shape of the demand function. Although the results of a shift in the demand function are indeterminate in general, Estrin discusses several cases of interest for empirical work. An elasticity-preserving demand shift leaves optimal output unaffected as it has no effect on the Lerner coefficient at the previous optimum. As Ireland and Law (1982) demonstrate, an elasticity-increasing demand shift leads to a higher optimal output for homothetic technologies. The Lerner coefficient at the old optimal level increases so that output must increase to equalize scale and this ratio at a new optimum.

The relationship between changes in elasticity and a parametric shift in demand have proved useful to the analysis of advertising decisions in a LMF. Intuitively, the parameter shifting the demand function now becomes a choice variable, advertising expenditures. The well-known Dorfman–Steiner optimality condition for the PMF involves equating advertising expenditures as a proportion of sales to the ratio of the elasticity of demand with respect to advertising expenditure divided by the absolute value of the price elasticity of demand. As Ireland and Law (1982) succinctly summarize, the comparison between the LMF and the PMF according to advertising expenditures has been debated in a lively fashion. Vanek demonstrates that the LMF would choose a lower advertising expenditure than the PMF for a given level of output. Meade (1972) queries the relevance of this since the LMF would also operate at a smaller scale thus leaving ambiguous the relationship between the Dorfman–Steiner ratio in the LMF and the PMF.

Alfred Steinherr (1975) attempts to extend the Vanek result to a comparison of advertising expenditures per unit of output because of its potential welfare importance when advertising expenditures yield no social benefits. However, as Ireland and Law (1977) show, Steinherr's conclusion that the LMF would do less advertising depends on overly restrictive assumptions. In general, firms operating on different portions of a given demand function will experience different values for the two elasticities rendering the ratio of advertising expenditures to sales revenue noncomparable. However, if these elasticities are constant (i.e., the demand function exhibits constant elasticities), Ireland and Law show that both the LMF and the PMF will spend the same proportion of their sales revenue on advertising. Since the PMF operates at a larger scale, its sales revenues will be larger and hence so will its advertising expenditures. Furthermore, a comparison of advertising expenditures per unit of output as Steinherr performed would yield in this constant elasticity case equal ratios when the advertising elasticity is unity and a larger (smaller) advertising expenditure per unit of output for the LMF when this elasticity is smaller (larger) than unity. Hence, no general case can be made for the superiority of the LMF on the grounds of lower advertising intensity.

In his treatise on the labor-managed economy, Vanek (1970) claims that, since a LMF operates at a smaller scale of output than the PMF twin when the latter earns positive profit, concentration ratios in oligopolistic industries will be smaller in the LME than in its imperfectly-competitive counterpart. Martyn Hill and Michael Waterson (1983) show that, in positive profit oligopolistic equilibria, the LME industry will have the same number of firms as its profit-maximizing counterpart and, because each LMF will produce less output than a PMF, product price will be higher in the LME. Hugh Neary (1984) constructs an example to show that the Hill–Waterson result is dependent upon the strong assumption of symmetry in both cost and demand across all firms (including potential entrants). In a homogeneous product industry with symmetric firm technological structure but non-symmetric fixed costs so that inframarginal firms earn positive profit in a free entry profit-maximizing industry, Neary's example shows that the LME industry may have more firms.

For the case of monopolistic competition where entry is free and firms produce heterogeneous products which are close but not perfect substitutes for each other, Neary (1984) demonstrates that the LME may provide a higher level of net social welfare than its profit-maximizing counterpart. Under these circumstances, a PMF can earn positive locational rents in long run equilibrium by proper selection of product characteristics. Since positive rent implies a smaller scale of operation for the LMF twin, Neary shows that the LME can support a greater variety of products in equilibrium. More product diversity may be sufficient to compensate for the smaller output per product and the LME may yield more net social welfare than its profit-maximizing counterpart.

While the monopolistic competition framework assumes free entry, many oligopoly models stress entry-deterring strategies. Yoshinari Miyamoto (1980) compares limit entry strategies for the

LMF and the PMF in an analytical structure based on work by Michael Spence (1977). Each firm uses a linear homogeneous production technology with fixed factor prices, and potential entrants face the same cost and production conditions. For the PMF the limit entry price would be that which makes profit nonpositive for any (all) entrant(s). Miyamoto argues that the equivalent condition for the LMF is that dividend be less than or equal to an alternative market wage, taken to be that paid by the twin PMF. Hence, he argues that the limit entry price would be the same for both enterprise types.

Miyamoto also considers, for the sake of comparison, an excess capacity strategy characterized by Spence. For the PMF, sufficient capacity is maintained to expand output to the point at which price would fall to its limit entry level, but the firm actually chooses a price above this to maximize short run profit. For the LMF, since positive rent can be earned with a similar strategy, the effects of dividend-maximizing behavior yield different allocational results. In essence, the LMF maintains sufficient capacity to expand and deter entry, but this requires more capital than the PMF due to the WDV factor distortion. In a non-competitive LME, the existence of an alternative market wage seems problematic casting doubt on the equivalence of the limit price and hence the required excess capacity. Presumably, the alternative dividend available to potential entrants (LMFs) would itself depend on the structure of the market.

Traditionally, in the economic literature, oligopoly theory has been treated as a strategic game between (usually) two participants (duopolists). The earliest Cournot–Stackelberg models derive reaction functions for PMFs based on the optimal quantity decision as a function of the rival duopolist's output. Cournot equilibria are compared with other types of strategic behavior (i.e., leader-follower). Similar analysis has been done for the LMF duopolist by Vanek (1970), Ireland–Law (1982), and Miyamoto (1982). For the Vanek case in which reaction functions for the two duopolists are upward-sloping in quantity space (i.e., the quadrant defined by the quantity chosen by each duopolist on one of the axes), Ireland-Law show that the LMF duopolist in contrast to its PMF counterpart may prefer to be a follower and allow the rival LMF to be a Stackelberg leader. Further differences due to organizational form are discussed in Miyamoto where reasonable conditions on technology and demand are given and shown to lead to downward-sloping reaction functions.

From our analysis of the workers' desire to diversify firm-specific earnings risk in the LMF, we conjecture that workers are likely to find product diversification strategies attractive. Therefore, we would expect to find incentives for horizontal mergers and the formation of large conglomerates in the LME. Whether such tendencies would lead to more or less entry barriers and to more or less industrial concentration seems to be a question for empirical investigation.

To isolate the influence of product market uncertainty in a Ward-type model, Timothy Muzondo (1979) takes the objective function to be the expected utility of the dividend. The usual assumptions of positive first and negative second derivatives are imposed on the utility function (i.e. simple risk-aversion is assumed). Product market uncertainty is modeled as a stochastic output price while the other elements of the simple Illyrian model are retained. Starting from a solution to Ward's dividend maximizing problem under certainty, Muzondo demonstrates a risk-hedging result. Since the fixed cost is certain while the return to production is uncertain, the LMF hedges by decreasing the certain fixed cost per worker and increasing the optimal number of worker/members. Hence, product price uncertainty leads to a larger output and more members in the LMF than would be the case under certainty.

It is well-known that the risk-averse PMF reacts to the same product market uncertainty by reducing output and employment (or stated another way; the risk-averse PMF produces less than the risk-neutral PMF). Uncertainty and risk-aversion thus modify PMF and LMF behavior in opposite directions. Naturally, one might wonder whether the LMF actually produces more output and achieves higher employment levels than the PMF in the presence of market uncertainty. The comparison requires a statement about the profitability of the PMF in a certainty-equivalent situation. If positive rents prevail under certainty, the outcome is ambiguous. Suppose instead that both the LMF and the PMF can earn only zero profits, and thus would produce the same output with the same level of employment, in the certainty situation. The introduction of product market uncertainty would then lead to the LMF producing more output with higher employment than the PMF as Muzondo demonstrates.

In general, the comparative static results with respect to prices and fixed charges derived for the certainty case are not affected by uncertainty when the usual assumptions are imposed. As Bonin (1980) shows in his correction of a mathematical error in Muzondo's paper, the LMF responds in a Ward-type way to changes in fixed costs and changes in the expected value of its output price if decreasing absolute risk-aversion is assumed. The LMF increases workers and output when fixed costs increase while the PMF under the same assumptions of risk-aversion would decrease employment and output. The analogue of the downward-sloping supply curve is also present as the LMF responds to an increase in the expected price by decreasing output and workers. The PMF exhibits a positive supply response in this situation.

Furthermore, Bonin shows that, when the sign of the effect can be determined, the response of the LMF to a change in a tax parameter is always opposite that of a PMF under equivalent risk-aversion assumptions. Jacob Paroush and Nava Kahana (1980) demonstrate that, since the utility function is assumed to be concave and the dividend is linear in the stochastic variable (price), the indirect utility function is concave in expected price. Consequently, they argue that the introduction of uncertainty is formally equivalent to a decline in price, and, therefore, the output response follows from the Ward supply response. Gabriel Hawawini and Pierre Michel (1979) show similar results using a mean-variance approach.

In a subsequent paper, Hawawini and Michel (1983) demonstrate that the choice of technology will be more labor intensive under uncertainty and risk-aversion in the LMF than under certainty. A similar result is shown by Rama Ramachandran, William Russell, and Tae Kun Seo (1979) for cases in which membership or capital are respectively fixed. Ramachandran–Russell–Seo also consider the impact of a minimum wage on the LMF facing price uncertainty (see also, Bonin (1977) for a discussion of the impact of a minimum wage on the collective farm). The minimum wage effectively truncates from below the distribution of return per capita and reduces downside risk; consequently, the optimal membership is reduced with the reduction in earnings variation. A convenient way of deriving many of the above comparative static results by direct comparison with the comparative statics of the PMF is shown in John Hey and John Suckling (1980).

3.4. Growth and macroeconomics in the labor-managed economy

Intertemporal comparisons of dividend-maximizing and profit-maximizing firms are made by A. B. Atkinson (1973) for equilibrium growth paths in a Marris-type environment: specifically, no choice of production technique is incorporated; rather, a fixed coefficient production function and exogenous labor-augmenting technical change are assumed. A steady-state growth rate is the essential choice variable as it is determined by the firm's once-and-for-all optimal choice of demand-expanding selling costs. Atkinson argues that only economies of scale induce growth in the LMF because he demonstrates that constant returns to scale lead to a choice of zero growth-inducing sales promotional costs, hence leaving the LMF to grow only at the exogenous rate due to technical change.

With increasing returns and wholly external financing of capital at a fixed rate of interest, Atkinson shows that the growth rate chosen to maximize the present value of dividends (i.e. net revenues after subtracting selling costs minus the cost of capital financing) by the LMF is a decreasing function of the effective discount rate which is the difference between the members' time discount rate and the exogenous growth rate of technical change. Atkinson turns to a comparison of the growth rates resulting from optimal choices by this LMF and a PMF twin. The PMF twin pays to its employees wages which increase over time at a fixed rate, finances capital formation wholly from retained earnings, and pays to its shareholders dividends which equal the difference between net revenues and the above costs. The assumed maximand for the PMF is the difference between the present value at a market rate of interest of the stream of dividend payments and the value of the initial capital stock.

Atkinson demonstrates that the LMF chooses a lower growth rate than its PMF twin when the effective discount rate for the LMF is larger than the interest rate which serves as the discount rate for the firm maximizing shareholders' wealth. Atkinson argues that such a relationship is likely because of an FPV effect even though he assumes wholly external financing of capital. This is a sufficient condition only as Atkinson (1975) makes clear in his response to a comment on his paper by Alfred Steinherr and Henk Peer (1975). In the opposite case, either the capitalist firm grows faster or it can not break-even (i.e. make a profit). Furthermore, Atkinson justifies his assumption by referring to the non-recoupability of dividends paid after the worker leaves the LMF. Essentially, present values are computed over infinite horizons because shareholders in the PMF can sell their ownership rights to the stream of returns. To adjust for the impossibility of workers selling their membership rights (or living forever), Atkinson uses a higher time discount factor than the market interest rate for present value calculations in the LMF.

Masahiko Aoki (1979) provides a behavioral rationale for growth in the LMF by postulating two groups of workers within the firm: junior workers and senior partners. Growth of the firm increases the probability of a junior worker being promoted to a senior partner so that the younger workers stand willing to support growth-stimulating strategies in the interest of lifetime income maximization. Andre Sapir (1980) models a training, or apprenticeship, period in a LMF for newly hired workers some proportion of whom will graduate (or be promoted) to full membership status. Assuming an infinite decision-making horizon and capital rental at a market rate, Sapir considers hired workers receiving on-the-job training which increases their productivity to that of a full member. While in training the workers are paid a wage, but members receive a dividend.

Sapir characterizes a steady-state solution in which promotion is just sufficient to replace members who are retiring voluntarily at some predetermined rate and the dividend received by members is constant. The steady-state solution is not globally stable so that the tenured management of the firm must determine the appropriate promotion rate given the initial membership. When the initial membership is below its optimal level, the members choose to hire a relatively large number of trainees and select a high promotion rate. Both the number of hired workers and the promotion rate must be reduced as the steady-state is approached. When the steady-state path is reached so that trainees are promoted in sufficient numbers to exactly replace retiring workers, the total size of the firm's workforce is smaller but a larger proportion are members than was the case in the initial situation. Sensitivity analysis indicates that a lower wage rate paid to hired workers, an increase in the retirement rate, or a narrowing of the productivity gap between trainees and members will lead to a long run steady-state increase in employment and the total workforce.

John Bonin (1983) compares the dividend maximizing firm with a profit-rate maximizing firm with regard to long-run technical change, both endogenous and exogenous. This stylized LMF chooses innovations which are more labor *saving* than the stylized PMF counterpart. Furthermore, if technical change of the Harrod-neutral sort is exogenous, the LMF chooses a more capital-intensive trajectory than the PMF. Thus, as membership is less of a constraint on labor adjustment due to an ability to adjust the long-run labor-capital ratio when technical change (either endogenous or exogenous) affects the production function, the Wardian tendency to observe a more capital-intensive production mode in the LMF is corroborated in this model. Branko Milanovic (1982) reaches similar conclusions in an Austrian model of the cooperative when he finds that the LMF does not expand employment as much as a capitalist (profit-rate-maximizing) counterpart in response to technological progress.

Eirik Furubotn (1976) focuses on optimal investment behavior in a multi-period model of the LMF in which the initial membership is assumed to be the decision-making group. Furubotn imposes a rather arbitrary upper bound on membership to preclude the incoming group from usurping the decision-making control of the initial group. Then, assuming no attrition, the initial membership is a lower bound. Within this range, labor can be varied and members taken on during the planning horizon have no decision-making rights. Furubotn derives the optimal consumption and investment plan over the finite planning horizon of the initial membership and demonstrates the FPV underinvestment result in this model.

John Bonin (1982) models a similar intertemporal problem by introducing membership adjustment costs which depend on the membership at the beginning of each period in a finite planning horizon. Consequently, newly hired workers are included in the membership base for purposes of calculating the dividend in each period which is adjusted for the estimated cost of their impact on the LMF (e.g. it may now be more difficult to reach consensus in decision-making). Furthermore, Bonin allows for a decrease in membership again with an associated adjustment cost which is similar to Meade's transfer compensation to dismissed members. With membership treated as a proper state variable and the capital decision modeled within a Yugoslav-type financial environment (e.g. investment is assumed to be irreversible due to the capital maintenance requirement), Bonin derives optimal input policies from maximizing the discounted adjusted dividend over time.

From sensitivity analysis of the effect of a change in the discount rate on optimal input policies, Bonin makes policy inferences about the influence of interest rate changes on membership adjustment over time and the consequent impact on employment in any period. If the LMF is experiencing expansionary conditions in its product market, lower interest rates are shown to stimulate current employment. On the other hand, in a contractionary product market situation, higher interest rates lead to more current employment by reducing dismissals and, in a sense, provide financial support for membership solidarity. By examining the sensitivity of optimal employment policies to the given finite decision-making horizon imposed initially on the problem, Bonin shows that shorter planning horizons result in less membership adjustment and hence more solidarity.

Realistically, the planning horizon for the LMF should be a choice variable decided by the current membership and should respond inversely to economic opportunities for members elsewhere in the economy (i.e., the planning horizon will be shorter, *ceteris paribus,* if members expect to leave soon for other jobs). Of course, the age composition of the membership will influence the horizon as well. As we have discussed before, Vanek and others stress the importance of public policy to encourage the formation of firms (i.e. entry) to combat some of the inefficiences attributed to the LMF. In a general contractionary situation where firms are dismissing workers, entry-encouraging policies will increase the mobility of already-employed workers and be further reinforced if planning horizons are shortened by members to take account of the new opportunities. In contractionary situations, shorter horizons lead to more current employment in the LMF. However, if existing firms are expanding yet employment opportunities are still not adequate, government-encouraged entry will be countervailed to some extent as members shorten planning horizons and take on fewer new members. In this situation, new firms are a partial substitute for job creation by existing firms.

From a microeconomic perspective, Bonin argues that the macroeconomic policy instrument chosen should be tuned carefully to the cyclical problem in the LME in ways that are often different from the appropriate policy prescriptions for the capitalist mixed economy. Milanovic (1982) argues from an Austrian microeconomic model of the cooperative that, if macroeconomic authorities maintain interest rates at a (subsidized) below-market-equilibrium level, employment performance of the LMF will be unsatisfactory. The spirit of Milanovic's result is captured in our earlier demonstration that the demand for labor is positively related to the fixed cost of non-labor inputs. Lower capital charges reduce the demand for labor and, consequently, unemployment problems in an LME may be exacerbated by such interference in capital markets.

Formal macroeconomic modeling of the LME began, and virtually ended, with the two seminal books on the LME; one by Benjamin Ward (1967) and the other by Jaroslav Vanek (1970). Both are essentially closed models in which the perverse microeconomic behavior of the LMF is grafted onto a simple traditional macroeconomic framework. Vanek claims that Ward uses a simplistic theory of the money market, i.e., the quantity theory, and takes too seriously the backward-bending product supply curve. Vanek's own theory is a Keynesian one in which one of four markets, goods, money, bonds, and "quasi-labor", may be ignored owing to Walras' law. The adjective "quasi" addended to labor indicates Vanek's concern that hired labor be forbidden in the LME.

In his book, Vanek also considers backward-bending product supply curves a potential problem although he prefers to think of them as simply less elastic than product supply curves in the CME. Although he has a chapter on investment disincentives, Vanek claims that the macroeconomic significance of this is slight as the aggregate investment function will still be negatively sloped with respect to changes in the interest rate. Furthermore, Vanek claims that there is no reason to believe that the fundamental nature of money and securities markets would be any different from that of these markets in the CME. Regarding the "quasi-labor" market, Vanek claims that the LME has a significant advantage over the CME because of the absence of wage-price rigidity. He appeals to entry to solve any short run unemployment problems arising from membership restriction.

Vanek argues that the *aggregate* product supply curve is vertical in the short run due in essence to a membership labor solidarity response to price increases and a binding full employment constraint when price decreases. This rids the macroeconomic model of the potential instability problem introduced by a Ward backward-bending aggregate supply curve. In the closed model, employment and output are fixed in the short run so that macroeconomic policy has no effect on any of the real variables and serves to influence only monetary variables. Monetary expansion (contraction) increases (decreases) the aggregate price level and decreases (increases) the interest rate. Vanek's criticism of Ward notwithstanding, a (crude) quantity theory seems to result from his own assumptions.

An expansionary fiscal policy, i.e., an increase in expenditures or a decrease in the general tax rate, increases the price level and the interest rate with the opposite changes brought about by contractionary fiscal policy. The long run implications of Vanek's macroeconomic framework include the usual growth response to both interest rate and money national income changes and a continual state of full employment of labor due to free entry. Finally, consideration of an open economy would introduce to the model the balance of payments on current account and exchange rate determination. However, as Vanek (1972) shows, these extensions generate no policy surprises nor does their inclusion alter the results concerning the real/money dichotomy discussed above.

Vanek's macroeconomic model remains too simplistic for use as a basis for policy prescriptions. When short-run disequilibrium occurs in the "quasi-labor-market", the implications of disequilibrium in some other market (which follows from Walras' law) are not considered. Nor are any of the FPV results from capital theory incorporated in the macroeconomic model. Lest the reader find these comments overly critical of Vanek's work, we should report that we know of no systematic attempts to incorporate any of the recent theoretical work on the LMF into an integrated macroeconomic model. Vanek's book still contains the most detailed discussion of macroeconomic theory of which we are aware.

The partial equilibrium approach to public finance is implicitly considered in many of the microeconomic models of the LMF when the effects of different types of taxes and subsidies are included in the sensitivity results. Jean-Jacques Laffont and Roger Guesnerie (1984) examine several tax policies in a general equilibrium model of the LME with a fiscal authority and conclude that lump sum taxation of consumers and producers allows the government to restore Pareto-optimality after some disturbance of a long-run equilibrium with zero rents and that the LME and the CME equilibria are initially equivalent. However, simply taxing the consumers with a combination of lump sum and excise taxes is shown to fail to bring about Pareto-optimality in general. Laffont and Guesnerie show that cases can be found in which all taxation instruments will fail to achieve Pareto optimality if the LMF is monopolistic.

Ward's original concern about stability in the LME is echoed by Drèze when he states that comparisons between the LME and the CME should deal not only with equilibrium allocations, but also

> with such issues as the ability of alternative systems to generate equilibria, or to generate satisfactory adjustments to equilibrium situations, or to generate alternative solutions (like underemployment or monopolistic equilibria).
>
> Drèze (1976, p. 1128)

The sole systematic attempt to deal with the stability of a general equilibrium model of the LME of which we are aware is undertaken by David Conn and Fernando M. C. B. Saldanha (undated manuscript). The authors assume a fixed number of firms so that the results are applicable to short run stability. They assume an exogenous "foreign" wage, which provides the opportunity cost basis for the calculation of membership share prices, and consider a non-tâtonnement Hahn-type adjustment process with the number of firms fixed.

In the Conn and Saldanha model, production takes place only after equilibrium in the membership shares market is reached (as in the general equilibrium model of Dow discussed in Section 1.6). A worker who joins a firm makes a commitment to share in the management, profits and work of the firm while he is a member.

However, the non-tâtonnement process allows a worker to join a firm during the groping toward equilibrium but leave it before production actually takes place and thus earn the appropriate Meade transfer compensation for not working in the firm. Consequently, income can be earned prior to production in a speculative manner due to the transactions which take place on the way to equilibrium. Under the naive expectations assumption that agents behave as if they expect equilibrium to occur at the particular prices prevailing at each moment, Conn and Saldanha demonstrate the stability of their adjustment mechanism.

Further theoretical work in these areas is necessary before we can talk confidently about the "macroeconomic theory of the LME". The recent work in the microeconomic theory of the LMF allays many of the concerns about perverse behavior at the enterprise level infecting macroeconomic performance. However, the incompleteness of a labor market in which workers are not treated as a commodity imparts a distinctive characteristic on the LME. If the essence of labor-management is the right of the worker to control his own work environment by democratic procedures, this right should not be "for sale". If worker control exacts a toll in capital financing arrangements due to moral hazard concerns, this is a price to be paid for worker democracy. Economic models must recognize these aspects of the LME so that meaningful welfare statements can be made. For this, we look to the future.

PART II: APPLICATIONS

4. SELF-MANAGEMENT THEORY AND THE YUGOSLAV ECONOMY

While isolated cases of worker-run enterprises within capitalist economies have probably existed for as long as capitalism itself, self-management did not elicit sustained attention from economists until one country, Yugoslavia, made the system its central principle of economic organization. "Workers' control," at the level of society as a whole, had been a nominal principle of other socialist economies, so Yugoslav claims to be implementing such control at the enterprise level only gradually gained the credence of outside observers, as evolving implementation deepened the reality of decentralization and worker influence. The background for this experiment could hardly have been more striking. Yugoslav workers inherited an industrial structure built by Soviet-style command planning on the backdrop of an underdeveloped and largely agrarian economy, in a nation only recently born from an amalgam of "nationalities," of different languages and religions, straddling the frontiers of centuries-old empires and spheres of religious influence.

As the sole national embodiment of self-management, Yugoslavia's impressive but flawed economic performance has been the object of much scrutiny. The country's industrial and GNP growth rates in the 1960's and 1970's compared very favorably with those of other developing nations, of the more developed capitalist economies, and of the various centrally planned economies. But to some East European observers, growing Yugoslav unemployment, inflation, and macroeconomic instability have illustrated the dangers of reliance on market mechanisms; and even some socialist *reformers* have concluded that the apparent defects of that economy should serve as a warning against altering conventional management systems at the enterprise level. From a Western perspective, the flaws in Yugoslav performance have been interpreted as evidence of allocative distortions inherent in self-management property rights.

Our earlier discussion has already illustrated the influence of

Yugoslav institutions on self-management theory, and has also warned against the blanket equation of self-management with such institutional particulars. In this section, we draw together some of the major implications of self-management theory for Yugoslav practice and performance, and review institutional and econometric evidence bearing on them.[39]

4.1. Self-management and Yugoslav market socialism

While a series of reforms since the early 1950's has lent increasing practical significance to the principle of ultimate control of Yugoslav manufacturing enterprises by their workers via elected workers' councils (or directly, for the smallest enterprises) and their appointed boards of management, Yugoslav economic organization and ideology has also been described by two other salient features: decentralized economic coordination by the market, and socialist property rights. The theories of self-management discussed in this paper have generally assumed a market environment, but at the same time, have suggested that incompleteness of some markets may be a general characteristic of LME's. With respect to Yugoslavia, not all of the abridgment and imperfection of markets can be attributed to self-management directly; it must be emphasized in addition that, while highly decentralized relative to its Soviet-type point of departure, the country continues to manifest substantial levels of price-setting and other interventions by authorities at federal, republican, and commune (local government) levels. Also, one can argue that the Yugoslav economy has ultimately become as much a system of allocation through *bargaining* among political and economic units as it has been one of allocation by a market mechanism.

Socialist property rights are manifested, in particular, in rules governing the control and accumulation of capital goods, and in the ideological interpretation given to those rules. While empowered by

[39] Those already familiar with the literature on Yugoslav economic experience will note at least three major areas of neglect in what follows. First, we pay little attention to regional differences; second, we provide little discussion on the international dimension of the economy. On the latter, the reader is recommended to consult Burkett, 1983, and references cited therein. Finally, we can make only passing references to the literature published in Yugoslavia itself.

self-management reforms to control production and employment decisions, Yugoslav enterprises are prohibited from distributing to individual members salable or heritable claims to the capital goods of their enterprise. Instead, these assets are viewed as the property of society as a whole, and workers' rights over the capital of their enterprises are limited to its use (on a collective basis) and to the distribution of resulting income streams according to internally determined income schedules. Moreover, before distribution of revenues, the law requires that depreciation funds be set aside to provide for replacement of existing capital goods with others of equal value. The book value of an enterprise's capital may thus grow, but can not decline unless another enterprise agrees to take on its capital maintenance obligation. Additions to the stock of enterprise capital goods can be financed by state allocations, on which interest charges are assessed;[40] through self-financing out of retained net earnings; or through loans from other enterprises or from banks also belonging to the "social" sector.[41] In all cases, the same rules of non-individual ownership of enterprise capital and of perpetual maintenance of the book value of that capital apply. "Private investment" in the "social" sector takes place indirectly, however, when individuals hold savings accounts with banks that in turn make loans to self-managed firms.

Socialist property rights have been perhaps the most constant feature of the Yugoslav system since the early 1950's. During the following three decades, the degree of enterprise autonomy, the definition of the enterprise, the financial system, and the level of market freedom or restriction have changed almost continuously. Nevertheless, simplifying periodizations such as that presented by Estrin (1983) seem to be acceptable to many experts on the Yugoslav economy.

Following Neuberger (1970), Estrin dubs the first dozen years after establishment of the workers' councils and of the legal principles of enterprise self-management (in 1950–52) the "Visible

[40] Since 1964–65, however, such direct allocations were made only to less developed regions.

[41] Because the self-management sector was created by direct transformation of the state sector of the former, centralized system, the terms "state", "self-managed," "social," and "socialized" refer to the same set of, e.g., manufacturing, service, and financial enterprises.

Hand" period.[42] Broadly speaking, investment remained centrally planned, production was guided by a mix of plans and market regulations, and the Soviet-type enterprise management structure was gradually reformed into one over which workers' representatives began to exercise some authority.[43] The "Market Self-Management" period of 1965–72/74 was ushered in by fundamental reforms which increased enterprise autonomy, dismantled central planning agencies, and relaxed market controls. The transition to this period also saw substantial replacement of the state's financing role by that of a decentralized state banking system.

The end of the middle period, between 1972 and 1974, manifested two trends that appear contradictory from the standpoint of workers' control. First, self-management in the political sense was potentially strengthened by redefining the enterprise unit as the smallest association of workers producing a product of ascertainable exchange value: the "basic organization of associated labor" (BOAL). This significantly reduced the average size of self-managing units, bringing enterprise democracy closer to the grass roots level by divisionalizing large enterprises by plant, workshop, etc. (Sacks, 1983). Second, however, some market controls were restored, and enterprise autonomy was restrained by "social compacts" and other agreements involving enterprises, government bodies, and other organizations.[44] Thus, the crucial external interactions for the enterprise shifted from the planning hierarchy, in the "Visible Hand" era, to the market, in the "Market Self-Management" era, to bargaining in the local polity, also referred to as "agreement," in the "Social Planning" era.[45] In view of these changes, applicability of self-management models may vary from period to period. Estrin and other theorists familiar with Yugoslav experience argue that only the middle period may be appropriate

[42] *Op. cit.*, pp. 57–77. See also Bicanic, 1973, Horvat, 1976, and Milenkovitch, 1971.

[43] A more refined periodization might give more emphasis to movement toward "indicative" planning and "income sharing" with the second Five Year Plan beginning in 1957–58.

[44] Since 1974, "self-management communities of interest" have extended self-management relations to the organization and financing of public services including health and education (Singleton and Carter, 1982).

[45] On Yugoslav self-management and bargaining, see Comisso 1979 and 1980.

for testing hypotheses rooted in the Western theoretical literature on LMF's.

4.2. Self-management theory and enterprise self-finance

As we have seen, theoretical considerations lead us to expect that capital maintenance and "non-ownership" will lead to low internal financing and to extensive reliance on bank funds where available. In practice, the level of bank financing rose rapidly in Yugoslavia during the 1960's, but this was essentially substituting for financing by various levels of government. Between 1960–63 and 1972, the bank share of finance rose from 3 to 42%, the state share fell from 60 to 20%, and enterprise shares were level at 30%.[46] Only between 1966 and 1969 was there an apparent trade-off between enterprise and bank financing, with the former falling from 39 to 28% of the total and the latter rising from 39 to 49%; but this short-term trend vanishes in the longer perspective, as just seen.[47] Total investment as a percentage of gross domestic product remained high by international standards from the early 1950's onwards, with perhaps a slight dip in the middle 1960's (when "market self-management" was vigorously implemented) followed by steady increases during the 1970's and another decline during the early 1980's recession. The share of investment obtained by self-financing may if anything have risen during the 1970's.[48]

There are a number of plausible explanations for observed enterprise investment behavior in Yugoslavia. In the first place, the appearance of sustained, positive self-financing in the face of the conflicting implications of self-management theory may be read as evidence that enterprise work forces were not entirely free to determine investment and consumption out of net revenues. Furubotn and Pejovich (1970) suggest that enterprise directors might be successful in selecting investment rates that give weights to the interests of both enterprise workers and outside political authorities. Historically, one might argue that the relative influence of the

[46] World Bank, 1975, reported in Estrin, 1983, p. 67. The remainder of finance was by "social organizations," and was also approximately level at 7 to 8%.

[47] *Ibid.*

[48] This seems to be the implication of data presented by Dimitrijevic and Masecich, 1983, p. 61, and brought to our attention by Will Bartlett.

latter was decisive up to the mid-1960's, that self-financing did decline as would be predicted by theory during the late 1960's, when workers' influence rose, and that self-financing rose rapidly in the 1970's when external influence was restored. Estrin and Bartlett (1982) cite several sociological studies by Yugoslav authors indicating seemingly disproportionate managerial influence in decision-making, and "a divergence between the formal self-management arrangements and their actual implementation."[49] Such findings, while not historically pegged to a scenario of the type just sketched, could be viewed as broadly consistent with the Furubotn–Pejovich conjecture.

Alternatively, one may note that while the shift from government to bank finance *decentralized* finance allocation, interest rates continued to be administratively maintained at low and sometimes negative real levels, so that available capital had to be rationed by criteria other than willingness to pay.[50] A procedure reported to be widely used was that bank finance would be approved only for projects that were also substantially self-financed by their enterprise. In the context of the imperfect and regulated Yugoslav capital market, this can be viewed as an administrative rule allowing the state to put additional pressure on enterprises for self-finance. Nevertheless, the reader may recall our discussion of similar phenomena in connection with uncontrolled capital markets. The venturing of its own savings by the enterprise workforce (or more conventionally, proprietors) is a signal that the entrepreneurs share the financiers' interest in selecting the best projects and in bringing them to successful operation. Such securing of loans by partial self-finance can be related to the "principle of increasing risk" discussed by McCain (1977), but even more directly to the Schlicht–von Weiszacker discussion of "commitment mechanism" (1977) that is formally developed by Gui (1983).

Tyson (1977) offers a further explanation of enterprise self-finance in Yugoslavia. According to Tyson, the investment theories of Furubotn, Pejovich, and Vanek, do not give adequate attention to the implications of enterprise investment decisions for an enterprise's competitiveness within its industry. Given limited

[49] P. 86. See Estrin and Bartlett for reference to these studies.
[50] For an early discussion, see Neuberger, 1959.

worker mobility between firms, a moderately long time-horizon of a relatively youthful workforce, and rapid investment in new technology by other firms in one's industry, the substantial negative consequences of failing to invest in one's own enterprise may convince workers to forego considerable amounts of current consumption. Tyson also suggests that the desire to minimize fluctuations in consumption that could otherwise be substantial for worker-enterpreneurial firms may lead enterprises to establish target levels for distributed income, and to allocate the fluctuating remainder of *ex post* (achieved) enterprise incomes to investment. While the target proportion of income to be invested would be a function of the concerns of competitiveness just indicated (along with more standard savings-consumption considerations), actual investment would then vary directly with net revenues, leaving distributed incomes relatively insensitive to revenue fluctuations. Tyson finds some support for this "permanent income hypothesis" in annual industry-level data for 16 Yugoslav industries in the period 1965–1974.

4.3. Self-management and Yugoslav inflation

What are probably the two most commonly mentioned "blemishes" on the Yugoslav economic record—the persistence of unemployment and of inflation—have been associated in the literature with two extensively discussed analytical constructs: the Ward underemployment tendency, and the Furubotn–Pejovich underinvestment tendency. The connection between unemployment and Ward effects or their long-run analogues is relatively direct, and will be discussed in the next section. The link between inflation and the Furubotn–Pejovich underinvestment predictions is less direct, but helps us to introduce inflation as the topic of the present section.

The "horizon problem" analysis of Furubotn and Pejovich was extensively treated in our discussions of the economic theory of self-management. Although the evidence on self-finance and on Yugoslav investment rates just presented lends little immediate support to that analysis *per se,* the authors have argued that policy measures undertaken to sustain high investment rates in the face of low saving *incentives* provide a direct explanation of inflationary tendencies in the Yugoslav economy. Furubotn (1974) argued that the Yugoslav "system enforces a structure of property rights that . . . limits severely the incentives for investment in the firm," from which restriction "*the retardation of voluntary saving in the economy as a whole* (p. 274, emphasis in original)" is expected to follow. On the demand side, however, Yugoslav worker-managers would seek bank financing for enterprise projects on which the internal rate of return exceeded the bank interest rate. The trouble, according to Furubotn, is that "too much new money is likely to be put into the system," producing an inflationary tendency. He concludes that "the structure of the labor-managed firm, as such, contributes significantly to the process of inflation (p. 275)."

Before commenting on Furubotn's argument, a few words about the magnitude of Yugoslav inflation. According to calculations by Tyson (1980), retail price inflation averaged 18.1% in Yugoslavia during 1971–77, as compared with between 5 and 7% in the U.S., West Germany, and Switzerland, 0.0 to 0.6% in the G.D.R., Czechoslovakia, Bulgaria, and Romania, and about 3.2% in Hungary and Poland. However, the Yugoslav inflation was quite similar to those of other middle-income Mediterranean economies, which ranged from 13.8 and 14.9% in Greece and Spain to 17.5 and 18.6% in Portugal and Turkey. During the same period, Italian and British inflation ran at 13.6 and 14.0%, respectively, and Japan experienced an 11.2% inflation rate. The contrast with the Soviet-type economies and similarity with other growing market economies suggests that the Yugoslav experience may provide more evidence of the workings of a market mechanism—and also, perhaps, of the effects of exposure to international markets—than of self-management as such.[51]

Tyson argues that like other market inflations, that of Yugoslavia may be understood in terms of demand, cost-push, and monetary

[51] Yugoslav inflation rates in the early 1980's were considerably higher than those reviewed by Tyson. While it is clear that this heating up of inflation can be related to the concurrent international recession and inflation, and that the echo of these trends in a deepening Yugoslav economic crisis was unusually severe, an attempt to separate out the influence of specific Yugoslav policy failures from problems endemic to self-management for this recent period would take us beyond the scope of our essay.

factors. The classical explanation of too many dollars (dinars) chasing too few goods applies in that both consumer demand and investment funding were expanding during the 1960's and '70's. Cost-push stems in particular from rising materials costs, some of these heavily influenced by world market prices, and rising earnings, insofar as target wages were treated as a cost by enterprises. Expansion of the money supply at least "accomodated" inflationary pressures, permitting if not causing sustained price increases.

Insofar as the banking system has pumped excessive funds into investment projects at artificially low interest rates, Furubotn's analysis contains some insight into the Yugoslav inflation. However, the fixed interest rate and the priority accorded to capital accumulation were government policies of a kind observed in other developing market economies; in accepting inflation financing of economic growth, they show no clear link to self-management. To the extent that the government lacked adequate control over growth of loans and of the money supply, it can be argued that this source of inflation was indeed endemic to Yugoslav institutions; but again, there is nothing to suggest an intrinsic link to self-management *per se*. Furubotn provides no reason why bank financing of investment by self-managed firms at a market-bearing interest rate in an economy with a responsible monetary authority would be inherently inflationary.

A less formally derived explanation linking inflation with self-management focuses on wage increases. A casual observer might conclude that inflation is an inevitable outcome of giving workers power to set their own wages. The problem with this argument is that the wage-setting power is only effective to the extent that there is some way to pay the wage bill. Yugoslav workers could have tended to pay themselves higher incomes and pass on price increases to their customers, insofar as they had market power. But there is evidence that much of the earnings expansion tendency in Yugoslavia has been due not to market power but rather to the operation of what Janos Kornai calls "soft budget constraints"—i.e., a situation in which the enterprise can assume that the government will make up for deficits by way of subsidies or other transfers. This phenomenon is indicative of the lingering milieu of central planning—albeit now in the absence of a plan as such—and whether any market socialist system can escape it remains an open question.[52]

Tyson (1980) finds possible explanations for the co-existence of inflationary earnings increases and aggregate unemployment in both (neoclassical) self-management theory, and in evidence of labor market segmentation. Self-management theory indicates that workers in a profitable industry may raise their earnings although there are unemployed job applicants outside willing to work for lower wages, because the employed workers have no interest in expanding employment at the expense of lowering their own earnings. Tyson suggests that this tendency may be considerably strengthened by the regional and sectoral segmentation of the underdeveloped Yugoslav economy. She goes on to argue that workers in less profitable firms and industries may successfully press for earnings increases imitating those achieved in profitable ones. If target wages are taken as a fixed cost by the firms, workers may succeed in their demands provided that their markets will bear price increases, that bank finance can be substituted for revenues allocated formerly to investment and now to distribution, or that the government will underwrite consequent losses. Insofar as imitative pay increases are linked (in the third scenario) to "soft budget constraints," Tyson's and Kornai's analyses are complementary. Related to them too is an important additional form that the "soft budget constraint" assumes in Yugoslavia: enterprise to enterprise loans, which frequently arise due to unpaid debts, and which now constitute a substantial proportion of outstanding credit in the country. The general point is that it may be misleading to think of Yugoslavia as a model of independent worker-run economic units competing in a true market environment. Instead, workers' control is observed in the context of a socialist economy that lacks both planners' and market discipline, and that is hostage to an ideology enshrining both worker's self-management and worker income security.[53]

[52] Kornai, 1984, has recently used World Bank data to argue that enterprises in Yugoslavia are still largely protected from the burden of market losses by a coddling government that will not permit bankruptcies or unmet payrolls. The data cited are from Knight, 1983.

[53] This is not to say that the political-economic lessons of Yugoslavia for potential self-managed economies are irrelevant to other countries. On the contrary, they will have a familiar ring and immediate recognition in countries in which capture of government to protect the threatened economic interests of firms, workers, or communities is a perennial problem.

4.4. Allocative efficiency and job creation

Unemployment has been another major "blemish"—or at least a perceived one—on the Yugoslav economic record. Faced with the "stylized fact" of substantial unemployment rates, economists interested in applying the theory of labor-managed firms to the Yugoslav economy have naturally focused on the Ward model's short-run comparative static prediction that profitable LMF's would use less labor than comparable capitalist firms. While application of the short-run model itself has been effectively critiqued by a long line of theorists including Estrin, whose argument is specifically geared to an analysis of the Yugoslav economy, Estrin himself (along with Ireland and Law, and others; see Section 2.1, above) demonstrates that results of a similar flavor are retained in long-run planning models in which both capital and labor are variable. Ward-type concerns about unemployment and capital-intensity may therefore be relevant to empirical studies of Yugoslavia if set in a more long-run framework of enterprise decision-making and allocative efficiency.

Yugoslav conditions give rise to special concerns about capital allocation. As we have seen, from the mid-1960's, the largest portion of Yugoslav investment finance has come from the banks, with internal self-finance and state (here, predominantly the republican governments) finance being the other significant sources of funding. Absence of a market-clearing interest rate has necessitated the use of administrative methods of capital allocation, which raises the question of the efficiency of this allocation as well as that of the income inequalities due to the rents earned on capital goods on which full scarcity charges are not assessed. Vanek has argued that an inefficient allocation of capital due to failure to assess a scarcity-reflecting interest rate is a major weakness of the Yugoslav economy; indeed, Vanek has proposed that the Yugoslav-type system be labelled something other than "labor-managed" to underscore this defect.[54] Concern about the allocative effects of low

[54] Vanek, 1978. The proposal to label the Yugoslav-type system as "worker managed" and the system with "fully-costed capital" as "labor managed" has not been adopted by other authors, to our knowledge. For his critique of Yugoslav practice, see also Vanek, 1973.

interest rates has been shared also by many Yugoslav economists.[55] At least until recently,[56] however, these economists have had little success in implementing reforms in accord with this analysis.

A number of attempts have been made to establish the effects of capital rationing empirically. For example, Vanek and Jovicic (1975) suggested that differences in administered capital allocation were the principal source of systematic dispersion in average incomes in nineteen Yugoslav industries during 1970–71. Vanek and Jovicic were able to demonstrate a significant positive relationship between per capita net product and capital-labor ratios across these industries, and they argued that the absence of significant relationships between the unexplained residual differences in net product and the industries' producer prices, concentration ratios, degree of price controls, and "newness" of fixed assets further singled out capital allocation as the only apparent economic explanation of the disperions. Capital rents per worker, which were imputed from the net product regression and hypothesized accounting identities, varied from 1,062 new dinars in the leather and leather products to 24,262 in the electrical generation and distribution industries, with an average of 4,118 and a standard deviation of 5,224. Estimated pure labor income was put at 25,050 new dinars in all industries.[57] Rivera-Batiz (1980) performed a similar exercise, but in addition to the capital-labour ratio, he proposed variables proxying for average firm size and market power as hypothesized determinants of net product per worker, all at industry level. He obtained a higher R-square for the regression and a lower imputed rent on capital (about 6% as opposed to 9%) than Vanek and Jovicic. In addition to capital-labor ratios, average firm size (but not

[55] Estrin (1983) and Estrin and Svejnar (1982) state that Vanek's position had considerable influence among Yugoslav economists, but this is disputed in the unpublished comments of Yugoslav readers, who assert that the view is indigenous and has been expressed for at least 15 years by Yugoslav economists, though largely without acceptance.

[56] Sharply rising interest rates since about 1982 may signal an end to the earlier mentioned phenomenon of low administered interest rates. This may also signal increased influence of Yugoslav economists having a greater market orientation, although the impact of the economic crisis and of the International Monetary Fund should certainly be cited.

[57] Labor was normalized to "unskilled labor equivalents" in these calculations.

market power) showed a positive and significant relationship to incomes.

Estrin and Bartlett (1982), Estrin and Svejnar (1982) and Estrin (1983) argue that the econometric work of Vanek and Jovicic, Rivera-Batiz, and others, has been based on an approach which they refer to as the "capital school," which emphaizes investment allocation and incentives to invest as the key source of inefficiencies in the economy and of differences in earnings of similar labor types.[58] These authors identify a contending "labor school," which instead emphasizes labor allocation and labor productivity factors as sources of inefficiency and as determinants of earnings dispersions. Wachtel's (1972, 1973) work, which shows average earnings to be closely related to labor productivity at industry level in each year from 1956 to 1968, is cited as belonging to this strand.

Estrin *et al.* argue that the empirical studies of the "capital school," while inspired by ideas derived in the static theory of self-management, cannot serve as direct tests of theoretical predictions, since they fail to distinguish between those factors which are endogenous and those which are exogenous from the standpoint of an enterprise's income-maximizing decisions. Estrin (1983) proposes that since Yugoslav markets exhibit imperfect competition, and since their capital stocks and labor forces may be more or less *equally* fixed for the short run and variable for a somewhat longer run than the enterprise long run, in which both capital and labor are variable but free entry and exit do not (yet) occur, is the appropriate analytical basis from which to derive testable hypotheses about enterprise behavior. While the costs of capital facing the firm should influence observed behavior, in such a framework, investment decisions would be seen as simultaneous with those determining long run employment and output levels, and would be influenced by both technological and market factors in ways specific to self-management theory.

As already reported, Estrin (1982, 1983) expands upon Vanek's (1970) model of the enterprise long-run planning problem, in which equilibrium is characterized by a position on the "locus of maximum

[58] Estrin *et al.* identify the ideas of Vanek and of Furubotn and Pejovich as the bases of this "school." In addition to the papers just cited, other tests of the relationship between capital intensity and incomes or output per head by Miovic (1975) and Staellerts (1981) are mentioned as sharing in its approach.

physical efficiency" where returns to scale are constant. He finds that capital-labor ratios decline uniformly with reductions of product price, and that the response of equilibium output to product price changes depends upon the relationship between returns to scale and factor proportions. In his empirical work, Estrin (1983) assumes a Cobb–Douglas, variable returns to scale technology, and derives equilibrium reduced-form equations for earnings per worker from the long run planning problem, for both perfectly competitive and monopolistic market situations. Adopting fixed Cobb–Douglas factor weights but variable minimum efficient scales and residual efficiency (or disembodied productivity) across industries, he finds that earnings depend upon product price, residual efficiency, the interest rate, the scale of output, and the degree of market power.[59] He then estimates this relation by a log-linear regression equation on industry level data from 19 Yugoslav industries for each year from 1964 to 1972, and finds that between 70 and 90% of the variance in earnings is explained by the variables derived from the long run model. The hypothesis that the industries were perfectly competitive (i.e., that the market power variable can be excluded) is rejected, as is the suggestion that average firm size does not matter. The latter finding is taken by Estrin as support for the variable returns to scale formulation of his own and Vanek's (1970) models.

In addition to the methodological advance of testing self-management theory on the basis of reduced form equations derived from a complete revenue-maximization problem, Estrin's argument advances the study of the Yugoslav system by focusing attention on predicted system-specific tendencies with respect to employment and factor proportions. While the employment-restricting tendencies of Ward's short run model have been discredited by sustained criticisms of the labor force variability assumption for the short run, Estrin (along with Meade, 1979, Sapir, 1980, and Ireland and Law, 1982) shows that similar system-specific effects are predicted for the long run, when labor force adjustments through attrition or job creation are more likely, provided that competitive general equilibrium in product markets has not been attained. In practice, as Estrin argues, Yugoslav firm-creation has been motiv-

[59] The last variable is defined as the ratio of marginal revenue to price, and is proxied by the industry four firm concentration ratio.

ated by regional and political considerations rather than profitability, although some industry concentration levels have fallen due to entry by existing firms into new markets in response to profit opportunities. Bankruptcies, on the other hand, are virtually ruled out because of the interventions of various authorities; the closest widely observed counterpart to bankruptcies is absorption of loss-making firms by profitable ones, often in response to political pressures rather than economic incentives. Thus, market equilibrium via entry and exit can hardly be assumed.[60] The policy implication is that either measures must be taken to encourage competition, or ways must be sought to mitigate the harmful effects of self-management labor misallocation—along lines such as those of the Ireland and Law incentive fund, discussed above—or both. However, Yugoslav policy-makers—both federal, and what is now more important, regional—show little sign of abandoning industrial policies centered on regional autonomy and on coordination via "agreement" or direct links rather than the market. Promotion of firm-creation and especially of competition as ends in their own right are thus little in evidence.

4.5. Economic development and structural factors

Bringing together labor and capital allocation concerns in a multi-sided study of Yugoslav institutions and economic experience, Tyson (1980) writes, "To scholars in both the West and the East, Yugoslavia's experience suggests that self-management may not be an effective institution for development because there is nothing in the behavioral rules of the self-managed firm operating in a market system to guarantee full employment (p. 57)." Tyson observes that "in the self-managed market system, the existence of unemployed workers . . . who can be hired at less than the incomes paid to employed workers . . . has no effect on the individual self-managed firm, which has no incentive to look for the cheapest labor available (p. 58)." In addition, she lists as possible explanations of the employment problem the failure of enterprises to be charged a scarcity price for capital, their ability to distribute capital returns to their workforces, and capital immobility. She further notes that the

[60] On the problem of entry in Yugoslavia, see Sacks, 1972 and 1973.

costs of labor itself have been artificially inflated by the taxation system, aggravating the tendency toward capital intensity. However, Tyson warns that comparisons of Yugoslav unemployment rates with those of East European neighbors are inappropriate, and that, in fact, "the available evidence seems to support the view that Yugoslavia's experience has been similar to that of other market economies of similar development levels (p. 61)."

A recent paper by Bartlett (1984) is also in the spirit of Tyson's conclusions. Reviewing the historical trend of Yugoslav output and employment growth, Bartlett disputes the assumption of a sharp change in these series coinciding with the self-management reforms of the mid-1960's. Attributing the observed discontinuity to a "credit squeeze" leading to "a complete cessation in . . . new job openings (p. 5)" between 1965 and 1967, he finds that excluding those years, there was a relatively small difference between the 4.5% average rate of employment growth in the socialized sector between 1957–64 and the 3.5% rate between 1968–75. Also, when the decade rather than pre- and post-reform marks are used to specify periods, the growth rate of manufacturing output, at 6.9% per year in 1970–79, compares respectably to that of 1960–69, which was 7.7%. In addition, Bartlett disputes Sapir's suggestion that Yugoslav manufacturing growth rates were gradually falling below international averages after the reforms. He cites World Bank evidence that whereas the Yugoslav output growth rate was exceeded in 19 out of 33 "middle income" developing countries and 8 of 12 "industrial market economies" in the 1960's, the corresponding rate was exceeded in only 9 of the former and none of the latter in the 1970's.

More directly appropos to the present discussion, Bartlett argues that the main cause of Yugoslav unemployment has been structural, namely the preservation of large urban-rural income differentials in the context of rapid industrialization and urbanization of a poor peasant economy. While Yugoslav policies favoring industry, capital intensity, and urban development generally may have contributed to urban-rural wage differentials, and while capital subsidization and other policies may have moderated the rate of job creation, Bartlett finds the Yugoslav employment creation record to be comparable with those of other "middle income" developing countries. The associated unemployment phenomenon is typical of dualistic development, where rural-urban migration in the presence of a persistent wage gap and non-zero probability of finding urban employment generates unemployment rates that may even increase in response to new job creation (as, e.g., in the well known model of Harris and Todaro, 1970). Indeed, structural unemployment in Yugoslavia might be attributed as much to the weaknesses of the *non-socialist* rural sector (as a "push" factor in rural-urban migration) as to the failings of the country's industrial LMF's. Moreover, unemployment rates vary substantially across regions, in some of which it makes little sense to speak of a special unemployment problem.[61] Attention to such structural features suggests to observers such as Bartlett that the resemblence of Yugoslav economic problems to the predictions of Ward's or Estrin's analysis may be largely or wholely coincidental.

5. COLLECTIVE FARMS AND COMMUNES

Collective farms and communes have been the dominant forms of agricultural production unit in the Soviet Union since the 1930's, and in Eastern Europe and China since the 1950's. Collective and cooperative farms and agricultural communes are also found scattered throughout the "First" and "Third" Worlds. Although for lack of true workers' control most collective farms fail to satisfy the full definition of self-managed enterprise or producers' cooperative, their income-sharing procedures lend themselves to analysis in the framework of PC models. This factor, plus their importance to the overall performance of the socialist economies, has led to the development of an important sub-literature on collective farms and communes.

[61] In common with Bartlett, Milenkovitch (1983, p. 15) writes: "the unemployment rates are very different across republics, ranging from 1.3 percent in Slovenia and 5.4 percent in Crotia, to 22 percent in Macedonia and 28 percent in Kosovo. This suggests that more of the unemployment may be explained by the level of development than by the system of self-management" [since] "[t]he failure of labor markets to clear is common in countries at similar levels of development . . ." In personal communication, Dr. Rusinow similarly points out that far from having a serious unemployment problem, relatively developed Slovenia has of late faced social problems due to the presence of large numbers of "guest workers" from other parts of Yugoslavia.

A key feature differentiating collective farms from most self-managed enterprises is the existence side-by-side of both joint (collective) and individual (private) production activities. This has added a dimension to the economic analysis of collective farms which has encouraged closer attention to incentive issues. It is not surprising, then, that the analytical literature on collective farms and communes has fed back into the mainstream self-management literature particularly in the field of work incentives. It is to that topic that we now turn.

5.1. Incentives and effort allocation in collective farms

Western observers have generally characterized collective farms as being inefficient and having low productivity, with the presumption that peasant members of collective farms have had little incentive to work industriously outside of their private plots. There were intuitive explanations for this in the forced nature of collectivization and in the low prices of procured products and consequently low incomes from collective work. However, some scholars were also tempted to see poor work incentives as eminating from the collective remuneration system itself. For example, it was argued that entitlement to a workday or workpoint constituted a poor incentive because the value of the workpoint was unknown during the production cycle, and would fluctuate with factors beyond the control of an individual peasant, including the quality and quantity of work provided by fellow collective farmers. Such arguments began to be examined rigorously following the development of formal models of collective farms, beginning in the 1960's.

Two important early contributions to the PC literature, to which we have referred in earlier sections, dealt explicitly with collective farms: an idealized Soviet *kolkhoz,* in Domar (1966), and a Chinese-type commune, in Sen (1966). Both authors departed from the Ward approach by *not* modelling the enterprise as facing a perfectly elastic labor supply curve. As we have already seen (in Section 1), Domar assumed an upward sloping supply curve of labor input from a given membership, with actual labor use being supply-constrained if the intersection of the labor supply and the net income per member or dividend curves occurred before the latter reached its maximum. Sen, on the other hand, assumed a given labor force, and he substituted the idea of member utility maximization (with respect to income and leisure) for that of member income maximization. In Sen's model, members had to anticipate the level of other members' labor inputs, and their pay-out from the joint firm could depend upon either work contributions, household needs (population), or both. Sen's paper foreshadowed the approach of subsequent collective farm models, although its inquiry into the possible role of altruism, which constitutes a major sub-theme, has not generally been incorporated in them.

The distinguishing feature of the coexisting private sector was first introduced in a 1968 paper by Oi and Clayton. This paper largely reverted to the Ward approach of treating membership as a short-run policy variable, and its major contribution, apart from encouraging two sector analysis, was in its discussion of quotas and two level pricing, to which we return below. Marriage of the two sector concern and the individual labor allocation approach took place in papers by Bradley (1971, 1973), Cameron (1973a, 1973b), and Bonin (1977), with attention restricted to the system of "distribution according to work" (equivalent to the Soviet workday system), and by Chinn (1979), reintroducing the alternative "needs" distribution system. Two papers by Markusen (1975, 1976) focused on distribution and incentives, and Israelsen (1980) looked at the contrast between "needs" and "work"-based incentives, both in one-sector settings. Putterman (1980, 1981) included both the two sector and the mixed distribution approaches, and studied voting choice over inter-sectoral land allocation and the degree of "needs" distribution.

Viewing membership as given has been an appealing approach in dealing with collective farms and communes, for which the membership decision is simultaneously a residence choice. In Soviet-type economies and China, peasant membership in a collective farm unit was made essentially mandatory, and which unit the household joined was most often simply determined by residence at the time of collectivization, and later, by birth and by spouse's residence. Even when Soviet peasants had the option of leaving the countryside, this presented collective farmers and farm managers with only limited means of influencing total membership. In China, where rural-urban migration has been sharply limited, migration and family planning policies and rules affecting establishment of new households may have impacted differentially upon localities, giving some units ways of influencing membership size. In both cases, however, labor input to a given collective farm would usually depend in the short and medium run upon time allocation by existing resident households among alternatives of collective and private work, and of leisure.

In the models of Bradley, Cameron, Bonin, and Chinn, the division of land between private and collective plots is assumed to be institutionally given, closely reflecting Soviet and Chinese realities.[62] Attention is turned to households permitted to maximize utility by allocating time either freely, or subject to a minimum collective labor time constraint.[63] In the free allocation case, subjective optimization requires equalization of the marginal return from each type of work and the marginal rate of substitution between income and leisure, which implies (assuming no price or production uncertainty) that the incomes yielded at the margin by collective and private labor are equalized by each household.[64] When collective labor time is constrained, only the marginal utility of the return from private work and of leisure are equated.[65] Since the marginal rate of substitution between income and leisure and the marginal return from collective work are equalized in the free allocation case, analysis of that case is identical for many purposes with that of the one-sector labor-managed firm or agricultural producers' cooperative (Sen, Markusen, Israelsen, Ireland and Law, etc.). That problem has already been treated above under work incentives in labor-managed firms (Section 1.8), so here we touch only on its special application to collective farms.

The two sector setting makes explicit the contrast between the incentives of independent (private) and of collective producers. The

---

[62] For a given size of membership, land allocation is also taken as institutionally fixed by Oi and Clayton who, however, allow the proportions of land in the sectors to vary by treating membership (as mentioned) as a short-term policy variable.

[63] Note the simplifying assumption that the household itself rather than its individual members is the utility-maximizing unit in all models of this genre. This makes the household of the collective farm models the analogue of the individual in the more general incentive literature.

[64] One cannot, however, rule out corner solutions, in which one or another type of labor falls to zero and the two marginal yields are not equated.

[65] Treatment of this case engendered contention between Bradley and Cameron. See, however, the remarks in Bonin, 1977, pp. 84–85.

independent producer has full claim to the marginal return on his labor, so there are no apparent incentive distortions.[66] As a collective member, the same peasant may have claims to the marginal value of collectively produced output either in proportion to his share of the total labor input, to his household's size (needs), or both. As already shown, the marginal return to collective labor will not equal the marginal value product except in special cases. Unless one accepts the assumption of Bradley's original model (1971) and of Bonin (1977) that each household expects other households to (proportionately) match its labor adjustment decisions, then as Cameron (1973a) first showed and as Israelsen (1980) and Putterman (1985b) emphasize, the marginal return to collective labor can be less than the marginal product for small values of the total labor input, and greater than the marginal product for large values of that input. This suggests a crucial role for expectations of other households' labor contributions. Expectations of low participation could be self-confirming, because with expected average net product of labor below marginal product, such expectations would be associated with sub-optimal incentives toward collective work. Accordingly, Cameron observed that a possible reason for enforced collective work requirements would be to push the collective out of the range of low labor input in which the sub-optimality problem is most serious.[67]

[66] Of course, distortions from *social* optimality could arise from externalities of production, administered prices, etc.

[67] As Cameron pointed out, with high fixed charges to the collective (including the tax implicit in quota deliveries at low prices), the net income yield on very low levels of labor could be negative, even though the net return curve had a respectable positive range for high levels of labor input. This explanation of the work quota bears some similarity to one offered by Oi and Clayton, which is that with a two level pricing system, attainment of a higher-output equilibrium may depend on forcing collective workers beyond a preferred low-output (and low price) equilibrium at which the quota would not be fulfilled. Whereas the Oi–Clayton scenario is one in which cooperators' welfare unambiguously falls with the imposition of the quota, however, the Cameron case could conceivably entail a welfare improvement resulting from moving the cooperative out of a "low-level expectations equilibrium trap." Recognizing this possibility need not imply that the motives or consequences of actual work quotas were benign; in various periods and regions, labor quotas merely pressed more barely-remunerated labor out of a captive labor force. Where labor quotas are not binding on Soviet collective farms (as is now reported to be general by Stuart, 1972, p. 118), Cameron's mechanism might be pertinent; but minimum wage guarantees will in general have obviated the problem as discussed here.

In spite of this possibility, most analysts have concluded from such formal investigations that poor incentives in collective farms do not stem from the collective payment system as such. If "cohesion" is "perfect" in Chinn's sense (elasticity of labor response $\eta = 1$), as in the models of Bradley (1971) and Bonin (1977), collective remuneration amounts to marginal value product remuneration, work input to the sector is optimal, and in the certainty case, responses to price and rent changes may be normal (see below) if individuals' labor supply curves are upward sloping (income effects are not stronger than substitution effects). If "cohesion" is "imperfect" (including the [Cournot] case in which the worker assumes others' choices to be independent of his own)[68], marginal payment approximates labor's average net product, so that in high ranges of aggregate labor input the incentive will be non-optimal and will tend to lead to a labor input that is socially *excessive* from a classical welfare standpoint, but that could be desirable from the standpoint of a Soviet-type regime.

While the abstract character of these models and, in particular, their exclusion of production uncertainty require emphasis, it is of at least theoretical interest that the previous observation suggests a rationale for the collective agricultural form in socialist states. Not only did adoption of this form, combined with imposition of delivery quotas and price controls, permit socialist governments to extract fixed quantities of output from their peasantries and to force the latter to bear the burden of agricultural fluctuations. In addition, the use of what is basically an average product reward scheme would—assuming an equilibrium in which average net product exceeds marginal product of labor—have coaxed more labor from collective farmers for less resources, since like fishers of a common fishing ground, each would be lured by shares of a catch the diminution of which does not enter his own calculations.

That binding collective work hours quotas still needed to be used during much of the development period in the Soviet Union suggests, however, that the incentive potential of collective remuneration was often inoperative. Soviet peasants at the time earned well over half of their incomes from their private farms.

[68] "Cohesion" or "reaction" expectations may or may not be required to be correct or rational, depending upon the analyst.

(Averaging around one acre per household, these were substantial compared to the private plots of most later Chinese counterparts, which averaged less than a tenth of an acre per household and which appear to have provided, along with husbandry and other private pursuits, no more than a fourth or at most a third of their total incomes.) With nominal delivery prices and other heavy obligations on the collectives, average net product claims for work in the collective sector were usually an insufficient attraction to voluntary labor. Indeed, the effective motivation for collective work would often have been unabashedly coercive, with the system as a whole most resembling a feudal manor in which labor is contributed to the manorial farm without economic compensation, the peasant being expected to support himself on the reserved household plots in the time remaining to him.[69] Certain crucial inputs to the private plots, such as feed for animals,[70] were also provided by the collective only if work obligations were fulfilled, thus constituting a kind of material incentive for participation. However, an accurate account of this system might deal as much with penalties as with rewards, and could differ in various other ways from the genre of model here under discussion. We are aware of no formal models along such lines.

Still other explanations of incentive failure in collective farming systems can be derived more directly from the framework of the existing formal models. For example, uncertainty would have influenced the allocation of work effort assuming farmer risk aversion. Both collective and household (private) plots would be subject to production uncertainty, so no differential impact on labor supply is apparent from that source. One could argue that group farming of amalgamated plots has a risk-pooling effect with respect to plot-specific output variation. The comparison of guaranteed (if low) state prices for collective products with fluctuating free market prices for private plot outputs might also favor collective produc-

[69] Evans, 1983 (p. 153), calls the Soviet collective farm system under Stalin "neomanorial" and writes: "Collective farm peasants looked on the requirement of labor in socialized agriculture as a levy to which they had to submit in order to obtain permission to engage in private plot farming. The peasant family relied on its private plot, primarily for satisfaction of its own consumption needs, and also to provide most of its modest cash income."

[70] See Karcz, 1966.

tion, from a risk-aversion standpoint. For the collective farm, however, production uncertainty might be compounded by uncertainty over the labor and managerial inputs of non-family members, and its interdependence with ones own household's decisions (Bradley, 1973; Cameron, 1973b; Bonin, 1977; Chinn, 1979; Putterman, 1980).

After their country abandoned collective crop production in favor of household farming of land "contracted out" by the collective in the early 1980's, Chinese spokesmen asserted that incentives were poor in the agricultural production teams due to poor monitoring and hence ineffective linking of work input to reward.[71] To the extent that monitoring is particularly difficult in agriculture (because of micro-climate and soil heterogeneity, the physically dispersed character of production, etc.) and that technical economies of scale are insufficient to overcome the resulting incentive "friction," this can provide a quite general explanation of poor incentives and performance of collective farms. Signs of substantially higher labor productivity following restoration of principally household-level production in China are consistent with such explanations, although it is presently impossible to distinguish between the effects of the change in production unit, of improved agricultural prices, of increased crop diversification, and of related policies.

One of the few attempts to test data on collective farm behavior for consistency with the theory of self-management and cooperation is by Wyzan (1983). Wyzan produces a table, based on Cobb–Douglas production function estimates using pooled 1960's and '70's time series and cross section data from nine Soviet republics, in which the marginal and average products of land and labor are compared in state farms (*sovkhozy*) and collective farms (*kolkhozy*). For the five crops reported (grain, sugar beets, cotton, potatoes, and vegetables), the estimates show average products of labor much further above marginal product in the *kolkhozy* than in the *sovkhozy* (with the exception of potatoes and vegetables in the latter). Although Wyzan finds these results *inconsistent* with "any tendency to conserve on hiring in the manner of a self-managed

[71] See Putterman, forthcoming.

enterprise,"[72] the marginal-average product relations exhibited by the *kolkhozy* are consistent with the super-optimal incentive tendencies of "collective" distribution discussed above. Of course, such consistency would be coincidental if labor input were predominantly determined by fiat rather than household choice, or if *kolkhoz* payment systems had little to do with *kolkhoz* performance, a possibility for this period to which we return below.

5.2. Incentives in pure communes

Earlier discussion of "distribution according to work," the system hypothetically characterizing the collective farm, and of "distribution according to needs," the system of the pure commune, suggested that while work incentives in the former might be adequate or even excessive, those in the latter would be woefully inadequate. But reality is stubbornly resistant to these predictions, if most observer's views of Soviet and Chinese collective farms,[73] on the one hand, and of Israeli *kibbutzim* and Hutterite communes,[74] on the other, are accurate. Of course, one has the list of disincentives attributed to the collective farms above, on the one side, and on the side of these particular communes, the fact that

[72] P. 192. Wyzan is aware that freedom to choose membership is an inappropriate assumption for the *kolkhoz*. However, he cites only Oi and Clayton (1968) and Sapir (1980) from the self-management literature, and both are examples of Ward–Vanek type theory. Wyzan argues as we have that the *kolkhoz* cannot be considered a self-managed firm in view of its limited real democracy and the degree of external control. Interestingly, however, he finds reason to believe that cooperative distribution principles remain in place to some degree even after the late-1960's moves toward a wage system. Wyzan also mentions a possible tendency toward *kolkhoznik* overwork, which is rooted in a farm manager's view of the collective farm member as "overhead": see Wyzan, p. 183, and for the same argument on Chinese communes, Chao, 1970, p. 47.

[73] The Chinese people's commune, in spite of its name, had as agricultural production unit from 1962 to 1978 (and later in some areas) the production team which followed a workpoint distribution system with some admixture of "distribution according to needs" (Nolan, 1983; Putterman, forthcoming). It is thus classified as a collective farm or at most a partial commune under the present scheme. (This definition of "collective" as producers' cooperative distributing "according to work" and of "commune" as one distributing "according to needs" follows Israelsen, *op. cit.*)

[74] For references to the Hutterite colonies, see Section 6.1.1. The *kibbutz* is discussed further in Section 6.3.

their memberships are voluntary, to a degree self-selecting, and bound together by strong ideologies. The definitive incentives in this comparison may have little to do with internal distribution rules. Still, we need not abandon altogether the attempt to relate communal work incentives to some variant of the utility calculus.

Sen has proposed three modifications of conventional preference structure that could explain sufficiency of work incentives in pure communes. First,[75] he shows that if commune members place as much weight on others' as on their own utility, on average, then "distribution according to needs" has incentive effects equivalent to those resulting from distribution to each worker of his or her marginal product. Second,[76] he argues that people as moral beings may have preferences (or "meta-preferences") over possible preference structures, including those based upon strict self-interest and those involving a high degree of social consciousness. Choice of the latter as a preferred preference may imply cooperative behavior in spite of self-interest. Third,[77] he shows that with a somewhat less drastic modification of the utility function, situations that present themselves to the egoist as prisoners' dilemmas may be transformed into "assurance games." While agents in the latter may wish to avoid being "suckered" by cooperating while others cheat, they prefer not to cheat when others are cooperating. Such agents need only be assured that others are doing their part before settling on cooperative behavior for themselves. In the commune as assurance game, expectations of cooperative behavior are self-fulfilling, and an equilibrium of "from each according to his ability" becomes possible.

Even these modifications may be unnecessary, according to an argument by Putterman (1983).[78] As has been seen earlier, inadequacy of incentives in communes is partly based on the assumption that members view their work inputs as independent of one another. This is an unrealistic supposition insofar as the work behavior (effort supply) of each individual has some influence on the effort equilibrium or "convention" that prevails. If one's effort

[75] In the paper cited (Sen 1966).

[76] In Sen, 1977. See also Sen, 1973.

[77] See Sen, 1967.

[78] See also the related discussions in Sections 1.8 and 1.10. above.

choices are made in strategic consideration of their impact on others' choices, and if individuals can bind themselves to reacting in predictable ways to changes in the behaviors of other agents, then pure self-interest may sustain an equilibrium of high incentives in the commune, because it is rational to commit oneself to a positive "matching" or tit-for-tat strategy. This notion provides one possible micro-foundation to the idea of "collective material incentives" employed by some writers on China.[79]

With such an abundance of ways in which communal distribution can be imagined to achieve incentive sufficiency, there may appear to be no reason for preferring one incentive system to another, or predicting different outcomes from them. Again, we are reminded of the importance of the historical and social variables. However, it is reasonable to suppose that those variables and the incentive structures interact. Purely communal incentives are unlikely to be effective unless the income sharing groups are small enough to have face-to-face contact and to establish trust relations, and unless they have the commitment to make the incentive system work either for ideological reasons or for a systemically or authoritatively imposed lack of alternatives. Thus, the "free supply" system of the huge Chinese people's communes of 1959 was ineffective, and widespread distribution of large fractions of team incomes on a physical ration basis between the mid-1960's and the late 1970's in that country can be assumed to have had a strong incentive-dampening effect there. On the other hand, "distribution according to work" can only be effective when the cooperative has the monitoring abilities—and the trust in those charged with the task—to implement a discriminating reward system that will not be perceived as arbitrary. This last point suggests the possibility of situations in which adoption of an equal sharing system by mutual agreement, supported by group policing of work obligations, is superior to work rewards that would generate dissention and the breakdown of mutual monitoring and cooperation.[80]

[79] See, e.g., Riskin, 1974. "Collective material incentives" are those generated by income raising opportunities facing a work team or group within which internal income differentiation is small.

[80] This point resurfaces below in our discussion of Espinosa and Zimbalist's findings on Chilean industrial democracy.

5.3. Responses to price, rent, and quota adjustments

As we have seen above, much of the self-management literature is concerned with enterprise responses to changing prices and costs because of the implications of these response patterns for efficiency and public policy in a labor-managed market economy, or in a mixed market economy in which some labor-managed firms participate. In the case of collective farms in centralized socialist economies, prices and rents are generally policy variables in their own right, while the concept of market equilibrium has little direct relevance. Analysts have been interested in examining the impacts on collective farm units of the policies chosen by the central authorities, so as to better understand the reasons for past policy decisions, their costs to peasants and national economies, and the likely effects of future policy changes.

Most of the theoretical papers mentioned above have given some attention to the effects of price and rent, and in some cases to quota, changes. However, with the partial exception of the sustained discussion involving Bradley, Cameron, and eventually Bonin and Chinn, analysts have treated the questions under rather different assumptions, and the literature lacks an overall synthesis or conclusion. For example, Domar treated the cases of perfectly elastic labor supply, of upward sloping supply curve of labor to the enterprise, and of a coop able to hire non-member labor, all for a one-sector model with certainty, while Oi and Clayton assumed variable membership, fixed labor input per member, and variable size of collective farm, in a two-sector setting with some emphasis on two-tier pricing. Both of the latter papers posited a dividend-maximizing manager. Among the papers taking membership as given but effort as freely chosen by individual households, Sen deals with one sector and does not directly attack the question of external policy instruments; Bradley (1971) and Bonin in distinction from Cameron, Chinn, Israelsen, and Putterman (and Bradley, 1973) assume (by way of their supposition on "cohesion" or "responses") that the marginal payment to labor equals the marginal product of labor; and Bonin is the only author to rigorously treat uncertainty. Sen, Chinn, and Putterman model producers' cooperatives employing "communal," "collective," and mixed distribution systems.

It is convenient to look first at the Oi and Clayton model, since its assumption of unlimited labor availability facing a dividend-maximizing management puts it in a common class with the Ward, Domar (Part I) and Vanek models that were the earliest to be extensively developed in the labor-management literature. As we have seen in Section 1, analyses of these models have shown that when labor is the only variable input, when a single output is produced, and when prices and rents are parametric to the firm, then a price change has the "paradoxical" effect of reducing membership and output, if positive, and increasing them if negative. An increase in fixed charges leads to increased membership and output, "to spread the costs or losses" over more members, and conversely for a decline. These results look promising indeed to a Stalinist policy-maker facing one-product peasant coops and an ample rural labor force, for the state can at a single stroke increase agriculture's physical output and reduce net monetary flows to the sector by reducing crop prices and increasing land rents or taxes.

The Oi–Clayton model in its non-quota, uniform price version, modifies such expected W–D–V results for two reasons. First, the responses of the collective sector are complicated by the addition of the private sector which is assumed to produce a different product or to face a different price for the same product. Since a given labor force can be shifted between sectors, the "paradoxical" response of the collective sector will tend to be muted or reversed by normal inter-sectoral labor shifts responding to the changing opportunity costs occasioned by altered price ratios.[81] Second, admission of new members or expulsion of existing ones alters the inter-sectoral allocation of land, because Oi and Clayton assume that both the size of the private plot per household and the total land available to the collective farm (including its private plots) are fixed. Admitting new members thus simultaneously increases the proportion of land farmed privately *and* the amount of labor that can be divided

[81] The same tendency, observed in Oi and Clayton in the context of a manager's decisions taken to maximize income per worker, is observed under individualized labor allocation in the models of Bradley, Cameron, *et al.* The phenomenon also resembles the modification and possible reversal of the price response "paradox" ("Ward effect") with the addition of a second output in the one-sector case analyzed by Domar, p. 739.

between the two sectors.[82] For example, when the price of private plot output rises, the collective farm may both increase membership and thus total labor input, so as to reduce collective and increase private land allocation, *and* increase the proportion of labor allocated to the collective sector.

With their assumptions regarding membership and inter-sectoral land allocation, Oi and Clayton's model results in an "expansion path" in product space,[83] for varying membership levels and given relative product prices, that bends "backwards" at higher levels of labor input. This occurs because the maximum product of the collective sector eventually declines as membership grows, as a result of new private plots automatically being carved out of the collective fields. Output responses to changes in the private output price are normal, but the output response of the collective crop to changes in its own price can retain its Wardian sign. Optimal membership varies negatively with collective output price, as in the Ward model, while it varies positively with private output price, as in conventional price theory and for the additional reasons suggested above. The effect of a change in fixed charges to the community, likewise, is the "paradoxical" increase in membership and collective output, for increasing charges along the normal range of expansion paths. Even private output increases with the charges, regardless of expansion path slope. Ward's results are modified in that collective output could rise in response to a price increase, as a possible result on a normal path and a certain result on a "backward" one; but most of the results retain their "paradoxical" flavor.

As we have observed, treatment of membership as a short-run variable, a practice already questionable for labor-managed firms in a market economy, is especially difficult to justify in the case of socialist collective agricultures. In the Soviet Union, relevant labor

[82] As in the Ward, Vanek, and Meade models, labor contribution per member (here, household) is fixed, by assumption. An alternative model permitting adjustment of intersectoral land allocation by voting, and assuming flexible labor input choice by each of a given number of households, is presented by Putterman (1980, 1981, 1986a chapter 3) and discussed briefly below.

[83] With collective and private output plotted on the two axes, and with total land fixed, this expansion path shows income-maximizing output levels for a constant output price ratio and varying membership sizes.

mobility has been almost entirely rural-urban (except for some seasonal flows back to agriculture), with the collective farm manager having at most limited influence over the rate of the exodus (Stuart and Gregory, 1977). In China, except during brief periods, rural-urban and rural-rural migration possibilities have been limited, and urban-rural migration has occurred almost exclusively as a political penalty. In both countries, collective farm membership has been essentially involuntary. It is thus more realistic to assume a given membership, changing principally in response to demographic factors that are themselves insensitive to short-term price changes. However, utility-maximizing labor contributions of given collective farm members may be sensitive to output and input prices, rent, and others factors that influence the return per unit of labor, provided that the member household is free to set its contribution level. If the collective sector provides the households' only income earning opportunities, and if households treat the return per labor unit as parametric for given prices, rents, and taxes, then labor input depends upon individual supply decisions based on labor-leisure preferences. Assuming that an upward sloping aggregate supply curve of labor to the cooperative is a binding constraint on its dividend-maximizing management,[84] Domar shows that higher output prices will increase labor input and crop output, while higher taxes or rents will reduce input and output, since the former change increases while the latter reduces the return per labor unit. "Normal" responsiveness to price changes is thus assured, although PMF-like insensitivity to fixed charges does not hold because laborers respond directly to the influence of these charges upon their effective "wage."[85]

In the remaining literature, Domar's variable-labor-input results are modified because (a) the household does not take return per labor unit as parametric; (b) in some cases, it does not take the labor input of other households as invariant with respect to its own contribution; (c) household decisions are the *only* determinant of aggregate labor input (i.e., managers either do not exist or act as if

---

[84] Domar does not specify whether this is an aggregation of the upward sloping supply curves of individuals, or of varying numbers of individuals each offering a constant amount of labor.

[85] Domar's contribution with respect to the effects of multiple products and multiple variable inputs, in the same paper, has already been treated in Section 1.

constrained to accept offered labor input in all cases); (d) the private sector, as mentioned, is explicitly reintroduced by many authors; and (e) some or all collective income is assumed to be distributed according to "needs" in certain models. With only (a) and (c) but not (b), (d) or (e) invoked, the results differ little from Domar's labor-supply-constrained case, especially if the membership is larger than a handful, because the marginal income yield determining labor input, although a weighted average of marginal and average net products, approaches average net product asymptotically as the share of the household in aggregate collective labor approaches zero. Thus, in the one-sector setting without labor interdependence or "cohesion," labor input and output tend to increase in response to rising prices and falling fixed charges when individual labor supply curves are upward sloping.[86]

Because of the great variety of assumptions and of results obtained, it is difficult to generalize about cases invoking "cohesion," a second sector, and/or "needs" distribution; it would, on the other hand, require too much space to review the results individually. Perhaps the most useful remark to make is that differences in the specifications on member household utility functions appear to generate different comparative static outcomes at least as frequently as do changes in other elements of the model. We can state in a very rough way that results resembling Domar's hold provided that income effects are absent or non-dominant, for this full range of cases, while Ward-type results hold when negative income effects dominate. However, the Slutsky-type decomposition of total effects into substitution and income effects for this problem is more complicated than that of conventional labor-supply problems. These substitution and income effects have not been formally solved for in the literature, so that more precise statements are difficult to make, and a complete comparison of the results obtained by different authors—for what are in principle sub-models nested in the same general model—cannot be provided. It may be noted that

[86] Israelsen's analysis of collective incentives restores many Wardian results, putting him at odds with Domar. (See especially his Table 3, p. 115.) The impression that their differences arise principally from the fact that Israelsen models individual utility maximization instead of an aggregate labor supply curve is partly erroneous, however. At least some of the sign reversals can instead be attributed to Israelsen's assumptions regarding member utility functions, which permit income effects that can generate backward bending individual labor supply curves.

even in the cases in which what we loosely label "strong income effects" generate Ward-type results, presence of the private sector alternative continues to provide a moderating tendency.

This leads us to two further topics in the price response literature, namely the effects of output quotas and of two-tier pricing, and the effects of price and/or output uncertainty. Theoretical insight into centrally-directed collective agricultural economies may be advanced by incorporating the fact that collective farm units often face quotas of crops that must be delivered to state channels at one price, with options to sell additional amounts (also to the state) at higher prices. The essential result here was obtained by Oi and Clayton, who showed that the incentive effects of the quota and price differential are equivalent to those of a lump sum tax equal to the added revenue that would have been obtained had all output sold received the above-quota price. If incentives are sufficient to generate over-fulfillment of the quota, this means, under the conditions of the Oi–Clayton model, that the state can again draw more work and output from the collective labor force for less remuneration, by implementing a high price differential. In that model, higher rents lead to larger optimal memberships (the Ward "loss-sharing" effect), while, since it is the *above-quota* price for collective crops that determines the income-maximizing mix of collective and private labor and output, higher above-quota prices can coax more collective labor out of that larger labor force. In the fixed-membership, individual utility-maximizing models (Bradley, Bonin, Israelsen, etc.), however, higher effective rents will increase labor supply only when there are strong "income effects," but higher marginal prices for collective output will increase the sector's share of labor and output only if "substitution effects" prevail, so that the combined Oi–Clayton effect of two-tiered pricing becomes less likely, although it is not entirely ruled out.[87] In particular, a simultaneous increase in above-quota price and decline in below-quota price can increase the value of dy_i/dl_i while lowering income at the original l_i, leading to an upward adjustment of labor input. The combined effect of more work for less income thus remains possible in the individual labor supply decision model.

[87] See for example Bonin, 1977, Table 1, which reports a positive rent effect and an indeterminate price effect.

This analysis is only slightly complicated by the possibility that forthcoming labor would not allow the output quota to be met without an additional quota on labor itself. As we have seen above, a binding labor quota can change the time allocation problem to one in which the leisure/private labor balance alone is optimized subject to meeting the required collective labor input. On the other hand, with above-quota prices higher than those for below quota output, and with a resulting discontinuity in the marginal return to collective labor schedule, it is conceivable that once quota output is reached by means of required labor minima, marginal incentives are high enough that voluntary above-quota labor is then forthcoming, producing a distinct above-quota equilibrium with optimization of all elements of time allocation. A similar result is illustrated in the Oi and Clayton model.[88] While there may be an unconstrained equilibrium at which the quota would not be met, once the quota is assumed to have been met by legal requirement, there may then exist a quota-exceeding equilibrium at which additional labor flows to the sector to satisfy the requirements of (constrained) income (Oi–Clayton) or utility (Bradley, *et al.*) maximization, responding to the higher above-quota price.

Bradley, Cameron, and Bonin discuss the changes introduced to the analysis by considerations of uncertainty. In particular, the prices received for private but not collective crops will be subject to uncertainty when the former are fixed administratively in advance of the production season and the latter are formed in local free markets. Also, the production functions themselves may contain stochastic elements due to the unpredictability of weather, disease, and similar factors. The one formal analysis, that of Bonin, is limited to the cases of production uncertainty in the collective sector and price uncertainty in the private sector. Two major positive results are derived. First, when both kinds of labor and leisure are variable, introduction of uncertainty makes it possible that an increase in fixed charges will reduce total labor input under utility specifications that lead unambiguously to the opposite result in the certainty case. Second, for a given total labor input, uncertainty means that a change in fixed charges to the collective sector will lead to a reallocation of labor between sectors. In particular, with

[88] Compare figures 3-A and 3-B on pp. 46 and 47 therein.

decreasing absolute risk aversion, increasing fixed charges to the collective sector imply a shift of labor out of that sector and into private production. Other results are derived for price effects when leisure is held constant, but all price effects become ambiguous, due to countervailing income and substitution effects, when leisure and the labor inputs are all variable.

In the absence of other studies, the significance of Bonin's uncertainty results is difficult to evaluate, because they can only be directly compared with the certainty results for his particular specifications on utility functions and the labor responsiveness term, η.[89] Thus, while the "counter-example" of rising fixed charges reducing labor input contrasts with a determinate result for the certainty case in his model, this same counter-result can follow a fixed charge change *under certainty* provided that "cohesion" is "imperfect" ($\eta < 1$) and that utility functions generate upward sloping individual labor supply (see above). The effect of fixed charges on intersectoral labor allocation occurs only under uncertainty in Bonin's model, because "complete emulation" means that the marginal return to labor has no average net revenue product component; this is not the case in the "incomplete emulation" models of Cameron, Chinn, and Putterman, for example. Thus, it seems too early to attempt a synthesis or overview of the effects of introducing uncertainty to the analysis of responses to price and rent changes.

To conclude and summarize our discussion of collective farm responses to changes in policy parameters, we may suggest that while many of the specific results reported are sensitive to modelling assumptions that have resisted standardization, the literature nevertheless provides reasons for believing that collective farms, insofar as they have autonomy to respond to exogenous variables and insofar as work incentives are not predominantly coercive, may behave somewhat differently from profit-maximizing firms. Like self-employed artisans or peasant laborers, the output responses of such collective farms are likely to be based upon households' utility-maximizing calculations, which take both income and leisure as arguments of the utility function.[90] Rather than selecting a

[89] Defined in equation (1.23) of Section 1.8, above.

[90] An excellent overview of peasant household models is provided by Strauss, 1986.

profit-maximizing employment level subject to a given wage rate, the collective farm thus takes membership as given but accepts variability of forthcoming labor from that workforce. How changes in fixed costs affect collective farm output, and whether price changes lead to normal or backward supply responses, will depend in large part upon the way in which income and leisure enter utility functions. Provided that it is understood that the problem of tracing a labor supply curve is substantially more complex here, and that the analysis has yet to be completed for the more general model in which the various analyses in the literature are nested, it can be said that utility functions consistent with upward sloping individual labor supply in conventional analysis are likely to generate "normal" responses to price changes, whereas backward bending curves can reproduce Ward-type effects, although for different reasons than those of the Ward model. Backward bending product supply curves are made less likely by multiple output production, or by the existence of a private sector. With positive responses to the impoverishing tendency of higher fixed costs *and* to higher marginal output prices simultaneously possible, procurement quotas and two-tier pricing may give the state a way to draw out labor and output while granting only minimal incomes to collective farmers.

5.4. Historical observations on the "classical" Soviet and Chinese collective farms

In both the Soviet Union and China, general collectivization of the peasantries was preceded by land reform, and by periods of relatively uncontrolled semi-commercial peasant agriculture with some voluntary cooperative farming. Vigorous nation-wide collectivization campaigns began in the Soviet Union in 1929, and in China in 1956. The Soviet campaign backtracked briefly in 1930, when Stalin accused local officials of overzealously pushing peasants into collective farms, and gave permission for voluntary withdrawals—whereupon the proportion of peasants in collective farms fell from 55 to 23 percent in three months. With pressure soon brought to bear again, over half of all peasant households were in collective farms by July 1931, and this figure rose continuously thereafter, reaching the 90% mark in 1936.[91] China's

[91] Nove, 1969, pp. 169–176.

campaign completed collectivization along Soviet-type lines in a still shorter period during 1955–57, went on to form peoples' communes in 1959, but retreated from large-scale communal farming and, in some areas, even collective farming, in the face of the disastrous agricultural years of 1960–61. Beginning in 1962, China consolidated collective farming on the basis of a system of three production tiers—production teams, brigades, and communes—plus small household plots and sideline activities.[92]

Both countries had relatively stable and organizationally comparable collective farming systems during "classical" periods, which can be associated with the years 1933–1966 in the Soviet Union, and 1962–1978 in China. In these "classical" periods, production was dictated by state plans, farmers were residual claimants of collective incomes after delivery of crops at low procurement prices, collective incomes were divided according to workday (*trudoden*) or workpoint (*gong fen*) systems, and substantial portions of household incomes came from private production activities. The "classical" period in its strict sense ended in the Soviet Union in 1966 when the workday payment system was modified by guaranteeing minimum collective farm wages.[93] The "classical" period ended far more radically in China in the early 1980's, when collective lands began to be "contracted" out to households for independent farming on the equivalent of a fixed rental basis.[94]

While it is beyond the scope of this essay to undertake a comprehensive review of the literature on the history and performance of collective farms in these countries, it is appropriate to discuss the application of the theoretical framework reviewed in this

---

[92] On the chronology of these institutional changes in China, see Chao, *op. cit.*, and Nolan, 1976. On the structure of the commune system, see Crook, 1975.

[93] A more gradualist view of this evolution in the U.S.S.R. could consider also the increase in procurement prices in 1953, the dropping of some quotas in 1957, amalgamation of collective farm units and increasing attention to capital investment beginning at least in the 1950's, abolition of machine tractor stations (separate and often effectively superior units that had served groups of collective farms) in 1958, and other changes. Also, since the 1966 reform set fixed minimum wages but left "full wage" to vary with net revenue when sufficient to cover these, the "collective" element does not entirely vanish at that point.

[94] The actual movement to "household contracting" took place at different times in different parts of the country, and there was experimentation with intermediate forms, such as production by smaller work teams, during the transition period. But the result had been relatively standardized by late 1983. See Nolan, 1983.

section to such questions as: Why did centralized socialist states carry out collectivizations? Why were the collective farm systems either modified or abandoned? And, was the collective farm experience of the Soviet Union and China indicative of the inherent attributes of these organizational forms, and of their best realizable performance?

The collectivizations in question must be placed in the context of the relative backwardness of Soviet Russia and China, the commitment of their leaders to rapid industrialization, the absence of significant external finance for the latter purpose in both cases, preference for directed structural change, beliefs in the existence of scale economies and in a socioeconomic stratification tendency in uncontrolled commercial agriculture, and determination to safeguard Communist Party monopoly on political power. The parties claimed that collective farming was in the self-interest of peasants, who could increase their productivity by grasping economies of scale and organizational advantages in the domain of technological change, and could share these benefits and income security by managing land jointly. In 1918, the year following the October revolution, approximately fifteen hundred agricultural communes were organized in the Soviet Union on the basis of voluntary membership, and the numbers of collective farms of various types grew rapidly until 1921, when perhaps 175,000 rural families belonged to over 15,000 *communes, artels,* and *tozes*; but numbers remained largely unchanged through 1927, when state policy began to switch from the relatively *laissez-faire* New Economic Policy toward universal collectivization.[95] More significantly, as many as 14% of China's rural households voluntarily joined producers' cooperatives up to 1956.[96] But these units differed from "advanced producers' cooperatives" or collective farms in that land, tools, and animals remained private property and were paid shares of cooperative net revenue alongside labor. Large-scale and full-fledged collectivization in both countries awaited central directives.

[95] See Wesson, 1963. Data given are based on the tables and discussion provided by Wesson on pp. 119–122. The three forms (*commune, artel,* and *toz*) differed by system of income distribution (more or less egalitarian), degree of collectivity of production and ownership, and other characteristics; for details, see Wesson. Other sources are Male, 1971, and Davies, 1980.

[96] Nolan, 1976; Selden, 1982; Shue, 1980.

In the Soviet Union, the collectivization process led in the short run not to rising but to declining farm incomes, due to forced grain procurements at low prices, to slaughtering of livestock by peasants entering the collectives, and to resistance toward collective farming. While its impact on the recovery and growth trend of the 1950's is debatable, collectivization in China certainly did not reduce rural output or incomes. However, both fell disastrously with the *communization* that followed shortly thereafter (during the "Great Leap Forward"), and many peasants' incomes failed to return again to 1950's levels until the late 1970's.

Rapid industrial growth was associated with both collectivizations, but there remains controversy as to whether either country actually succeeded in increasing the flow of "economic surplus" from agriculture.[97] Certainly, both countries secured grain requirements for their urban populations at lower prices than would have to have been paid in a free market. In the Soviet case, rural poverty also promoted rural-urban migration, consistent with state industrialization plans, in spite of still low urban wages.[98] However, there were also substantial backward resource flows, especially in the Soviet Union, where machine traction had to be supplied to agriculture to replace depleted animal draft power. While the original justification of collectivization, that of stable grain supply to the industrial sector, may eventually survive historical criticism, partial explanations of the policy may have to be sought also in the domain of ideology and of Party preferences with regard to rural socio-political structure.

In view of these histories of forced and at least partially welfare-depressing collectivizations, it is worth remarking that just as the formal theory discussed above fails to support the common assumption of incentive failure in collectives, so too do similar analyses fail to corroborate the idea that voluntary collectivization

---

[97] With respect to the Soviet Union, the debate centers on the first Five Year Plan (1928–32), and the principal participants are James Millar and Michael Ellman. See Millar, 1970, Ellman, 1975, and Millar's review (1983) citing additional sources. On China, see Lardy, 1983.

[98] A similar effect occurred in China during the "Great Leap Forward," but the government returned most of the migrants to the countryside when its ability to generate high-productivity industrial jobs, and the costs of urban services, were subjected to more sober evaluation as the "Leap"'s failure began to be evident.

by self-interested peasants is inconceivable. An analysis by Putterman (1980, 1981), assuming production and price certainty and foreknowledge of work participation rates, shows that utility-maximizing peasants deciding democratically on the allocation of land to collective versus household-level farming and on the degree of "needs" as opposed to "work"-based distribution of collective income, would select a division of the land efficiently responding to production possibilities, and a mixed remuneration system generating an approximation to marginal product returns. "Voluntary collectivization" occurs automatically, in this framework, if there are economies of scale in production and if household production is restricted to households' own labor forces.

This leaves open any number of reasons why large scale collectivizations have not been voluntary. Peasants may have preferences over the form of production organization and property ownership, independent of income and leisure consequences. There may simply be no economies of scale in relevant production technologies, beyond those that can be grasped by the household itself.[99] Households with advantages in capital accumulation, technical and marketing know-how, landholdings, etc., may, on the other hand, be able to build profitable larger farms on a private basis, in which case they are likely to resist uncompensated pooling of their land under collective control—the main barrier to movement from "elementary" to "advanced" producers' cooperatives in China.

There are other reasons why collective production may not be advantageous even if there are scale economies and if there exist no inequalities among households. The systems of "distribution according to work" used on collective farms generate work incentives as analyzed above only on assumption that labor input can be accurately monitored. In practice, monitoring is costly and necessitates classification of tasks according to conditions of soil, climate, and ecology that vary from plot to plot and from day to day even in a given locale. If awarded workpoints or workdays only approximately reflect real labor input, there is an added source of uncertainty regarding one's prospective return from collective labor. Combined with risk-aversion, this might tend to reduce real labor

[99] On scale economies in Soviet collective agriculture, see Bradley and Clark, 1972, and Wyzan, 1981.

input to the collective sector, and produce a decline in the sector's observable productivity. In practice, the collective needs to exhibit not only higher returns for given factors, but higher returns in spite of the reduced real factor inputs that will be associated with the "incentive frictions" of imperfectly monitored labor.[100]

6. OTHER EXAMPLES

6.1. Cooperation, employee ownership, and participation in the West

6.1.1. Overview. Although the Móndragon and U.S. plywood cooperatives are at present the most studied, they are by no means the only examples of workers' cooperatives in Western industrial economies. Isolated cases of producers' cooperatives can be found in most Western countries beginning at least as early as the 19th century. A rough "census" of producers' cooperatives in some Western countries is provided by Estrin, Jones and Svejnar (1983), who define producers' cooperatives (PC's) as enterprises in which "many" workers are also "members" who participate in firm control and management, share in distribution of net income, and earn a limited return on capital.[101] According to these authors, the Mondragon network of PC's, providing about 16,000 industrial jobs, placed Spain's cooperative sector only third among Western nations after Italy, in which about 200,000 jobs were provided by over 20,000 PC's, and France, in which 35,000 jobs were provided by about 700 PC's in the late 1970's to early 1980's. The U.S. and Britain were at the same time estimated to have had 10,000 jobs in

[100] For an argument on monitoring and supervision problems in Soviet collective farms, see Bradley and Clark, *op. cit.* For a theoretical discussion, see Putterman, 1986b.

[101] On the principle of "limited return," see below. Note that these authors include among PC's, firms having unspecified proportions of non-member workers. In addition, while "one-member-one-vote" is said to be the usual basis for control, some "PC's," as defined by these authors, follow a "one-share-one-vote" formula. Share ownership may be unequally distributed among worker-members, the stated proviso being that "there is an absence of concentration." Such firms fail to satisfy our pure definition of self-management, but they may well exhibit many features of the pure model.

100 PC's and 6,700 jobs in an unspecified number of PC's, respectively. These figures exclude considerably larger numbers of enterprises in many countries exhibiting forms of profit-sharing, of employee ownership, and of worker participation in decision-making (such as "co-determination").[102] Also excluded are cooperative farmers, of whom the approximately 22,000 members of Hutterite colonies in western Canada and the northern plains of the U.S. are undoubtedly the most numerous.[103]

Among the PC's described by Estrin and co-authors, there was considerable variation in size, industrial sector, and capital intensity, both within and across countries. For example, the Mondragon cooperatives, whose most important products are consumer durables (but which, as a group, are significantly diversified), had an average capital intensity of about $24,000 per worker, produced an average of $18,000 value added per worker per year, and had an average of 224 workers per coop. French consulting cooperatives generated a similar value added of $17,000 using only $2,600 in capital per worker, in enterprises averaging 14 members. The Italian sector included some very large construction cooperatives ranking among the largest Italian enterprises and affiliated in a powerful Federation (Lega). In addition to the plywood industry, significant number of PC's were found in reforestation, taxi, and garbage collection industries in the U.S. British PC industries included clothing, footwear, and printing. With respect to worker membership, average figures ranged from 99 to 100% of the workforce having membership in Mondragon and U.S. reforestation cooperatives, to 65–75% worker membership in French consulting, printing, and service, Italian manufacturing and construction, and British footwear cooperatives, and to about 60% in French electrical and U.S. plywood cooperatives, and 40–45% in French construction and British clothing and printing cooperatives.

While not captured in the formal models discussed above, an idea

[102] For example, Whyte and Blasi, 1984, report the existence of over 500 U.S. firms in which employees are majority owners, as well as over 5,000 in which employees are minority owners through employee ownership plans.

[103] The Hutterite colonies are pure agrarian communes each consisting of approximately 100 persons, which Bennett (1977, p. 65) describes as being "organized in virtually identical fashion . . . [to] the *kibbutzim* of Israel . . . although with very different historical traditions and duration". For references, see Bennett. For a fascinating institutional account bearing on organization and incentives, see Bullock and Baden, 1977. On the *kibbutz,* see Section 6.3 (1977, p. 65).

that pervades many empirical studies is that the social and organizational arrangements of self-management may have direct effects upon factor productivities. The basic idea is that when organizational parameters are allowed to vary, the technological production function linking inputs with outputs in a deterministic fashion may no longer be valid. An early argument to the effect that effective labor and managerial inputs may vary substantially depending upon motivational factors was put forward by Leibenstein (1966) without particular reference to cooperatives. A similar idea occurs in Jensen and Meckling's 1979 paper on labor-managed firms and codetermination, where the authors argue that the neoclassical production function needs to be augmented with information on property rights and institutional constraints. While Jensen and Meckling's argument suggests a negative impact of workers' participation on productivity, the idea that workers' participation in decision-making will have a *positive* effect on productivity has been put forward by a number of authors, one of the earlier contemporary treatments being that of sociologist Paul Blumberg (1968).

Estrin, Jones and Svejnar found the cooperatives in their PC studies to have been similar to one another in control structures in that ultimate authority rested in an assembly of members which appointed a board of directors. However, relationships between policy-making bodies, organs concerned with day-to-day executive decisions, and the general meetings of members differed considerably. For example, whereas many European cooperatives delegated substantial authority to boards that in turn selected managers from among cooperative members, U.S. plywood PC's appointed non-member top managers by general vote, and U.S. PC's tended to reserve more major decisions to the full membership.

In most PC's, although one-worker-one-vote rule was practiced, membership was legally tied to holding a capital stake in the firm, and not only to status as a worker. In turn, by far the greatest part of enterprise capital derived from member subscriptions and retained earnings, with the latter, in some cases, being attached to individual members' accounts or share values, in others entering enterprise collective reserves. Some PC's permitted non-workers—especially retired worker-members or family members—to hold shares and sometimes voting rights. Following a widely influential principle of the International Cooperative Alliance, capital once invested with PC's earned only a limited return, often fixed in advance. This means that profit-sharing was more directly reflected in the wages or total compensation received by worker-members than in the return on share capital. Profitability was also captured in share values in a few cases which included the U.S. plywood cooperatives, where these values were market-determined, and the Mondragon cooperatives, where they were not, but where the authors reported that "the value of an individual member's stake rises (and may fall) depending on the fortunes of the firm." Although none of the cooperatives were reported to be able to borrow funds in external capital markets, some had access to loans from specialized financial institutions, and most did some borrowing from their own members. On the whole, however, external finance provided a small proportion of capital to these PC's.

6.1.2. Participation and productivity. Estrin *et al.* summarize the results of studies of the French, Italian, and British cooperative sectors by Estrin and Jones (1983), Jones and Svejnar (1983), and Jones (1982). These studies used enterprise level data from the late 1970's in the French and Italian cases and from 1945–68 for the British firms. Their purpose was to distinguish the effects upon factor productivity of differences in the levels of profit-sharing, decision participation, individual share ownership and loans, collective ownership, and age of firm. To do this, they estimated an equation of the form

$$V = V(K, L, X, Z)$$

where V is value added, K and L are capital and labor inputs, X is a vector of industry and enterprise-specific "environmental" variables, and Z is the vector of variables representing various elements of "cooperation." The results of these studies suggested that profit (surplus) sharing, as proxied by the absolute size of the average bonus per worker, had significantly positive effects on productivity; that participation, as proxied by the proportion of workers who are members, had in some cases a positive effect and in others no effect on productivity; and that collective capital ownership had negative effects on productivity, at least for the large Italian sector. No systematic effects of individual ownership and loans were found.

In the authors' interpretation, the studies by Estrin *et al.* imply that profit-sharing, as opposed to decision-participation and ownership stakes, is the principal source of productivity effects of cooperation. They also interpret the results as being suggestive of a negative impact of collective ownership on factor productivity. Only limited conclusions can be drawn from these studies, however. Since the sample group includes cooperatives only, no conclusions about the effects of substituting cooperation for conventional forms of enterprise are possible. In addition, the variable used to measure participation in decision-making is inadequate, since it attains a maximum when all workers are members regardless of what percentage of members are workers, and since it gives no reading on the actual involvement of, control over, or identification with decisions on the part of rank-and-file workers. The studies are also not designed to detect interaction of the sources of higher productivity, such as enhancement of the effects of decision-participation by the addition of profit sharing, or the reverse. Finally, it is even unclear that the association between bonuses and productivity indicates a causality running from the incentive system to net earnings, and not in the opposite direction; moreover, since bonuses can be viewed as a rather arbitrarily determined portion of total net revenue shares, unambiguous interpretation of any kind may be impossible.

Some evidence attributing productivity effects to participation in decision-making is presented for U.S. plywood PC's by Bellas (1972) and reviewed by Conte (1982). Results of Internal Revenue Service challenges to pre-tax distribution in several highly productive plywood cooperatives (Berman, 1976) supported the coops' arguments that their abnormally high wages were a legitimate reflection of labor productivity as much as 20–50 percent higher than average, rather than returns on capital being distributed in evasion of tax provisions. Bellas compared two groups of plywood PC's, one composed of six firms having hourly wages 25–35% above industry average, and the other composed of the remaining fifteen cooperatives, the hourly incomes of which were slightly above or below industry averages. He found the distribution of firms across these two groups to be significantly correlated with measures of decision participation, proportion of workers among owners, proportion of members among workers, and capital per worker. The decision participation result, which was the strongest at 0.005

significance, used a participation index combining indicators of worker membership on boards of directors and committees, frequency of board and general meetings, and effectiveness of communication of board minutes to worker-members. Since the ratio of worker-members to owners and the ratio of worker-members to workers can also be taken as measures of the degree of workers' control, their correlations with the labor productivity proxy (hourly incomes) are another indication of a productivity-participation association. However, higher capital-labor ratios can be expected to be associated with higher worker productivity, so the final correlation might be viewed as undermining the argument for the latter association except insofar as high capitalization is itself a result of participation—a suggestion which is at odds, as we will see below, with the views of Jaroslav Vanek and some other authors.

Other studies permitting comparison of cooperative with conventional enterprises in the same industry include Zevi's (1982) study of the Italian PC sector and Thomas and Logan's (1980) study of the Mondragon cooperatives. Zevi found enterprise growth rates and profit divided by assets and by turnover to be substantially higher for PC's than for non-PC's in a given industry, but his findings regarding relative productivity of labor were ambiguous. Thomas and Logan found value added per worker substantially higher in Mondragon cooperatives than in Spanish industry as a whole, but slightly lower than the average for the 500 largest Spanish enterprises, in the early to mid-1970's.

Data for 1972 derived from a productivity study by the Caja Laboral Popular, the cooperative bank of the Mondragon group, are also reviewed by Levin (1983). Levin argues that their concentration in capital-intensive manufacturing sectors such as iron and steel, consumer durables, and industrial refrigeration equipment, implies that the Mondragon cooperatives are more comparable to the 500 largest Spanish industrial enterprises than to other industrial enterprises in Spain. In this comparison, the 500 are found to use about four times as much capital per worker, but to produce only 20% more value-added per worker and only about 1/3 as much value-added per peseta of fixed capital. Although total productivity cannot be assessed without providing specific factor weights, Levin asserts—perhaps with some range of factor shadow prices in mind—that total factor productivity can indeed be judged to be higher in the Mondragon enterprises.

6.1.3. Effects of co-determination. The productivity implications of participation have also been studied in the context of co-determined firms. The Federal Republic of Germany's Codetermination Law of 1951 provided for equal representation by workers and shareholders on the Boards of Directors of firms in the German iron, steel, and coal-mining industries. The 1952 Works Constitution Act gave worker representatives a third of the seats on the Boards of Directors of firms with 500 or more employees in the remaining German industries, and also mandated the establishment of works councils having grievance handling, negotiating, and information rights, in all plants with over five employees. The 1972 Works Constitution Act gave the works councils full co-determination (or equal say with management) over job evaluation, employment policies, layoffs and working hours, and related issues.

Svejnar (1982) tested for the effects of the legislated institutional changes in the F.R.G. on industry level data for the period 1950–1976, by estimating both Cobb–Douglas and Kmenta production functions, where the latter provide approximations to constant elasticity of substitution production functions. Dummy variables were added for industry or period coverage of the 1951, 1952, and 1972 laws. For the full multi-industry sample, he found statistically insignificant effects of the 1951 law and the 1952 act, and a statistically significant 3% productivity decline associated with the 1972 act. Svejnar argued that data limitations call the significance of the 1972 result into question, however. He then tested two presumably more homogeneous sub-samples, one composed of coal, iron ore, potash and rock salt, and other mining industries, the other composed of iron-making, iron and steel foundries, steel-drawing and cold-rolling, and nonferrous metals industries. In the mining industries, the 1951 law showed no significant productivity effect; the 1952 law was associated with an "almost significant" 6 to 7% decline in productivity; and the 1972 law coincided with a significant 8–9% fall in productivity. For the metal industries, estimation resulted in a negative estimated coefficient of capital. Since this would imply negative marginal productivity of that factor, Svejnar re-estimated the question in a restricted form in which a positive lower bound was imposed on the capital coefficient. With the restriction adopted, a 12.6% positive effect was estimated for the 1952 law in these industries, but Svejnar stated that its meaning is unclear given the restricted estimation procedure. The estimated effects of the other laws were all insignificant for the metals sample. Svejnar summarized his results as indicating that the 1951 and 1952 laws had no perceptible effects on productivity, and that the effect of the 1972 Act was either insignificant or mildly negative.

In addition to firms covered by co-determination laws and related legislation, West Germany contained over 700 voluntary "industrial partnerships," involving varying degrees of worker participation in decision-making and/or profit-sharing, around 1980. Cable and FitzRoy (1980) analyzed data obtained from a survey of 42 of these firms for the years 1974–76. In a first exercise, they estimated the effects of individual incentive pay, profit distribution, employee-owned capital, and degree of decision participation as "factors" in a Cobb–Douglas production function alongside capital and white and blue-collar labor. The estimated effects of profit-sharing and capital-ownership were found to be insignificant, and those of "incentive pay" were significant and *negative* (corroborating Cable and FitzRoy's suggestion that individualistic incentives are production *disrupting*). Consistent with their hypothesis, however, the estimated coefficient on participation was strongly positive and significant.

In a second exercise, Cable and FitzRoy divided the sample into "high" and "low" participation firms, and looked for effects of participation on differences in estimated factor productivities. Their results suggested slightly lower marginal productivity of labor and substantially higher marginal productivity of capital in the "high" as compared to "low" participation firms. Overall, "the high participation firms on average out-performed the low group by 5 percent, 177 per cent, and 33 per cent respectively in terms of output per man, output per unit of capital, and profitability (rate of return on capital employed)" during the period studied.[104]

A more qualitative discussion of the greater than three decades of German experience with co-determination, by Streeck (1984),

[104] p. 153. In a more recent study, FitzRoy and Kraft, 1984, have looked at the effects of profit sharing on productivity in a sample of 65 West German firms having conventional works councils but not "industrial partnership." The authors hypothesize that profit sharing leads to a more cooperative effort and mutual (horizontal) monitoring response among workers, and hence to increased productivity. While their regression analysis shows a positive relationship between profit sharing and both profitability and productivity, they are unable to rule out reverse causality (from profitability to profit sharing).

provides interesting evidence on issues raised earlier in this paper.[105] Streeck argues, although entirely without reference to the economic theory literature, that co-determination has imparted "syndicalist" characteristics to enterprise behavior in the sense that (a) it has made labor nearly as fixed a factor to the firm as is fixed capital, (b) it has accordingly changed labor utilization patterns and the considerations behind the hiring decision, and (c) it has isolated the firm from the labor market, and segmented the interests of workers within and outside of the firm. The author cites the report of a government-appointed commission on co-determination (Mitbestimmungskommission, 1970) as suggesting that capital-labor "parity," rather than leading to confrontation and inefficiency, had proved itself to be a source of mutual internalization of the others' interests by both capital and labor, and an efficient organizational adaptation fully consistent with the general nature of the (capitalist) economy. He also suggests that while co-determination is only one of several forces (others of which are common to the advanced industrial economies) that have raised the costs of treating labor as a variable factor, it is unique among these forces in also providing a solution to the problem of labor immobility that it creates: namely, an institutionalization of cooperative relations, instead of antagonistic ones, between capital and labor within the firm.

Since Streeck does not claim that the co-determined firm is absolutely more efficient than the conventional firm, the implication is that the increase in organizational effectiveness due to co-determined industrial relations more or less offsets any static efficiency losses due to reduced flexibility of factor utilization. Indeed, Streeck expresses concern about static efficiency when he writes:

> a co-determined manpower policy is costly since it may involve extended delivery terms in times of peak demand, stockbuilding during demand slumps, internalization of training costs, and even the postponement or modification of investment plans to fit the constraints of the existing manpower structure. These short-term costs may well be offset by long-term gains deriving from fewer disruptions, swifter introduction of new technology, and higher quality. But this is not always certain, and foreign competitors may sometimes be advantaged by their higher ability to exploit short-term changes in the market price and the market power of labour. (p. 417)

[105] For a parallel discussion which raises many of the same issues, see Aoki, 1984, especially pages 156–162.

At the same time, Streeck's expressed concern over the increased probability that high cost stable employment within the firm can coexist with macroeconomic unemployment under the system, is remarkably similar to the terms of analysis of, and sometimes also the expressions of concern by, such authors as Tyson and Estrin with respect to Yugoslavia.

West Germany is by no means the only country that has instituted co-determination laws. Pejovich (1978) writes that

> Codetermination is a major postwar social experiment in Western Europe. It is being introduced into the social life of West European countries via a series of laws and regulations. The common trait of all codetermination laws . . . [is]: labor representatives are being allowed to participate in decision-making processes of business firms.

Pejovich lists Denmark, France, the Netherlands, Norway, and Sweden along with Germany as countries that were "actively promoting "industrial democracy" through the use of codetermination schemes" (p. 3). Since Pejovich wrote, various versions of the Meidner plan, under which ownership of large industrial firms would gradually pass into the hands of national pension plans, have been discussed in Sweden; a socialist government with at least nominal commitment to democratizing workplaces came into power in France; and Britain's Labor Party, albeit in a politically weakened position, has declared support for some form of "industrial democracy."

6.1.4. Co-operatives in market economies: further issues. From generalizations about the record of cooperatives, profit-sharing, and co-determination in market economies, a number of theorists have drawn conclusions about either the relative efficiency of self-management or the pre-requisites for successful self-management. For example, Jensen and Meckling (1979) have argued that the dominance of conventional firms in market economies, in which producers' cooperatives have an equal opportunity to compete, indicates the superiority of the former not only in terms of profitability and productive efficiency but also with respect to the ability to foster workers' welfare. They also argue that the trend towards implementation of co-determination by legislation, rather than in response to the demands of workers in individual firms, suggests that decision participation does not benefit workers.[106] Other authors have questioned these arguments. For example, Ben-Ner (1984), as mentioned, attempts to show that labor-managed firms will "degenerate" into capitalist firms when exposed to conventional labor markets, in spite of the fact that worker-members (hence LMFs) might be unambiguously more productive than ordinary workers (and thus PMFs). Another example is Putterman (1984), who takes issue with Jensen and Meckling's conclusion that implementation of co-determination through legislation rather than at the firm level indicates that such participation does not benefit workers. Putterman argues that when a single firm attempts to replace voting with non-voting shares, or dilutes the voting power of shareholders by implementing a worker participation scheme, this raises the cost of finance to the firm and may threaten its workers' wages, jobs, or both. The cost to those workers of introducing participation through social legislation applying simultaneously to all firms, or to all firms in particular sectors, may be lower than the cost of single-firm implementation by an amount sufficient to make change by legislative means a welfare improvement while that at the firm level is not.

Like Jensen and Meckling, Alchian and Demsetz (1972)[107] also take the dominance of capitalist firms as evidence of their organizational superiority. Nevertheless, their theory of the firm suggests conditions under which partnerships and profit-sharing might be likely to exist. The Alchian–Demsetz explanation of the superiority of capitalist firms centers on the idea that monitoring of effort inputs, a critical requirement of team production, is best induced by assigning to a central agent or agents exclusive claims to the enterprise residual, along with rights to hire and fire workers. In some situations, however, monitoring is extraordinarily costly because workers must apply great discretion to their tasks, so that a supervisor may be able to evaluate the worker's effort only by also doing the task himself—the preparation of a legal case is offered as an example. Under these conditions, Alchian and Demsetz say,

[106] Pejovich (1978) argues that the chief beneficiaries are intellectuals who derive utility from instituting personally preferred social changes. Presumably, this small population group manages to exert extraordinary leverage in a good number of democratic polities.

[107] See the discussion in Section 1.9.

partnerships and profit-sharing may be the most viable organizational forms, since if the number of members is small enough, the profit share itself may be a sufficient inducement to conscientious effort.[108] This line of reasoning leads Alchian and Demsetz to speculate that partnerships and profit-sharing will be observed in legal and medical practice, artistic work, and other professional fields involving a high skill content, idiosyncratic work, and relatively minor economies of scale.

Alchian and Demsetz's conjecture about the differential incidence of cooperatives and cooperative-like forms has been supported, extended, or modified by the work of a number of authors. Pauly and Redisch (1973) have presented an influential model of the American-style not-for-profit hospital as a physicians' cooperative maximizing residual per physician over a given membership. Neuberger and James (1981) have similarly modelled the university department as a professors' cooperative. Russell (1985) adopts an Alchian–Demsetz-like theoretical perspective to analyze not only large legal partnerships, but also two other populations of American cooperatives: those in the taxi industry and in "scavenger" garbage collection. The last two, while not "professional," are nevertheless described by Russell as jobs requiring a large amount of almost unmonitorable on-the-site initiative by the worker.[109]

Vanek (1971a) argued that worker-managed firms in Western countries have historically lacked access to external capital sources,

---

[108] The same relationship between monitoring costs and profit-sharing is suggested by Stiglitz (1974).

[109] In cities with worker-run garbage collection firms, the relationship with existing and prospective customers, which is developed by the individual collector, is said to have a strong entrepreneurial aspect.

It seems relevant to mention here that a number of radical economists (such as Bowles, 1985) have suggested an "inverse" implication or extension of the monitoring problem identified by Alchian and Demsetz: namely, that organizers of capitalist workplaces have an incentive to modify production processes and organization in such a way that most jobs are left with minimal scope for the exercise of judgment or initiative. A corollary mentioned occasionally in the literature on self-management is that worker-run firms by virtue or their alternative control or monitoring structures, might make use of different and possibly more satisfaction-giving and/or more productive technologies.

For another perspective on the origins of cooperative firms in market economies, see Ben-Ner, 1986. On the relations between the employee ownership, workplace democracy, and quality of working life as sources of interest in self-management in the United States, see Blasi, Mehrling and Whyte, 1983.

and have therefore been largely worker-owned and financed. He went on to suggest that this may explain the numerical weakness of such firms, in view of what we have above termed Furubotn–Pejovich–Vanek (FPV) underinvestment theory. Assuming a production function with smoothly varying, first increasing and eventually decreasing returns to scale, and assuming collectively owned capital on which the firm fails to assess itself explicit rents, Vanek argues that a worker-managed firm will tend to operate in the zone of still increasing returns to scale and to use an inefficiently labor-intensive technology. Elsewhere, Vanek (1970: Chapter 15, and 1971b) suggested that an institution overarching individual worker-run firms, which he terms the National Labor Management Agency, is needed to facilitate external financing of the firms. The "N.L.M.A." could also undertake market and technical research, promote the creation of new cooperatives, and otherwise support the development of a cooperative sector in a market economy.

An early test of Vanek's ideas on finance was performed by Jones and Backus (1977) using data on British footwear cooperatives. These authors reported a negative association between collective ownership of capital and capital-labor ratios, consistent with Vanek's hypothesis. They also reported a link between collective ownership and suboptimal (sub-minimum-efficient-) scale in the footwear PC's, which again supports Vanek's analysis. Elsewhere, however, Jones (1979) has challenged the assumption that PC's in market economies are typically shorter-lived than their capitalist small business counterparts. Adopting a life-cycle view of the histories of PC's (see also Jones, 1984a), he attempts to show that these firms regularly manifest a pattern of birth, growth, decline, and death, but that this may not not differ either in character or in average duration from those of capitalist firms of comparable size, which are usually family businesses or partnerships.

A number of authors find support for the idea that a "sheltering organization," akin to Vanek's "N.L.M.A.," is either beneficial or essential to cooperative firms in market economies. The case of the Mondragon cooperative network, and the roles played there by second-tier banking, research, and technical training cooperatives, is mentioned in this context by several studies, including that of Thomas (1982). Zevi (1982) and Estrin, Jones and Svejnar (1983) also see the federations of cooperatives as successfully playing this role in Italy. (Outside the Western economies, Blasi, Mehrling and Whyte, 1984, see support for the "sheltering organization" concept in the Israeli *kibbutz* movement and in the Yugoslav economy.)

6.2. Cooperatives in socialist countries

Aside from collective farms, cooperatives play relatively minor roles in the economies of the socialist countries of Eastern Europe and Asia, and little has been written in the Western literature concerning producers' cooperatives in those countries. In several cases, however, socialist cooperative sectors are "minor" only in comparison to state sectors in the same countries; in comparison with cooperatives in Western economies, those in many East European countries, in particular, are quite numerous. Thus, Campbell (1981a) reports that there are large numbers of producer cooperatives in all countries of the European Soviet bloc, with the exception of the German Democratic Republic and the Soviet Union. The Polish movement, in particular, has been the subject of recent discussions by Campbell (1981b) and Jones (1985) in which it is compared in organizational dimensions and degree of success with the Mondragon cooperatives. Some remnants of the large pre-1949 cooperative movement in China also persisted to the late 1970's, at which time the role of producers' cooperatives began to be endorsed and promoted by the government. A review of the Chinese experience from 1919 to 1981 was recently provided by Lockett (1984).

According to Jones, as many as 1500 producers' cooperatives were formed between 1945 and 1948 largely as a means of job creation by unemployed craftsmen.[110] Subsequently, the Polish state fostered the growth of PC's as a complement to state enterprises. The absolute number of PC's rose to 3400 in the early 1960's before falling to a little over 1500 in 1978. Throughout the period, however, employment in the sector grew steadily, with average workforce per cooperative rising from 70 in 1948 to over 500 in

[110] While Jones states that these were formed "essentially on a voluntary basis and without a supporting institutional framework," Montias, 1962, holds that there was an overwhelming policy tilt against private firms in the form of special taxes, confiscation of licenses, and other measures, which played a possibly decisive role in making cooperatives economically viable.

1978, or about 15% of total Polish industrial employment in the later year. This means over 750,000 PC workers in Poland compared with 200,000 in the largest Western European PC sector, that of Italy. The corresponding numbers of PC members for other East European countries were 170,000 for Czechoslovakia, and 300,000 each for Hungary and Roumania, according to Campbell (1981a).

An outstanding feature of the Polish (but also other East European) cooperative sector(s) is its employment of large numbers of handicapped workers. Most Polish manufacturing PC's are found in light industries, such as textiles, clothing, and leather, in which capital-labor ratios are relatively low. However, they are also found in agriculture and in a wide variety of industrial activities, including metal, precision instruments, electronics, and chemicals, in each of which they account for over 5% of total industrial output. As of the late 1970's, most industrial PC's were multiplant, *averaging* five manufacturing plants and 17 service facilities per cooperative. Membership is restricted to workers in the enterprise, and while not all workers need elect to be members, in practice 80 to 90% membership is reported.

Jones (1985) examined evidence on factor use, technical efficiency, and income distribution in Polish producers' cooperatives and state enterprises. He found workers' incomes, labor productivity, and capital per worker to be substantially higher in the state as compared with the cooperative sector. However, since fixed assets per worker in the cooperative sector may have averaged less than 15% of those in the state sector during the period studied (the 1970's), Jones expressed the judgment that "in terms of total factor productivity, PCs probably have outperformed state owned firms during this period." He also cited a study by Skowronski (1979) which found non-labor costs per unit of output to be lower, and average quality of output to be higher in four clothing-producing PC's as compared with four state enterprises in the same industry. Skowronski (as reported by Jones) attributed the better performance of the cooperatives to better organization and management and less waste.

The potential for ambiguity in the status of producers' cooperatives in socialist countries is highlighted by the history of China's collective sector. Comprising from one fifth to one quarter of urban employment in that country in the 1960's, '70's, and early 80's, it would be by far the largest non-agricultural cooperative sector in the world, but its cooperative status is open to question. Handicraft cooperatives were promoted in Communist base areas as early as the 1920's, and over 2,000 cooperatives were created in both Nationalist and Communist controlled areas during the second world war in the war effort-related Chinese Industrial Cooperative ("*Gung Ho*") movement. After 1949, producer cooperatives became the cornerstone of the "socialist transformation" of handicrafts.

According to Lockett (1986), the rules governing PC's corresponded fairly closely to the standards of the International Cooperative Alliance; for example, the members' general meeting held ultimate authority over the enterprise and elected management and supervisory committees every one to two years. At the same time, the government put in place a variety of regulations constraining the behavior of cooperatives, and exercised indirect controls, for example, through its influence as purchaser of 56% of the output value of industrial cooperatives in 1952. While the worker membership of handicraft cooperatives had in 1955 reached 850,000—a number consistent with a gradual cooperativization process—political pressures soon led to a more rapid push during the "high tide of socialist transformation" in 1956. This brought the great majority of all handicraft production into what were formally producer cooperatives by 1957.

Cooperatives, insofar as the term can be legitimately applied, have continued to be highly susceptible to the vicissitudes of China's political winds since the 1950's. During the Great Leap Forward, they suffered widespread "upgrading" to state and to rural commune ownership, and such cooperatives as continued to exist tended to come under the control of local government organs, to lose profit distributing rights, etc. Although there was some restoration of cooperative autonomy following the failure of the G.L.F., the radical 1960's and '70's saw the transformation of former cooperative enterprises into big and small "collectives" that differed from state enterprises in being more nearly self-financing and in receiving lower priority in materials and personnel allocation, and that (contrary to cooperative principles) came under locally-appointed management and paid fixed wages on scales set by local government and not related to enterprise performance.

In the context of the increasingly positive attitude toward market forces and individual initiative displayed by the emerging Chinese leadership beginning in 1978, a new role has been envisaged for producers' cooperatives. Government figures cited by Lockett show new job creation in urban collectives running ahead of that in state enterprises in all years since 1978; indeed, it is hoped that cooperatives will play a major role in solving the employment problem that the government now not only recognizes to exist but also expects to see solved partly by non-governmental efforts.

With the wind of "market socialism" and even individual enterprise blowing strong in China, there may not only be a growing role for small-scale PC's; one might also speculate on the attraction of the Yugoslav model of "self-management" in the *state* sector.[111] At this time, however, it seems safe to conclude that Chinese "market socialism" will be more Hungarian than Yugoslav insofar as internal enterprise management is concerned. Even the large collectives, while gaining autonomy from higher levels of government and being directed to pursue profits, will continue to be managed hierarchically, usually under municipal control. True cooperatives are most likely to be formed where private enterprises or partnerships outgrow government-set limits on size. It remains to be seen whether cooperativization in such cases will not generally represent either a formality legalizing a private enterprise, on the one hand, or the absorption of the former private enterprise into the publicly controlled collective sector, on the other.

We may conclude by returning to Eastern Europe, where the evolution of cooperative forms and ideas within socialist environments is of particular interest. Yugoslavia, the only nation embracing "self-management" as an economic system, did so by decision of a ruling Communist party. Moves toward greater reliance upon "market forces" in other East European economies are often said to have been opposed by workers on grounds that security of employment, wages, and price stability would be threatened by "marketization."[112] While it might therefore be surmised that self-management lacks broad appeal in these countries, two important phenomena represent evidence to the contrary.

[111] See Lockett, 1983.
[112] Bornstein, 1977.

First, while clearly not introduced in the first instance in response to worker or broad public demands, Yugoslav self-management has by many accounts proved to be a highly effective factor in the *legitimation* of the country's political and economic system. In this sense, the leadership gambit of introducing self-management as a means of strengthening its internal support in the face of Cominform ostracism and the possibility of a Soviet-backed invasion, is widely perceived to have succeeded. With the initial external threat receding, and the present danger having shifted to internal economic problems that had reached a crisis level by the early 1980's, and to the political problems of regional strain and of the post-Tito integrity of the Federation, the effectiveness of the concept of self-management in continuing to provide legitimacy (if not wild popularity) to the system has impressed many observers.[113]

Secondly, the Polish Solidarity movement of the early 1980's, which had initially represented workers' more narrowly *economic* interests in a distressed centrally planned economy, emerged in 1981 as the proponent of a far-reaching plan of enterprise self-management. (This was embodied, in particular, in the document Solidarity (1981) which became a central pillar of the movement's position on economic reform after adoption by a meeting of 1000 representatives of existing "self-managements" of enterprises from all parts of Poland in July of that year.[114]) While it is impossible to know how well the commitment to self-management reflected the preferences of the approximately 13 million members of Solidarity, Kolarska (1984) argues that the demand emanated from factory level committees, rather than from either the national leadership of Solidarity or its advisers. In any case, the Solidarity experience, although ultimately largely terminated by a declaration of martial law,[115] is of special interest in having suggested a scenario of "transition from state to self-management socialism" that has not

[113] See, for example, Rusinow (1978) and Tyson (1980), p. 108.

[114] A chronology and discussion of the political-economic context is provided by Kolarska (1984).

[115] At least formal remnants of the movement for enterprise self-management remain in place in the system implemented under martial law. See Gomulka and Rostowski, 1984.

frequently appeared in Western discussions of the social relevance of the self-management concept.[116]

6.3. Cooperation in the Third World

Both agricultural and non-agricultural producers' cooperatives, and participatory and worker-owned firms, are found in great variety almost throughout the less developed nations of Africa, Asia, and Latin America. We have neither the ability nor, in this survey, the space in which to provide a thorough survey of the incidence of cooperation in the Third World. While providing some broad brush indications of where cooperatives are found and references to relevant studies, this section will focus primarily on a few cases that are relatively well-documented, and particularly those that have been examined by economists making use of frameworks discussed in other parts of this paper.

In agriculture, if we limit ourselves to *producers'* cooperatives and exclude from consideration household farmers cooperating on irrigation, input supply, credit, or marketing, the greatest incidence *in non-socialist countries* occurs in Latin America and Africa, while Asia would dominate in the number of collective farms if China, North Korea, and Vietnam were admitted.[117] In Latin America, cooperatives have been formed after government appropriation of haciendas and large agricultural estates, most prominently in Cuba and Mexico and, more recently, Chile, Peru, the Dominican Republic, and Nicaragua. In Africa, Soviet-type collectivization has

[116] It is oversimplifying matters to assume that all movements towards self-management at the enterprise level are also movements in favor of markets, or even of decentralization. The term "no-plan no-market" has had currency in Poland, for example, and one might even look to the post-1974 Yugoslav system of coordination by bargaining or "agreement" for an example of such an economy. A distinction between democratic and conventionally managed enterprises within a centrally planned system, although not addressed in the formal theoretical literature, also need not be dismissed out of hand. In any case, and even if the phenomenon be self-defeating, demands for self-management by various groups are by no means always coupled with a desire to adopt the market mechanism. (For an example of a platform favoring self-management without markets, see Knight and Roca, 1975.)

[117] Asian socialist countries are represented, if thereby only partially, by our discussions of Chinese collective farming and manufacturing cooperatives in Sections 4 and 6.2.

been emulated on a smaller scale or in a modified fashion by countries such as Algeria, Mali, Mozambique, and Tanzania, and has most recently been embraced by Ethiopia.

In the industrial sphere, small scale producers' cooperatives seem to exist, and to be promoted by governments to differing degrees, in a large number of developing countries. Formal promotion of participation or co-determination schemes has occurred, at least ephemerally, in such diverse countries as Bangladesh, Turkey, and Jamaica. The experience with industrial cooperation in Chile in the early 1970's has received particular attention, and will be discussed below.

Finally, an important group of cooperatives that combine features of community and of enterprise, and that engage in roughly equal measure in agricultural and industrial activities, are the Israeli *kibbutzim*. References to these settlements have been made elsewhere in this paper, but some brief remarks on their empirical manifestation will conclude the present section.

The case of agricultural cooperation and participation in Tanzania illustrates many of the problems surrounding the promotion of cooperatives in the Third World. The thrust towards agricultural collectivism in Tanzania was based, at least in part, on an assumption of scale economies for which little if any direct evidence existed or now exists. As in the Soviet case, promotion of collective agriculture may have partly reflected desires to *control* the peasant and some portion of his output. The ability of the Tanzanian state and party[118] to "penetrate" the countryside and enforce village organization during a brief span of years in the mid-1970's surprised many foreign observers. The victories in this drive for control were largely pyrrhic, however. Weakness of effective government control over farm *output*, and the inefficiency of the parastatal monopolies set up to handle marketed output, contributed to an outcome in which not only total output—as in the Soviet and Chinese cases—but even that part of output coming under state control (i.e., official marketed output) *fell* for many crops during the 1970's. Failure to collectivize production or to control marketed output in spite of

[118] In mainland Tanzania, the Tanganyika African National Union or, after 1977, the Party of Revolution (Swahili acronym C.C.M.).

spatial "villagization" led political economists such as Goran Hyden (1980) to speak of the Tanzanian peasantry as "uncaptured."

A Latin American case of equal scope but illustrating the enormous differences in social and developmental context is that of Peru, where an agrarian reform begun in 1969 under the military government of General Juan Velasco Alvarado affected nearly half of the country's agricultural land, eliminated nearly all large scale private holdings, and placed legal checks on parcelization so as to favor consolidated collective or state-managed operation of former haciendas and estates in both coastal and highland regions. While the Peruvian reform succeeded in maintaining joint operation of many large farms, effective self-management and collective production emerged in but a minority of cases. Far more cases have been marked by government domination of reform enterprise management, conflicts between member and non-member groups, and parcelization by successful invasion of estate lands from the outside or, especially of late (and under an anti-collectivist government), as an expedient to circumvent collective management problems.

An interesting difference between the Tanzanian case and earlier collectivizations was that while the force of the government was eventually used to attain peasant compliance with the requirement of residing in registered villages, the level of collective as opposed to household-based crop production (including the proportion of land in private as opposed to collective plots) remained at least formally subject to villagers' internal choices, so that hypotheses regarding the determinants of choice of farm scale and organizational form[119] as well as those regarding individual households' degrees of participation in village versus "own" production, could in principle be tested on intra- and inter-village data samples, as was done by Putterman (1986a) on data collected in 43 villages in 5 of the country's 16 regions between 1977 and 1982. Among the major results of this study are the finding of apparent links between (on the one hand) the proportion of collective out of total farming, across villages, and (on the other hand) (a) the use of material incentives (distribution of collective revenues according to work

[119] Note that scale and form were necessarily linked, since all large-scale farming in the villages was legally required to be by the village as a cooperative enterprise.

input), (b) relative factor productivities in the collective as compared with household production sectors, and (c) village population (negatively related to the degree of "collectivity"). The study also generated some evidence that participation in collective activity was linked to education, mobility, and exposure to wage employment, findings contradicting an understanding of cooperation in Tanzania as principally a residue of a supposed "traditional African socialism."[120]

As mentioned earlier, while not ruling out the conclusion that collective production generally failed in Tanzania because of either (a) limited scale economies, or (b) intrinsic incentive problems of collective team production, Putterman argues that much of the blame might also be borne by such "extrinsic" factors as (a) inadequacy of internal democratic control, (b) frequent failure to use differentiated material rewards, (c) the tendency to appropriate collective output for collective "accumulation" and services while failing to tax private earnings, and (d) government pricing and marketing policies which led to the decline of trade through official channels. Based on both the Tanzanian and Chinese experiences, he labels (1985a) as "anti-incentivism" the twin political-ideological tendencies to (a) minimize material incentives within collective production units, and to (b) minimize price incentives to collective production units, and argues that this set of factors may be sufficient to destroy any otherwise attainable benefits of cooperation for producers, and thus their willingness to enthusiastically participate in cooperative production. In any case, in spite of a sample purposely including the most successfully cooperating villages in several districts and regions, the data set shows lower productivity of both land and labor in collective as opposed to household plot production in 19 of 20 villages,[121] so that peasant *unwillingness* to allocate more than 5% of labor time or village land to collective

[120] Unfortunately, no convincingly systematic explanations of inter-household differences in collective work participation were discovered. Also, the results on the collectivism-incentives link are ambiguous, since distribution of collective income could have been a result of greater success in revenue generation, rather than the other way around. Finally, since the sample of villages was not entirely random, unambiguous statistical inference is ruled out.

[121] If villages for which data were available for one but not the other productivity measure are included, this becomes 26 of 27 for land productivity and 18 of 21 for labor productivity.

production, in spite of government and party promotion, probably was rational.

Since most Tanzanian collective farms represented only a fraction of village farming and were partly politically motivated, since time series data for individual collective farms are unavailable, and since price data for these series would have to be supplemented by even less available detailed data on black market conditions, reliability and timing of government pick-ups and payments, and similar factors, it is impossible to test theoretical propositions about price (and similar parameter) responsiveness of these farms. However, one theoretical problem that can be expected to have had little bearing on them, *a priori,* is that of limited employment, the reason being that, as in the models of collective farms discussed earlier, membership itself has essentially been given to the villages, while virtually all peasants were made members of one village or another by administrative fiat. To find apparent illustrations of the Wardian employment problem, mingled with the tendency to substitute non-member for member labor as identified by Ben-Ner (1984) and others, we may look, however, at Latin American cooperatives which gave membership to former permanent estate workers while excluding members of adjacent rural communities.

In Peru and Chile, cooperatives were created through agrarian reform efforts during the 1960's and early 1970's, membership was limited to the ex-hacienda workers, and benefits to rural landless families were limited because of the failure of the cooperatives to generate much additional employment or to invite in new members. According to Kay (1982, p. 156), coastal cooperatives drew a quarter of their labor from non-member *eventuales* who tended to "work more hours per day, do the most irksome tasks and receive considerably lower wages than the *socios*[members]."

> In the cotton and rice co-operatives members tend to reduce the number of days and hours per day worked for the cooperative's central enterprise by substituting *eventual* labor for their own. This occurs because *socios* tend to increase the proportion of land individually worked as a way of increasing their private profits.

Kay goes on to argue that these and related practices helped to bring on "a process of creeping State intervention in the affairs of the co-operatives."

According to McClintock, Podesta, and Scurrah (1984), who

survey a number of studies, the cooperatives were generally able to improve the incomes of their own members, and their economic performance was mixed but "not unfavorable." McClintock *et al.* also cite a large number of studies as showing that members worked harder on their private plots than on enterprise land, because of faulty work incentives in the co-operatives. The authors suggest that such problems might be tackled over time when they write

> In Peru, as this problem became evident, most co-operatives moved to pass "work codes" that rationalized compensation and promotion norms, and gradually members' energies were refocused upon the enterprise. In Chile, however, there was no time for such adjustments.

In a similar vein, Carter (1984, 1985) has recently argued that rather than supporting any simple hypothesis about the superiority or inferiority of collective production, the performance of Peruvian agricultural cooperatives, especially the better-endowed coastal Agricultural Production Cooperatives (CAP's), indicate that success will vary with the effectiveness of strategies for solving the unique internal incentive problems of democratic group enterprises.[122] Studying samples of CAP's and small and medium-sized non-cooperative farms drawn from coastal Peru, he finds substantially greater variability of productivity, or of latent "effort" measures, within the cooperative as opposed to non-cooperative farms. While Cobb–Douglas estimates indicated that cooperative producers averaged only 71% as much rice and 85% as much corn per unit of observed inputs, at least similar productivity differentials in favor of the smaller producers would be expected due to farm size differences alone, judging by other studies. Unless it is possible to compare productivity across organizational forms holding farm size constant, as Carter observes, definite conclusions about the efficiency of collective farming cannot be drawn. Nonetheless, by the early 1980's, Carter (1985) finds a marked tendency to parcelize cooperatives reflecting a belief that this will circumvent motivational (and perhaps management) problems of collective production. He

[122] Carter's argument on the inappropriateness of uniform efficiency predictions parallels that of Estrin, Jones, and Svejnar (1983), while his emphasis on internal organizational and incentive features is remarkably similar to that of Putterman (for example, 1982 and 1986a).

accurately compares the parcelization process to the Chinese "de-collectivization" of the same period, and speculates on whether an intermediate solution maintaining the economies of certain joint operations but using the incentives of household or individual responsibility for specific plots, might be superior to complete individualization in the Peruvian case.

If identification of the producers' cooperative with entire rural communities, as in China and Tanzania, is one way to avoid unwanted employment effects, another method is suggested by the experience of the "proportional profit farms" in Puerto Rico of the 1950's. As described by Edel (1962, 1963), these were large sugar estates taken over by the government, which appointed a manager to run them using the existing wage labor forces. The government considered itself to be in "partnership" with the workers, who received a share of profits in addition to their fixed wages. Management, however, remained under the strict control of the government, which also owned the land and received a rent for its use. Edel finds the government to have maintained employment in the farms and to have picked up losses in some years, so that the farms were only in part productive ventures, and in part employment programs run at positive cost to the government. Edel argues that the net cost to society was probably negative, since without the proportional profit farms, the government would have been faced with supporting the workers, unemployed, through social welfare programs.

Various Caribbean and Latin American examples are also pertinent to the frequently expressed beliefs that the desire to own land privately and the absence of economies of scale in production tend to rule out voluntary collective farming. These studies show that joint farm operation is more likely to be maintained "on estates where operations had been centrally managed prior to . . . agrarian reform and where substantial economies of scale existed";[123] and that in such cases, joint farming has often been supported by reform beneficiaries. Thus, in a study of Jamaican sugar cooperatives, Stone (1978, p. 15) found that a majority of workers on three of four

[123] Horton, 1973. The immediate reference is to the irrigated cotton and wheat zones of north-western Mexico, and to the henequen (sisal) plantations of the Yucatan, also in Mexico. See also Kay, *op. cit.*

cooperative farms formed by the government on bought-out estates "favoured the collective structure of land tenure." In his study of haciendas, plantations, and collective farms in Peru and Cuba, Martinez-Alier (1977, p. 29) argued that

> "Land hunger" is not a specifically "peasant" feeling. "Peasants" who are given good alternative employment lose their "land hunger" (as has happened to millions of them in industrialized countries) . . . [they] desire land of their own in order to have an assured supply of food and an assured opportunity of work. They will cease to desire land if such things are assured to them in some other way.

At the same time, Martinez-Alier found that attitudes toward cooperative farming among rural populations differed according to their status as small farmers, estate workers, or landless laborers.

Both Cuba and, more recently, Nicaragua have found small farmers resistant to collectivization, and have in the first instance proceeded towards "socialization" of agriculture by way of (para)-state farms created out of confiscated large estates. During a turbulent history of first attempting rapid diversification out of exports, then massive emphasis upon politicized labor mobilization toward sugar production, Cuba's policy was to tolerate and in various ways control the 20% of farmers remaining in the private sector, while encouraging the sale of private farms to the government. In the late 1970's, however, having adopted a more "moderate" overall policy giving place to technological development and expertize, material incentives, and a limited role for free markets, Cuba's government began inducing private farmers to join small production cooperatives which, after paying compensation for contributed non-labor inputs, would own land and distribute net incomes according to labor contributions. By early 1980, about 10% had joined these cooperatives (Forster, 1982).

With a smaller percentage of its land in the confiscated estate sector,[124] Nicaragua found that redistribution of parcels in the private sector of agriculture had led to seasonal labor-supply problems for the new parastatal farms. The Nicaraguan government has moved to establish formal organs of worker representation in the management of these farms, but whether this is to be a route to

[124] Unlike Cuba, Peru and Chile, Nicaragua did not appropriate farms exceeding a fixed hectare limit, but only acquired estates previously owned by the family and close associates of the deposed dictator Somoza.

their evolution into true producers' cooperatives remains unclear (Peek, 1983).

Thanks to its book-length treatment by Espinosa and Zimbalist (1978), the Chilean experience with workers' participation under the government of President Salvadore Allende is probably the Third World industrial case that is best known to students of self-management. Between 1970 and 1973, 420 firms accounting for 40 percent of the value of industrial output and employing about 30 percent of the industrial workforce of Chile were brought under state ownership and/or control, but with provisions for the firms to be run by administrative councils having five worker-elected and five state-appointed members, plus a state-selected administrator (McClintock, *et al.*; Espinosa and Zimbalist). Using data from surveys carried out in 35 of the industrial firms, Espinosa and Zimbalist tested hypotheses concerning the sources and consequences of differences in the levels of workers' participation in decision making. They found labor productivity to have increased or remained constant after the implementation of workers' participation in 23 of the 35 firms, among which an increase of over 6% a year was found in 14. Within the sample, productivity growth was also positively correlated with the authors' index of level of participation, as was the rate of investment in fixed productive assets. Productivity growth took place in spite of a "marked tendency for social area firms to expand employment" (p. 185).

According to Espinosa and Zimbalist, political and ideological factors were dominant in explaining the level of participation: 65% of the variance in the index of participation was explained by (a) labor mobilization and consciousness, (b) political ideology and attitude toward participation of worker leaders, and (c) political party composition (p. 183). The authors also found a positive relationship between participation and egalitarianism within the firms, and in turn, between egalitarianism and productivity.

Disparities between high and low wages were reduced. The number of wage grades was sharply diminished, and the incentive system was put progressively on a more collective basis, as opposed to individual piece rates. These changes in wage structure connoted a sense of solidarity, team work, high morale, and work spirit which had salutary effects on enterprise performance. Independent from and complementary to the influence of higher levels of participation, the move toward more egalitarian and collective forms of remuneration significantly promoted decreases in thefts and defective products and increases in innovative behavior, investment, and productivity.[125]

If Espinosa and Zimbalist are correct, emphasis on egalitarianism within successful Chilean democratic firms, like that in Israeli *kibbutzim,* presents a counter-example to the contention that self-managed firms must solve their potential "free-rider" problem by reliance on individual material incentives. One framework for interpretation is that of Carter (1985), who suggests that democratic work organizations might create successful work incentives either by emulating conventional firms in metering individual contributions, or by forging "multi-stranded ties" of mutual social obligation and commitment. Carter follows Oliver Williamson (1975) and others in suggesting that excessive metering can be counter-productive by encouraging calculative and opportunistic behavior; yet he argues from case studies that success may be based on either or both approaches. The solution by way of limited income differentiation and mutual commitment may be preferred when it is consistent with the ideological orientation of members and/or when metering with insurmountably high levels of inaccuracy will be counter-productive to incentives and work morale.

The *kibbutzim* themselves today number roughly 250 settlements with a combined population in excess of 115,000 adult members and children. The first of these strictly communal and at that time entirely agricultural settlements were founded between 1907 and 1920. Population and numbers have grown continuously, although the *kibbutz* share in Israel's population declined in the midst of the largest waves of European and Middle Eastern immigration, to stabilize at about 3.5%. The period since the 1960's has seen rising industrialization in these rural communities, with industry surpassing agriculture as an income source in many cases.

The *kibbutz* represents a pure case of self-management with the exception of some labor and hiring (usually a small fraction of the member labor force) and volunteer-temporary and candidate mem-

[125] *Op. cit.,* pp. 184–5.

bership categories.[126] A decline in the communal aspects of *kibbutz* life, including the rearing of children in common "children's houses" and the taking of meals in a common dining hall, have been observed in many of the settlements during recent decades. However, the communal principle of livelihood, according to which housing, food, clothing, and indeed all other goods and services, are allocated to members without regard to work role or measured labor input, continues to be maintained as a defining principle in all of the settlements.[127]

References

Alchian, Armen A. and Harold Demsetz, 1972, "Production, Information Costs, and Economic Organization," *American Economic Review* **62:** 777–795.

Aoki, Masahiko, 1979, "Worker Management and Worker-Owner Sharing in the Hierarchical Organization," *Economic Analysis and Workers' Management,* **XII:** 93–107.

Aoki, Masahiko, 1980, "A Model of the Firm as a Stockholder-Employee Cooperative Game, *American Economic Review* **70:** 600–610.

Aoki, Masahiko, 1984, *The Co-operative Game Theory of the Firm.* London: Oxford University Press.

Archibald, G. C. and H. M. Neary, 1983, "Achieving Pareto-Efficient Outcomes in the Labour-Managed Firm," University of British Columbia Working Paper No. 83-25.

Arrow, Kenneth, J., 1974, *The Limits of Organization.* New York: W. W. Norton.

[126] The *kibbutz* movements embrace "self-labor," the principle that individuals should not be enriched or be spared unpleasant work by employing others. In addition to exceptions made for skilled labor not available in the *kibbutz* population, the principle was violated on a significant scale when the state pressed the *kibbutzim* to contribute to employment creation after periods of mass immigration. There has also been slippage on the principle especially in the area of factory jobs. However, at least one of the *kibbutz* movements taxes settlements that hire outside labor and applies the funds to seeking ways to mechanize production so as to decrease the hired work force in *kibbutz* enterprises.

Resident non-members who join the *kibbutzim* for shorter periods numbered about 18,000 in 1983, bringing the combined kibbutz population to 134,000. (*Statistical Abstract of Israel, 1983,* Central Bureau of Statistics, Jerusalem; reported in *Kibbutz Studies* [*Yad Tabenkin,* Efal, Israel], April, 1984.)

[127] Most non*kibbutz* agriculture in Israel takes the form of cooperative settlements in which household-level production is combined with joint marketing, input supply, services, and common ownership of certain infrastructure and large equipment. Israel also has the world's largest *union-owned* industrial sector under its Histadrut labor movement. An economic overview of the *kibbutz* is provided by Barkai, 1977. Other discussions include Ben-Ner and Neuberger, 1982, Ben-Ner, 1982, and Morawetz. 1983.

Atkinson, A. B., 1973, "Worker Management and the Modern Industrial Enterprise," *Quarterly Journal of Economics* **LXXXVII:** 375–392.
Atkinson, A. B., 1975, "Worker Management and the Modern Industrial State: A Reply," *Quarterly Journal of Economicx* **LXXXIX:** 670–672.
Azariades, Costas, 1975, "Implicit Contracts and Unemployment Equilibria," *Journal of Political Economy* **83:** 1183–1202.
Baily, Martin N., 1974, "Wages and Unemployment Under Certain Demand," *Review of Economic Studies* **41:** 37–50.
Barkai, Haim, 1977, *Growth Patterns of the Kibbutz Economy.* Amsterdam: North Holland.
Bartlett, William, 1984, "Unemployment, Migration and Industrialization in Yugoslavia, 1958–1982," European University Institute Department of Economics Working Paper No. 90.
Bellas, C. J., 1972, *Industrial Democracy and the Worker-Owned Firm: A Study of Twenty-One Plywood Companies in the Pacific Northwest.* New York: Praeger.
Ben-Ner, Avner, 1982, "Changing Values and Preferences in Communal Organizations: Econometric Evidence from the Experience of the Israeli Kibbutz," in Jones and Svejnar, eds., 1982.
Ben-Ner, Avner, 1984, "On the Stability of the Cooperative Type of Organization," *Journal of Comparative Economics* **8:** 247–260.
Ben-Ner, Avner, 1986, "Producer Cooperatives: Why do They Exist in Capitalist Countries?" in Walter W. Powell, ed., *The Non-Profit Sector: A Research Handbook.* New Haven: Yale University Press.
Ben-Ner, Avner and Egon Neuberger, 1982, "Israel: The Kibbutz," pp. 186–213 in Frank H. Stephen, ed., *The Performance of Labor-Managed Firms.* New York: St. Martin's Press.
Bennett, Elaine and Myrna Wooders, 1979, "Income Distribution and Firm Formation," *Journal of Comparative Economics* **3:** 304–318.
Bennett, John W., 1977, "The Hutterian Colony: A Traditional Voluntary Agrarian Commune with Large Economic Scale," pp. 65–88 in Peter Dorner, ed., *Cooperative and Commune: Group Farming in the Economic Development of Agriculture.* Madison: University of Wisconsin Press.
Berle, Adolf A. and Gardiner C. Means, 1932, *The Modern Corporation and Private Property.* New York, Macmillan.
Berman, Katrina, 1976, "Comparative Productivity in Worker-Managed Cooperative Plywood Plants and Conventionally Run Plants." Mimeo. University of Idaho.
Berman, Matthew D., 1977, "Short-run Efficiency in the Labor-managed Firm," *Journal of Comparative Economics* **1:** 309–314.
Bicanic, R., 1973, *Economic Policy in Socialist Yugoslavia.* Cambridge, Cambridge University Press.
Blasi, Joseph, Perry Mehrling, and William Foote Whyte, 1983, "The Politics of Worker Ownership in the United States," in Frank Heller, *et al.,* eds., *International Yearbook of Organizational Democracy, Vol. I.* Sussex, England: John Wiley & Sons.
Blasi, Joseph, Perry Mehrling and William F. Whyte, 1984, "Environmental Influences on the Growth of Worker Ownership and Control," pp. 289–313 in Wilpert and Sorge, eds., 1984.
Blumberg, Paul, 1968, *Industrial Democracy: The Sociology of Participation.* New York: Schocken Books.
Bonin, John P., 1977, "Work Incentives and Uncertainty on a Collective Farm" *Journal of Comparative Economics* **1:** 77–97.
Bonin, John P., 1980, "On the Theory of the Labor-Managed Firm Under Price Uncertainty: A Correction," *Journal of Comparative Economics* **4:** 331–337.

Bonin, John P., 1981, "On the Theory of the Labor-Managed Firm from the Membership's Perspective with Implications for Marshallian Industry Supply," *Journal of Comparative Economics* **5:** 337–351.

Bonin, John P., 1982, "Optimal Employment Policies for a Multi-Period Labour-Managed Socialist Cooperative," *Jahrbuch de Wirtschaft Osteuropas* **10:** 9–47.

Bonin, John P., 1983, "Innovation in a Labor-Managed Firm: A Membership Perspective," *The Journal of Industrial Economics* **XXXI:** 3313–329.

Bonin, John P., 1984, "Membership and Employment in an Egalitarian Cooperative," *Economica* **51:** 295–305.

Bonin, John P., 1985, "Labor Management and Capital Maintenance: Investment Decisions in the Socialist Labor-Managed Firm," pp. 55–69 in Derek C. Jones and Jan Svejnar, eds., *Advances in the Economic Analysis of Participatory and Labor-Managed Firms, Vol. I.* Greenwich, CT: Jai Press.

Bonin, John P. and Wataru Fukuda, 1986, "The Multi-Factor Illyrian Firm Revisited," *Journal of Comparative Economics* **10:** 171–180.

Bornstein, Morris, 1977, "Economic Reform in Eastern Europe," pp. 102–132 in *East European Economies Post Helsinki.* Washington, D.C.: U.S. Congress Joint Economic Committee.

Bowles, Samuel, 1985, "The Production Process in a Competitive Economy: Walrasian, Neo-Hobbesian, and Marxian Models," *American Economic Review* **75:** 16–36.

Bradley, Keith and Alan Gelb, 1981, "Motivation and Control in the Mondragon Experiment," *British Journal of Industrial Relations* **19:** 211–231.

Bradley, Michael E., 1971, "Incentives and Labour Supply on Soviet Collective Farms," *Canadian Journal of Economics* **4:** 342–352.

Bradley, Michael E., 1973, "Incentives and Labour Supply on Soviet Collective Farms: Reply," *Canadian Journal of Economis* **6:** 438–443.

Bradley, M. and M. G. Clark, 1972, "Supervision and Efficiency in Socialized Agriculture," *Soviet Studies* **23:** 465–73.

Brewer, A. A., and M. J. Browning, 1982, "On the "Employment" Decision of a Labour-Managed Firm," *Economica* **49:** 141–146.

Browning, Martin, J., 1982, "Cooperation in a Fixed-Membership Labor-Managed Enterprise," *Journal of Comparative Economics* **6** (3, September) 235–247.

Bullock, Kari and John Baden, 1977, "Communes and the Logic of the Commons," pp. 182–199 in Garrett Hardin and John Baden, eds., *Managing the Commons.* San Francisco, W. H. Freeman.

Burkett, John, 1983, *The Effects of Economic Reform in Yugoslavia: Investment and Trade Policy, 1959–76.* Berkeley: University of California Press.

Cable, John and Felix FitzRoy, 1980, "Co-operation and Productivity: Some Evidence from West German Experience," pp. 141–160 in Alasdair Clayre, ed., *The Political Economy of Co-operation and Participation.* Oxford University Press. (Earlier version in *Economic Analysis and Workers' Management* **14** (1980): 163–180.)

Cable, John R. and Felix R. FitzRoy, 1980, "Productive Efficiency, Incentives and Employee Participation: Some Preliminary Results for West Germany," *Kyklos* **33:** 100–121.

Calvo, Guillermo and Stanislaw Wellisz, 1978, "Supervision, Loss of Control and the Optimum Size of the Firm," *Journal of Political Economy* **86:** 943–952.

Cameron, Norman E., 1973a, "Incentives and Labour Supply in Cooperative Enterprises," *Canadian Journal of Economics* **6:** 16–23.

Cameron, Norman E., 1973b, "Incentives and Labour Supply on Soviet Collective Farms: Rejoinder," *Canadian Journal of Economics* **6:** 442–445.

Campbell, Alastair, 1981a, "Producer Cooperatives in Eastern Europe: Lessons for the West," Leeds: Industrial Common Ownership Movement.

Campbell, Alastair, 1981b, "Polish Mondragon," Scottish Co-operatives Development Committee.

Carter, Michael R., 1984, "Resource Allocation and Use Under Collective Rights and Labour Management in Peruvian Coastal Agriculture," *Economic Journal* **94:** 826–46.

Carter, Michael R., 1985, "Revisionist Lessons from the Peruvian Experience with Cooperative Agricultural Production," pp. 179–194 in *Advances in the Economics of Labor Managed and Participatory Firms, Vol. I.*

Chao, Kang, 1970, *Agricultural Production in Communist China, 1949–65.* Madison, University of Wisconsin Press.

Chinn, Dennis L., 1979, "Team Cohesion and Collective-Labor Supply in Chinese Agriculture," *Journal of Comparative Economics* **3:** 375–394.

Comisso, Ellen T., 1979, *Workers' Control Under Plan and Market.* New Haven, Yale University Press.

Comisso, Ellen T., 1980, "Yugoslavia in the 1970s: Self-Management and Bargaining," *Journal of Comparative Economics* **4:** 192–208.

Conn, David and Fernando M. C. B. Saldanha, no date, "Stability of General Equilibria in Labor-Managed Economies: A Non-Tatonnement Approach," Department of Economics, University of Arizona.

Conte, Michael, 1982, "Participation and Performance in U.S. Labor-Managed Firms," pp. 213–237 in Jones and Svejnar, eds., 1982.

Crook, Frederick W., 1975, "The Commune System in the People's Republic of China, 1963–74," pp. 366–410 in U.S. Congress Joint Economic Committee, *China: A Reassessment of the Economy.*

Dahl, Robert, 1985, *A Preface to Economic Democracy.* Berkeley: University of California Press.

Davies, R. W., 1980, *The Soviet Collective Farm, 1919–1930.* Cambridge, Mass., Harvard University Press.

Davy, Samuel J., 1983, "Employee Ownership: One Road to Productivity Improvement," *Journal of Business Strategy* **4** (1)**:** 12–21.

Demsetz, Harold, 1967, "Toward a Theory of Property Rights," *American Economic Review* **57:** 347–73.

Dimitrijevic, D. and G. Macecich, 1983, *Money and Finance in Yugoslavia—A Comparative Analysis.* New York, Praeger.

Domar, Evsey, D., 1966, "The Soviet Collective Farm as a Producers' Cooperative," *American Economic Review* **56:** 734–757.

Dow, Gregory, 1983, "Labor Management in a Competitive Society," *Institution for Social and Policy Studies Working Paper No. 10008,* Yale University, New Haven, CT (forthcoming in *Journal of Comparative Economics*).

Dow, Gregory, 1986, "Control Rights, Competitive Markets, and the Labor Management Debate," *Journal of Comparative Economics* **10:** 48–61.

Drèze, Jacques, 1976, "Some Theory of Labor Management and Participation," *Econometrica* **44:** 1125–1139.

Dubravcic, Dinko, 1970, "Labor as Entrepreneurial Input: An Essay in the Theory of the Producer Cooperative Economy," *Economica* **37:** 297–310.

Edel, Matthew, 1962, "Land Reform in Puerto Rico, 1941–1959, Part One," *Caribbean Studies* **2** (3)**:** 26–60.

Edel, Matthew, 1963, "Land Reform in Puerto Rico, 1941–1959, Part Two," *Caribbean Studies* **2** (4)**:** 28–50.

Ellerman, David P., 1984, "Theory of Legal Structure: Worker Cooperatives,"

Journal of Economic Issues **18:** 861–891.

Ellman, Michael, 1975, "Did the Agricultural Surplus Provide the Resources for the Increase in Investment in the USSR During the First Five-Year Plan?" *The Economic Journal* **85:** 844–863.

Espinosa, Juan G. and Andrew S. Zimbalist, 1978, *Economic Democracy: Workers' Participation in Chilean Industry 1970–1973.* New York, Academic Press.

Estrin, Saul, 1982, "Long-Run Supply Responses under Self-Management," *Journal of Comparative Economics* **6:** 363–378.

Estrin, Saul, 1983, *Self-management: Economic Theory and Yugoslav Practice.* Cambridge: Cambridge University Press.

Estrin, Saul, 1985, "Self-Managed and Capitalist Behavior in Alternative Market Structures," pp. 71–86 in *Advances in the Economic Analysis of Participatory and Labour-Managed Firms, Vol. I.*

Estrin, Saul and William Bartlett, 1982, "The Effects of Enterprise Self-Management in Yugoslavia: An Empirical Survey," in Jones and Svejnar, eds., 1982.

Estrin, Saul and Derek C. Jones, 1983, "The Effects of Worker Participation upon Productivity in French Producer Cooperatives," European University Institute (Florence) Working Paper No. 68.

Estrin, Saul, Derek C. Jones and Jan Svejnar, 1983, "The Varying Nature, Importance and Productivity Effects of Worker Participation: Evidence for Contemporary Producer Cooperatives in Industrialized Western Economies," paper presented at the annual meeting of the American Economic Association, San Francisco.

Estrin, Saul and Jan Svejnar, 1982, "Wage Determination Under Labor-Management: Theory and Evidence from Yugoslavia," Working Paper No. 292, Department of Economics, Cornell University.

Eswaran, Mukesh and Ashok Kotwal, 1984, "The Moral Hazard of Budget-Breaking," *Rand Journal of Economics* **15:** 578–581.

Evans, Alfred, Jr., "Changes in the Soviet Model of Rural Transformation," pp. 143–158 in Stuart, ed., 1983.

Fellner, W., 1947, "Prices and Wages Under Bilateral Monopoly," *Quarterly Journal of Economics* **61:** 503–552.

FitzRoy, F. R. and K. Kraft, 1984, "Productivity, Profitability, and Profit-Sharing," mimeo, International Institute of Management, Berlin.

Forster, Nancy, 1982, "The Revolutionary Transformation of the Cuban Countryside," Universities Field Staff International Reports.

Friedman, James W., 1977, *Oligopoly and the Theory of Games.* Amsterdam, North Holland.

Fukuda, Wataru, 1980, "The Theory of the Labor-Managed Firm Under Uncertainty," *Kobe University Economic Review* **26:** 49–61.

Fukuda, Wataru, 1983, "On the Output and Employment Decisions of an Egalitarian Labor-Managed Firm," *Kobe University Economic Review* **29:** 51–67.

Furubotn, E., 1974, "Bank Credit and the Labor-Managed Firm: The Yugoslav Case," *Canadian-American Slavic Studies* **8:** 89–106.

Furubotn, E., 1976, "The Long-Run Analysis of the Labor-Managed Firm: An Alternative Interpretation," *American Economic Review* **66:** 104–124.

Furubotn, E., 1980a, The Socialist Labor-Managed Firm and Bank-Financed Investment: Some Theoretical Issues," *Journal of Comparative Economics* **4:** 184–191.

Furubotn, E., 1980b, "Bank Credit and the Labor-Managed Firm: Reply," *American Economic Review* **70:** 800–804.

Furubotn, E. and S. Pejovich, 1970, "Property Rights and the Behavior of the Firm in a Socialist State: The Example of Yugoslavia," *Zeitschrift fur Nationalokonomie* **30:** 431–454.

Gomulka, Stanislaw and Jacek Rostowski, 1984, "The Reformed Polish Economic System," *Soviet Studies* **36:** 386–405.

Greenberg, Joseph, 1979, "Existence and Optimality of Equilibrium in Labor-Managed Economies," *Review of Economic Studies* **46:** 419–434.

Greenwald, Bruce C., 1979, "Existence and Stability Problems of Economies of Labour-Managed Firms and Their Relationship to Those of Economies with Strong Unions," *Economic Analysis and Workers' Management* XIII: 73–90.

Grossman, Sanford J. and Oliver D. Hart, 1980, "Takeover Bids, the Free Rider Problem, and the Theory of the Corporation," *Bell Journal of Economics* **11:** 42–64.

Gui, Benedetto, 1985, "Limits to External Financing: A Model and an Application to Labor-Managed Firms," pp. 107–120 in *Advances in the Economic Analysis of Participatory and Labor-Managed Firms, Vol. I.*

Guttman, Joel and Michael Miller, 1983, "Endogenous Conjectural Variations in Oligopoly," *Journal of Economic Behavior and Organization* **4:** 249–264.

Harris, John R. and Michael P. Todaro, 1970, "Migration, Unemployment and Development: A Two-Sector Analysis," *American Economic Review* **60:** 126–142.

Hawawni, Gabriel A. and Pierre A. Michel, 1979, "Theory of a Risk Averse Producer Cooperative Firm Facing Uncertain Demand," *Annals of Public and Cooperative Economy* **50:** 43–61.

Hawawini, Gabriel A. and Pierre A. Michel, 1983, "The Effect of Production Uncertainty on the Labor-Managed Firm," *Journal of Comparative Economics* **7:** 25–43.

Hey, John D. and John Suckling, 1980, "On the Theory of the Competitive Labor-Managed Firm Under Price Uncertainty: Comment," *Journal of Comparative Economics* **4:** 338–342.

Hill, Martyn and Michael Waterson, 1983, "Labor-Managed Cournot Oligopoly and Industry Output," *Journal of Comparative Economics* **7:** 43–52.

Hirschman, Albert O., 1970, *Exit, Voice and Loyalty*. Cambridge: Harvard University Press.

Holmstrom, Bengt, 1979, "Moral Hazard and Observability," *Bell Journal of Economics* **10:** 74–92.

Holmstrom, Bengt, 1982, "Moral Hazard in Teams," *Bell Journal of Economics* **13:** 324–340.

Horton, Douglas, 1973, "Haciendas and Cooperatives: A Preliminary Study of Latifundist Agriculture and Agrarian Reform in Northern Peru," Land Tenure Center Research Paper No. 53, University of Wisconsin, Madison.

Horvat, Branko, 1971, "Yugoslav Economic Policy in the Post-War Period: Problems, Ideas, Institutional Developments," *American Economic Review* **61:** 69–169.

Horvat, Branko, 1976, *The Yugoslav Economic System: The First-Labor-Managed Economy in the Making*. New York, International Arts and Sciences Press.

Hyden, Goran, 1980, *Beyond Ujamaa in Tanzania: Underdevelopment and an Uncaptured Peasantry*. Berkeley, University of California Press.

Ichiishi, Tatsuro, 1977, "Coalition Structure in a Labor-Managed Market Economy," *Econometrica* **45:** 341–360.

Ireland, Norman, 1981, "The Behavior of the Labor-Managed Firm and Disutility from Supplying Factor Services," *Economic Analysis and Workers' Management* **XV**: 21–43.

Ireland, Norman, 1983, "On the Codetermined Firm and the Horizon Problem," unpublished manuscript, Department of Economics, University of Warwick, Coventry, U.K.

Ireland, Norman and Peter Law, 1978, "An Enterprise Incentive Fund for Labor Mobility in the Cooperative Economy," *Economica* **45:** 143–151.

Ireland, Norman J. and Peter J. Law, 1981, "Efficiency, Incentives, and Individual Labor Supply in the Labor-Managed Firm," *Journal of Comparative Economics* **5:** 1–23.

Ireland, Norman J. and Peter J. Law, 1982, *The Economics of Labor-Managed Enterprises*. New York, St. Martin's Press.

Ireland, Norman and Peter Law, 1985a, "Management Design under Labour Management," paper presented at the Fourth International Conference on the Economics of Self-Management, Liege, revised October 1985.

Ireland, Norman and Peter Law, 1985b, "Maximum Return Firms and Codetermination," pp. 21–40 in *Advances in the Economic Analysis of Participatory and Labor-Managed Firms, Vol. I.*

Israelsen, L. Dwight, 1980, "Collectives, Communes, and Incentives," *Journal of Comparative Economics* **4:** 99–124.

Jensen, Michael C. and William H. Meckling, 1979, "Rights and Production Functions: An Application to Labor-Managed Firms and Codetermination," *Journal of Business* **52:** 469–506.

Jones, Derek C., 1979, "U.S. Producer Cooperatives: The Record to Date," *Industrial Relations* **18:** 342–357.

Jones, Derek C., 1982, "British Producer Cooperatives, 1948–1968: Productivity and Organizational Structure," pp. 175–198 in Jones and Svejnar, eds., 1982.

Jones, Derek C., 1984, "American Producer Cooperatives and Employee-Owned Firms: A Historical Perspective," pp. 37–56 in Robert Jackall and Henry M. Levin, eds., *Worker Cooperatives in America*. Berkeley: University of California Press.

Jones, Derek C., 1985, "The Economic Performance of Producer Cooperatives Within Command Economies: Evidence for the Case of Poland," *Cambridge Journal of Economics* **9:** 111–126.

Jones, Derek C. and David Backus, 1977, "British Producer Cooperatives in the Footwear Industry: An Empirical Test of the Theory of Financing," *Economic Journal* **87:** 488–510.

Jones, Derek C. and Jan Svejnar, eds., 1982, *Participatory and Self-Managed Firms: Evaluating Economic Performance*. Lexington, Mass.: Lexington Books.

Jones, Derek C. and Jan Svejnar, 1983, "Participation, Profit Sharing, Worker Ownership and Efficiency in Italian Producer Cooperatives," Cornell University Department of Economics Working Paper No. 293.

Karcz, Jerzy, F., 1966, "Seven Years on the Farm: Retrospect and Prospect," pp. 383–450 in *New Directions in the Soviet Economy*. Washington: U.S. Congress Joint Economic Committee.

Kay, Cristobal, 1982, "Achievements and Contradictions of the Peruvian Agrarian Reform," *Journal of Development Studies* **18:** 141–170.

Knight, Peter T., 1983, "Yugoslavia: Financial Discipline and Structural Adjustment," unpublished paper, World Bank, April.

Knight, Peter T. and Santiago Roca, 1975, "Synthesis of the Principal Conclusions of the Workshop on Implementation of Self-managed Systems in the Third World (Cornell University, June 9–27, 1975)," *Economic Analysis and Workers' Management.*

Kolarska, Lena, 1984, "The Struggle About Workers' Control: Poland, 1981," pp. 425–441 in Wilpert and Sorge, eds., 1984.

Kornai, Janos, 1984, "Soft vs. Hard Budget Constraints: Relation Between State and Firm," faculty seminar on change in socialist societies, Yale University, March 22.

Laffont, Jean-Jacques and Roger Guesnerie, 1984, "Indirect Public Control of Self-Managed Monopolies," *Journal of Comparative Economics* **8:** 139–158.

Lardy, Nicholas R., 1983, *Agriculture in China's Modern Economic Development.* New York: Cambridge University Press.

Law, Peter J., 1977, "The Illyrian Firm and Fellner's Union-Management Model," *Journal of Economic Studies* **4:** 29–37.

Lazonick, William, 1982, "Production, Productivity and Development, Theoretical Implications of Some Historical Research," Discussion Paper No. 876, Harvard Institute of Economic Research.

Leibenstein, Harvey, 1966, "Allocative Efficiency and X-Efficiency," *American Economic Review* **56:** 392–415.

Leibenstein, Harvey, 1982, "The Prisoners' Dilemma in the Invisible Hand: An Analysis of Intrafirm Productivity," *American Economic Review* (Papers and Proceedings) **72:** 92–97.

Levin, Henry M., 1983, "Raising Employment and Productivity with Producer Co-operatives," pp. 310–328 in Paul Streeten and Harry Maier, eds., *Human Resources, Employment and Development. Volume* 2: *Concepts, Measurement and Long-Run Perspective* (Proceedings of the Sixth World Congress of the International Economic Association held in Mexico City, 1980). London: Macmillan.

Lewis, Tracy, 1980, "Bonus and Penalties in Incentive Contracting," *Bell Journal of Economics* **11:** 292–301.

Lockett, Martin, 1983, "Enterprise Management—Moves Towards Democracy?" pp. 224–256 in Stephan Feuchtwang and Athar Hussain, eds., *The Chinese Economic Reforms.* London, Croom Helm.

Lockett, Martin, 1986, "Producer Cooperatives in China: 1919–1981," in Joseph Blasi, ed., *Worker Ownership and Participation in International Perspective.* Norwood, Mass.: Norwood Editions. (Italian version: "Cooperative di Produzione in Cina: 1919–1981," *Rivista della Cooperazione* **11** (1983): 35–73.)

MacLeod, W. Bentley, 1984, "A Theory of Cooperative Teams," CORE Discussion Paper No. 8441, Universite Catholique de Louvain.

McCain, Roger A., 1973, "A Critical Note on Illyrian Economics," *Kyklos* **26:** 380–386.

McCain, Roger, 1977, "On the Optimal Financial Environment for Worker Cooperatives," *Zeitschrift fur Nationalokonomie* **37:** 355–384.

McCain, Roger, 1982, "Empirical Implications of Worker Participation in Management," in Derek C. Jones and Jan Svejnar, eds., 1982.

McClintock, Cynthia, Bruno Podesta and Martin J. Scurrah, 1984, "Latin American Promises and Failures: Peru and Chile," pp. 443–471 in Wilpert and Sorge, eds., 1984.

Malcolmson, James M., 1984, "Work Incentives, Hierarchy, and Internal Labour Markets," *Journal of Political Economy* **92:** 486–507.

Male, D. J., 1971, *Russian Peasant Organization Before Collectivization.* Cambridge, England: Cambridge University Press.

Manne, Henry, G., 1965, "Mergers and the Market for Corporate Control," *Journal of Political Economy* **73:** 110–120.

Markusen, James R., 1975, "Efficiency Aspects of Profit-Sharing Systems versus Wage Systems," *American Journal of Agricultural Economics* **57:** 601–612.

Markusen, James R., 1976, "Profit-Sharing, Labour Effort and Optimal Distributive Shares," *Economica* **43:** 405–410.

Martinez-Alier, Juan, 1977, *Haciendas, Plantations and Collective Farms: Agrarian Class Societies—Cuba and Peru.* London: Frank Cass.

Meade, James E., 1972, "The Theory of Labour-Managed Firms and of Profit-Sharing," *Economic Journal* **82:** 402–428.

Meade, James E., 1979, "The Adjustment Processes of Labour Co-operatives with Constant Returns to Scale and Perfect Competition," *Economic Journal* **89:** 781–788.

Meran, Georg, and Elmar Wolfstetter, 1984, "Optimal Risk Shifting vs. Efficient Employment in Illyria: The Labor-Managed Firm Under Asymmetric Information," unpublished manuscript, Discussion Papers on Political Economy, Number 21, Free University, Berlin.

Milanovic, Branko, 1982, "The Austrian Theory of the Cooperative Firm," *Journal of Comparative Economics* **6:** 379–395.

Milenkovitch, Deborah D., 1971, *Plan and Market in Yugoslav Economic Thought.* New Haven, CT: Yale University Press.

Milenkovitch, Deborah D., 1983, "Self-Management and Thirty Years of Yugoslav Experience," *Association for Comparative Economic Studies Bulletin* **25** (3): 1–26.

Millar, James R., 1970, "Soviet Rapid Development and the Agricultural Surplus Hypothesis," *Soviet Studies* **22:** 77–93.

Millar, James R., 1983, "Views on the Economics of Soviet Collectivization of Agriculture: The State of the Revisionist Debate," pp. 109–117 in Stuart, ed., 1983.

Miovic, P., 1975, "Determinants of Income Differentials in Yugoslav Self-Managed Enterprises," Ph.D. Dissertation, University of Pennsylvania.

Mirrlees, James A., 1976, "The Optimal Structure of Incentives and Authority Within an Organization," *Bell Journal of Economics* **7:** 105–131.

Mitbestimmungskommission, 1970, *Mitbestimmung im Unternehmen.* Stuttgart: W. Kohlhammer.

Miyamoto, Yoshinari, 1980, "The Labor-Managed Firm and Oligopoly," *Osaka City University Economic Review* **16:** 17–31.

Miyamoto, Yoshinari, 1982, "A Labour-Managed Firm's Reaction Function Reconsidered," unpublished manuscript, Faculty of Economics, Osaka City University, Osaka, Japan.

Miyazaki, Hajime, 1984a, "Internal Bargaining, Labor Contracts, and a Marshallian Theory of the Firm," *American Economic Review* **74:** 381–393.

Miyazaki, Hajime, 1984b, "On Success and Dissolution of the Labor-Managed Firm in the Capitalist Environment," *Journal of Political Economy* **92:** 909–931.

Miyazaki, Hajime and Hugh M. Neary, 1983, "The Illyrian Firm Revisited," *Bell Journal of Economics* **14:** 259–270.

Montias, John Michael, 1962, *Central Planning in Poland.* New Haven, CT: Yale University Press.

Morawetz, David, 1983, "The Kibbutz as a Model for Developing Countries or On Maintaining Full Economic Equality in Practice," in Frances Stewart, ed., *Work, Income and Inequality.* London: Macmillan.

Muzondo, Timothy R., 1979, "On the Theory of the Competitive Labor-Managed Firm Under Price Uncertainty," *Journal of Comparative Economics* **3:** 127–144.

Neary, Hugh, M., 1984, "Labor-Managed Cournot Oligopoly and Industry Output: A Comment," *Journal of Comparative Economics* **8:** 322–327.

Neuberger, Egon, 1959, "The Yugoslav Investment Auctions," *Quarterly Journal of Economics* **73:** 88–115.

Neuberger, Egon, 1970, "The Yugoslav Visible Hand System: Why Is It No More?" S.U.N.Y. Stony Brook Department of Economics Discussion Paper 23.

Neuberger, Egon and Estelle James, 1973, "The Yugoslav Self-Managed Enterprise: A Systemic Approach," pp. 245–284 in Morris Bornstein, ed., *Plan and Market: Economic Reform in Eastern Europe*. New Haven, CT: Yale University Press.

Neuberger, Egon and Estelle James, 1981, "The University Department as a Non-Profit Labor Cooperative," *Public Choice* **36:** 585–612.

Nolan, Peter, 1976, "Collectivization in China: Some Comparisons with the U.S.S.R.," *Journal of Peasant Studies* **3:** 192–220.

Nolan, Peter, 1983, "De-collectivization of Agriculture in China, 1979–1982: A Long-Term Perspective," *Cambridge Journal of Economics* **7:** 381–403.

North, Douglas C., 1981, *Structure and Change in Economic History*. New York: Norton.

Nove, Alec, 1969, *An Economic History of the U.S.S.R.* Harmondsworth, England: Penguin.

Oi, Walter Y. and Elizabeth Clayton, 1968, "A Peasant's View of a Soviet Collective Farm," *American Economic Review* **58:** 37–59.

O'Keeffe, Mary, W. Kip Viscusi and Richard J. Zeckhauser, 1984, "Economic Contests: Comparative Reward Schemes," *Journal of Labor Economics* **2:** 27–56.

Paroush, Jacob and Nava Kahana, 1980, "Price Uncertainty and the Cooperative Firm," *American Economic Review* **70:** 65–73.

Pateman, Carole, 1970, *Participation and Economic Theory*. Cambridge: Cambridge University Press.

Pauly, Mark and Michael Redisch, 1973, "The Not-for-Profit Hospital as a Physicians' Cooperative," *American Economic Review* **63:** 87–100.

Peek, Peter, 1983, "Agrarian Reform and Rural Development in Nicaragua, 1979–81," pp. 273-306 in Ajit Kumar Ghose, ed., *Agrarian Reform in Contemporary Developing Countries*. New York: St. Martin's Press.

Pejovich, Svetozar, 1969, "The Firm, Monetary Policy and Property Rights in a Planned Economy," *Western Economic Journal* **7:** 193–200.

Pejovich, Svetozar, 1973, "The Banking System and the Investment Behavior of the Yugoslav Firm," in Morris Bornstein ed., *Plan and Market: Economic Reform in Eastern Europe*. New Haven, CT.: Yale University Press.

Pejovich, Svetozar, 1978, "Codetermination: A New Perspective for the West," pp. 3–21 in Svetozar Pejovich, ed., *The Codetermination Movement in the West*. Lexington, Mass.: Lexington Books.

Pfouts, Ralph W. and Steven Rosefielde, 1986, "The Firm in Illyria: Market Syndicalism Reconsidered," *Journal of Comparative Economics* **10:** 160–170.

Putterman, Louis, 1980, "Voluntary Collectivization: A Model of Producers' Institutional Choice," *Journal of Comparative Economics* **4:** 125–157.

Putterman, Louis, 1981, "On Optimality in Collective Institutional Choice," *Journal of Comparative Economics* **5:** 392–402.

Putterman, Louis, 1982, "Some Behavioral Perspectives on the Dominance of Hierarchical over Democratic Forms of Enterprise," *Journal of Economic Behavior and Organization* **3:** 139–160.

Putterman, Louis, 1983, "Incentives and the Kibbutz: Toward an Economics of Communal Work Motivation," *Zeitschrift fur Nationalokonomie* **43:** 157–188.

Putterman, Louis, 1984, "On Some Recent Explanations of Why Capital Hires Labor," *Economic Inquiry* **22:** 171–187.

Putterman, Louis, 1985a, "Extrinsic Versus Intrinsic Problems of Agricultural Cooperation: 'Anti-incentivism' in Tanzania and China," *Journal of Development Studies* **21:** 175–204.

Putterman, Louis, 1985b, "On The Interdependence of Labor Supplies in Producers' Cooperatives of Given Membership," pp. 87–105 in *Advances in the Economic Analysis of Labor-Managed and Participatory Firms, Vol. I.*

Putterman, Louis, 1986a, *Peasants, Collectives and Choice: Economic Theory and Tanzania's Villages.* Greenwich, CT., JAI Press.

Putterman, Louis, 1986b, "Work Motivation and Monitoring in a Collective Farm," Brown University Department of Economics Working Paper No. 84-28, Revised December 1986.

Putterman, Louis, forthcoming, "The Incentive Problem and the Demise of Team Farming in China," *Journal of Development Economics.*

Putterman, Louis and Marie DiGiorgio, 1985, "Choice and Efficiency in a Model of Democratic Semi-Collective Agriculture," *Oxford Economic Papers* **37:** 1–22.

Ramachandran, R., W. R. Russell and T. K. Seo, 1979, "Risk-Bearing in a Yugoslavian Labor-Managed Firm," *Oxford Economic Papers* **31:** 270–282.

Riskin, Carl, 1974, "Incentive Systems and Work Motivations. The Experience in China," *Working Papers for a New Society* **1:** 27–31, 77–92.

Rivera-Batiz, Francisco L., 1980, "The Capital Market and Income Distribution in Yugoslavia," *Quarterly Journal of Economics* **44:** 179–184.

Robinson, Joan, 1967, "The Soviet Collective Farm as a Producer Cooperative: Comment," *American Economic Review* **57:** 222–223.

Ross, Stephen, A., 1974, "On the Economic Theory of Agency and the Principle of Similarity," in M. S. Balch, D. L. McFadden and S. Y. Wu eds. *Essays on Economic Behavior Under Uncertainty.* Amsterdam, North Holland.

Rusinow, Dennison, 1978, *The Yugoslav Experiment 1948–1974.* Berkeley, University of California Press.

Russell, Raymond, 1985, "Employee Ownership and Internal Governance," *Journal of Economic Behavior and Organization* **6:** 217–241.

Sacks, Stephen R., 1972, "Changes in Industrial Structure in Yugoslavia, 1959–1968," *Journal of Political Economy* **80:** 561–574.

Sacks, Stephen R., 1973, *Entry of New Competitors in Yugoslav Market Socialism.* Berkeley, University of California Institute of International Studies Research, Series 19.

Sacks, Stephen R., 1977, "Transfer Prices in Decentralized Self-Managed Enterprises," *Journal of Comparative Economics* **1:** 183–193.

Sacks, Stephen R., 1983, *Self-Management and Efficiency: Large Corporations in Yugoslavia.* London: George Allen and Unwin.

Sapir, Andre, 1980, "A Growth Model for a Tenured-Labor-Managed Firm," *Quarterly Journal of Economics* **95:** 387–402.

Schlicht, E., and C. C. Von Weizsacker, 1977, "Risk Financing in Labour Managed Economies: The Commitment Problem," *Zeitschrift fur Gesamte Staatwissenschaft* **133:** 53–66.

Selden, Mark, 1982, "Cooperation and Conflict: Cooperative and Collective Formation in China's Countryside," in Mark Selden and Victor Lippit, eds., *The Transition to Socialism in China.* Armonk, N.Y.: M. E. Sharpe.

Sen, Amartya K., 1966, "Labour Allocation in a Cooperative Enterprise," *Review of Economic Studies* **33:** 361–371.

Sen, Amartya K., 1967, "Isolation, Assurance, and the Social Discount Rate," *Quarterly Journal of Economics* **81:** 112–124.

Sen, Amartya K., 1973, "Behavior and the Concept of Preference," *Economica* **40:** 241–259.

Sen, Amartya K., 1977, "Rational Fools: A Critique of the Behavioral Foundations of Economic Theory," *Philosophy and Public Affairs* **6:** 317–344.

Sertel, Murat R., 1982, *Workers and Incentives*. Amsterdam: North-Holland.

Shapiro, Carl and Joseph E. Stiglitz, 1984, "Equilibrium Unemployment as a Worker Discipline Device," *American Economic Review* **74:** 433–444.

Shavell, Steven, 1979, "Risk Sharing and Incentives in the Principal and Agent Relationship," *Bell Journal of Economics* **10:** 55–73.

Shue, Vivienne, 1980, *Peasant China in Transition: The Dynamics of Development Toward Socialism, 1949–56.* Berkeley: University of California Press.

Simon, Herbert A., 1951, "A Formal Theory of the Employment Relationship," *Econometrica* **19:** 293–305.

Simon, Herbert A., 1971, "Decision Making and Organizational Design," in D. S. Pugh, ed., *Organization Theory*. New York: Penguin Books.

Singleton, F. and B. Carter, 1982, *The Economy of Yugoslavia.* London, Croom Helm.

Skowronski, S., 1979, "The Effectiveness of Economic Activity in Big and Small Enterprises (Productive Co-operatives)," *Cooperative Scientific Quarterly* (2): 12–16.

Solidarity (Network of "Solidarity" Organizations in Leading Factories), 1981, "Position on Social and Economic Reform of the Country," *Solidarnosc* (Gdansk) Nr 29/59/81.

Solow, Robert and Ian M. MacDonald, 1981, "Wage Bargaining and Employment," *American Economic Review* **71:** 896–908.

Spence, Michael A., 1977, "Entry, Capacity, Investment and Oligopolistic Pricing," *Bell Journal of Economics* **8:** 534–544.

Staellerts, R., 1981, "The Effect of Capital Intensity on Income in Yugoslav Industry," *Economic Analysis and Workers' Management* **15:** 501–516.

Steinherr, Alfred, 1975, "Profit-Maximising vs. Labor-Managed Firms: A Comparison of Market Structure and Firm Behavior," *Journal of Industrial Economics* **24:** 97–104.

Steinherr, Alfred and Henk Peer, 1975, "Worker Management and the Modern Industrial Enterprise: A Note," *Quarterly Journal of Economics* **LXXXIX:** 662–669.

Steinherr, Alfred and J-F Thisse, 1979, "Are Labor-Managers Really Perverse?" *Economic Letters* **2:** 137–142.

Stephen, Frank H., 1980, "Bank Credit and the Labor-Managed Firm: A Comment," *American Economic Review* **70:** 796–799.

Stiglitz, Joseph E., 1974, "Incentives and Risk Sharing in Share-cropping," *Review of Economics Studies* **41:** 219–255.

Stiglitz, Joseph E., 1981, "The Allocation Role of the Stock Market: Pareto Optimality and Competition," *Journal of Finance* **36:** 235–251.

Stone, Carl, 1978, "An Appraisal of the Co-operative Process in the Jamaican Sugar Industry," *Social and Economic Studies* **27:** 1–20.

Strauss, John, 1986, "The Comparative Statics of Agricultural Household Models," in I. Singh, L. Squire and J. Strauss, eds., *Agricultural Household Models: Extensions, Applications, and Policy*. Baltimore: Johns Hopkins University Press.

Streeck, Wolfgang, 1984, "Co-determination: The Fourth Decade," pp. 391–422 in

Wilpert and Sorge, eds.
Stuart, Robert C., 1972, *The Collective Farm in Soviet Agriculture*. Lexington, Mass., Lexington Books.
Stuart, Robert C., ed., 1983, *The Soviet Rural Economy*. Totowa, N.J.: Rowman and Allanheld.
Stuart, Robert C. and Paul R. Gregory, 1977, "A Model of Soviet Rural-Urban Migration," *Economic Development and Cultural Change* **26:** 81–92.
Svejnar, Jan, 1982, "Codetermination and Productivity: Empirical Evidence from the Federal Republic of Germany," pp. 199–212 in Jones and Svejnar, eds., 1982.
Svejnar, Jan, 1982, "On the Theory of a Participatory Firm," *Journal of Economic Theory* **27:** 313–330.
Thomas, Hendrik, 1982, "The Performance of the Mondragon Cooperatives in Spain," pp. 129–151 in Jones and Svejnar, eds., 1982.
Thomas, Hendrik and C. Logan, 1980, *Mondragon Producer Cooperatives*. The Hague, Netherlands: Institute of Social Studies.
Thomson, William, 1982, "Information and Incentives in Labor-Managed Economies," *Journal of Comparative Economics* **6:** 248–268.
Tugan-Baranovsky, Mikhail I, 1921, *Sotsialnyia Osnovy Kooperatsii*. Berlin: Slowo Verlagsgesellschaft.
Tyson, Laura D'Andrea, 1977, "A Permanent Income Hypothesis for the Yugoslav Firm," *Economica* **44:** 393–408.
Tyson, Laura D'Andrea, 1979, "Incentives, Income Sharing, and Institutional Innovation in the Yugoslav Self-Managed Firm," *Journal of Comparative Economics* **3:** 285–301.
Tyson, Laura D'Andrea, 1980, *The Yugoslav Economic System and Its Performance in the 1970's*. Berkeley: Institute of International Studies, University of California, Berkeley.
Vanek, Jaroslav, 1969, "Decentralization Under Workers' Management: A Theoretical Appraisal," *American Economic Review* **59:** 1006–1014. (Reprinted in Vanek, 1977).
Vanek, Jaroslav, 1970, *The General Theory of Labor-Managed Market Economies*. Ithaca: Cornell University Press.
Vanek, Jaroslav, 1971a, "The Basic Theory of Financing Participatory Firms," Cornell Department of Economics Working Paper No. 27 printed in Vanek ed., 1975 and Vanek, 1977.
Vanek, Jaroslav, 1971b, "Some Fundamental Considerations on Financing and the Form of Ownership under Labor Management," Cornell Department of Economics Working Paper No. 16, reprinted in Vanek, 1977.
Vanek, Jaroslav, 1972, "The Macroeconomic Theory and Policy of an Open Worker-Managed Economy," *Ekonomska Analiza* 3/4 reprinted in Vanek, 1977.
Vanek, Jaroslav, 1973, "The Yugoslav Economy Viewed through the Theory of Labor Management," *World Department* **1** (9): 39–56, reprinted in Vanek, 1977.
Vanek, Jaroslav, ed., 1975, *Self-Management, Economic Liberation of Man*. Baltimore, Penguin.
Vanek, Jaroslav, 1977, *The Labor-Managed Economy: Essays by Jaroslav Vanek*. Ithaca, N.Y.: Cornell University Press.
Vanek, Jaroslav, 1978, "Self-Management, Worker's Management, and Labour Management in Theory and Practice: A Comparative Study," *Economic Analysis and Workers' Management* **12** (1-2): 5–24.
Vanek, Jaroslav and Milena Jovicic, 1975, "The Capital Market and Income

Distribution in Yugoslavia: A Theoretical and Empirical Analysis," *Quarterly Journal of Economics* **89:** 432–443.

Wachtel, Howard, 1972, "Workers' Management and Inter-Industry Wage Differentials in Yugoslavia," *Journal of Political Economy* **80:** 540–560.

Wachtel, Howard, 1973, *Workers' Management and Workers' Wages in Yugoslavia.* Ithaca, N.Y.: Cornell University Press.

Ward, Benjamin, 1958, "The Firm in Illyria: Market Syndicalism," *American Economic Review* **68:** 566–589.

Ward, Benjamin, 1967, *The Socialist Economy: A Study of Organizational Alternatives.* New York: Random House.

Webb, Sidney and Beatrice, 1920, *A Constitution for the Socialist Commonwealth of Great Britain.* London: Longmans, Green.

Wesson, Robert G., 1963, *Soviet Communes.* New Brunswick, N.J.: Rutgers University Press.

Whyte, William Foote and Joseph R. Blasi, 1984, "Worker Ownership and the Unions: A Perspective on Industrial Policy," *Annals of the American Academy of Political and Social Sciences.*

Williamson, Oliver E., 1975, *Markets and Hierarchies: Analysis and Anti-Trust Implications.* New York: Free Press.

Williamson, Oliver E., 1980, "The Organization of Work: A Comparative Institutional Assessment," *Journal of Economic Behavior and Organization* **1:** 5–38.

Williamson, Oliver E., 1985, *The Economic Institutions of Capitalism: Firms, Markets, Relational Contracting.* New York: Free Press.

Wilpert, Bernhard and Arndt Sorge, eds., 1984, *International Yearbook of Organizational Democracy, Vol. II: International Perspectives on Organizational Democracy.* Chichester: John Wiley & Sons.

Wolfstetter, Elmar, Murray Brown and Georg Meran, 1983, "Optimal Employment and Risk Sharing in Illyria: The Labor-Managed Firm Reconsidered," unpublished manuscript, *Discussion Papers on Political Economy* No. 10, Free University, Berlin.

World Bank, 1975, *Yugoslavia: Development with Decentralization.* Baltimore, Johns Hopkins University Press.

Wyzan, Michael L., 1981, "Empirical Analysis of Soviet Agricultural Production and Policy," *American Journal of Agricultural Economics* **63:** 475–83.

Wyzan, Michael L., 1983, "The Kolkhoz and the Sovkhoz: Relative Performance as Measured by Productive Technology," pp. 173–198 in Robert C. Stuart, ed., 1983.

Wyzan, Michael L. and Utter, Andrew M., 1982, "The Yugoslav Inflation," *Journal of Comparative Economics* **6:** 396–405.

Zafiris, Nicos, 1982, "Appropriability Rules, Capital Maintenance, and the Efficiency of Cooperative Investment," *Journal of Comparative Economics* **6:** 55–75.

Zevi, Alberto, 1982, "The Performance of Italian Producer Cooperatives," pp. 239–251 in Jones and Svejnar, eds.

INDEX

For Product Safety Concerns and Information please contact our EU representative GPSR@taylorandfrancis.com Taylor & Francis Verlag GmbH, Kaufingerstraße 24, 80331 München, Germany